Options

plain & simple

Options

plain & simple

Successful strategies
without rocket science

LENNY JORDAN

London · New York · San Francisco · Toronto · Sydney
Tokyo · Singapore · Hong Kong · Cape Town · Madrid
Paris · Milan · Munich · Amsterdam

PEARSON EDUCATION LIMITED

Head Office:
Edinburgh Gate
Harlow CM20 2JE
Tel: +44 (0)1279 623623
Fax: +44 (0)1279 431059

London Office:
128 Long Acre
London WC2E 9AN
Tel: +44 (0)207 447 2000
Fax: +44 (0)207 240 5771
Website: www.business-minds.com

———————————————

First published in Great Britain in 2000

© Pearson Education Limited 2000

The right of Lenny Jordan to be identified as author
of this work has been asserted by him in accordance
with the Copyright, Designs and Patents Act 1988.

ISBN 0 273 63878 5

British Library Cataloguing in Publication Data
A CIP catalogue record for this book can be obtained from the British Library

10 9 8 7 6 5 4 3 2 1

Typeset by Pantek Arts Ltd., Maidstone, Kent
Printed and bound in Great Britain by Biddles Ltd, Guildford and King's Lynn

The Publishers' policy is to use paper manufactured from sustainable forests.

This book is dedicated to the memory of my grandfather, George S. Kuhter (1882–1976), who first taught me the principles of business.

Acknowledgements

The author would like to thank the following:

FutureSource – Bridge (futuresource.com)
PM Publishing website (pmpublishing.com)
Santo Volpe
Warwick Gück
Ron Lindenberg
Catherine

Contents

Preface • ix
About the author • x
About this book • xi
Introduction • xiii

Part 1 Options fundamentals
1 Options in everyday life • 3
2 The basics of calls • 6
3 The basics of puts • 21
4 Pricing and behaviour • 38
5 Volatility and pricing models • 52
6 The Greeks and risk assessment: delta • 63
7 Gamma and theta • 71
8 Vega • 81

Part 2 Options spreads
Introduction • 89
9 Call spreads and put spreads, or one by one
   directional spreads • 93
10 One by two directional spreads • 111
11 Combos and hybrid spreads for market direction • 127
12 Volatility spreads • 136
13 Iron butterflies and iron condors: combining
   straddles and strangles for reduced risk • 148
14 Butterflies and condors: combining call spreads
   and put spreads • 159
15 The covered write, the calendar spread and
   the diagonal spread • 181

Part 3 Thinking about options
16 The interaction of the Greeks • 193
17 Options performance based on cost • 207

18 Options talk 1 • 212

19 Options talk 2: trouble shooting and common probems • 216

20 Volatility skews • 222

Part 4 **Basic non-essentials**

21 Futures, synthetics and put-call parity • 239

22 Conversions, reversals, boxes and options arbitrage • 252

23 Conclusion • 263

Glossary • 265

Suggestions for further reading • 270

Index of underlying contracts • 271

Index • 272

Preface

What an option is

The difference between a commodity, a futures contract, and an options contract is illustrated in the following three paragraphs, which will take you $1\frac{1}{2}$ minutes to read.

Suppose you're in the market for an oriental rug. You find the rug of your choice at a local shop, you pay the shopkeeper $500, and he transfers the rug to you. You have just traded **a commodity**.

Suppose instead you wish to own the rug, but you prefer to purchase it in one week's time. You may be on your way to the airport, or maybe you need the short-term use of your money. You and the shopkeeper agree, verbally or in writing, to exchange the same rug for $500 one week from now. You have just traded **a futures contract**.

Alternatively, you may like the rug on offer, but you may want to shop around before making a final decision. You ask the shopkeeper if he will hold the rug in reserve for you for one week. He replies that your proposal will deny him the opportunity of selling the rug, and as compensation, he asks that you pay him $10. You and the shopkeeper agree, verbally or in writing, that for a fee of $10 he will hold the rug for you for one week, and that at any time during the week you may purchase the same rug for a cost of $500, excluding the $10 cost of your agreement. You, on the other hand, are under no obligation to buy the rug. You have just traded **an options contract**.

About the author

Lenny Jordan currently trades options at the London International Financial Futures and Options Exchange. Formerly he traded at the Chicago Board of Trade. He gives options training seminars, and is a risk consultant.

About this book

Options Plain and Simple is a straightforward and practical guide to the fundamentals of options. It is plain because it includes only what is essential to basic understanding. It is simple because it presents options theory in conventional terms, with a minimum of jargon. It is thorough; it is not simplistic.

The purpose of this book is to give you, the private investor, a basis from which to trade most of the options products listed on most of the major exchanges. It will also benefit those who serve the industry: administrative staff, accountants, attorneys, and others. When you have finished the book, you will be prepared for advanced options topics.

Like all investment strategies, options offer potential return while incurring potential risk. The advantage of options trading is that risk can be managed to a greater degree than with outright buying or selling. This book continually discusses the link between risk and return. It will help you choose justifiable and manageable strategies. Reading it will develop an awareness of the risks involved.

This book is the product of my training courses for new traders and support staff. My method has been tested and revised over the years. It has proved successful for those whose livelihoods depend on thorough understanding and flawless execution under circumstances that allow no error. Because I am an options trader, the strategies presented here are the very same that I have traded time and again, day by day, year after year.

In fact, you and I have the same goals: to make money and to manage risk.

This book is also the product of many informal discussions I have had over the years, on the golf course and at social gatherings, with investors outside professional investment circles: dentists, accountants, and business men and women, people who follow the markets and who want to know more about options. I have tried to include my answers to most of their questions.

Many theoretical concepts are included, but the focus of this book is on practice, not theory. While it is impossible to coach an investor at a distance, it is possible to recount many of the situations that often arise in the marketplace, and to discuss ways of approaching them.

The mathematics in this book involve only addition, subtraction, multiplication and division. These four functions plus a pricing model are all that we professionals use in order to trade most of the options products on the major exchanges.

The focus of this book is options: it is not a comprehensive guide to trading. As professional traders know, trading technique is only gained through experience. For this, you should engage a professional adviser to help you to decide the best strategies to use.

Acronyms

The following acronyms are used:

CBOT	– Chicago Board of Trade
CBOE	– Chicago Board Options Exchange
OEX	– Options Exchange Index or Standard and Poor's 100 index, the options on which are traded at the CBOE
CME	– Chicago Mercantile Exchange
FTSE-100	– Financial Times Stock Exchange 100 index
LIFFE	– London International Financial Futures and Options Exchange
OTC	– Over the Counter
NYMEX	– New York Mercantile Exchange
DJIA	– Dow Jones Industrial Average
S&P 500	– Standard and Poor's 500 index
SPX	– Options on the S&P 500 also traded at the CBOE

Introduction

Why options are useful

A word I often hear when people are discussing options is 'risky'. The other evening at dinner, a friend used this word in this context. An hour later, I was sorry to hear him say that he had recently lost 84 per cent of an investment in emerging markets.

It is an unfortunate and costly reality that few investors know how to protect their investments from downside risk. Their sole investment strategy is to select a stock to buy, or a fund to buy into. Over the long term, and if value is found at the time of purchase, this strategy makes sense. It also makes sense for those who entrust the management of their portfolios to financial advisers. But for those who take a more active role in their investments, options offer the two advantages of flexibility and limited risk.

For those new to day-trading the markets, call and put purchases are excellent ways of developing market awareness and building confidence. This is because with these strategies traders can take either a bullish or bearish position while limiting their maximum loss at the outset. Because the cost of options is paid for up front on most exchanges, the options buyer is forced to be more disciplined than traders who must simply post margin.

Because options have lives of their own, they are indicators of market sentiment. Implied volatility often anticipates changes in price activity in the underlying contracts. Simply knowing about options can improve your market awareness.

Options strategies are only 'risky' when, like other investments, their potential return does not justify the risks taken, or when the parties involved do not know the fundamentals. This book presents a sensible approach to profit opportunities with a manageable degree of risk.

How to use this book

This book is designed for readers whose time is limited, and for those seeking different levels of expertise. A basic understanding of calls and puts, for those who do not wish to trade, can be obtained by reading Part One. For investors willing to enter the market, Parts One and Two provide enough information to take positions in most market conditions. Part

Three presents more sophisticated ways of approaching options. Part Four covers basics that are not essential for most private investors, but which may be useful. It is recommended that those willing to commit capital read the whole book.

Each chapter presents explanatory material followed by a section with questions/examples. Use the latter as additional material from which to learn; don't expect to know all the answers the first time you go through the book.

An understanding of stocks, bonds or commodities is advisable before you start. You should also understand the simple mechanics of buying and selling through a broker or an exchange. Because stocks, bonds and commodities are often traded as futures contracts, a basic explanation of a futures contract is given in Part Four, which also explains the nature of a short position.

The substance of this book is accessible to all who have a basic understanding of one of the principle markets mentioned above. Occasionally subjects are presented that are at a slightly more advanced level than the immediate context in which they appear. These subjects are not difficult; they may merely require rereading after later portions of the book have been assimilated.

The examples in this book are drawn from exchange listed products. These products serve the needs of most investors, and their prices are reported in most daily business journals, on the Internet and through many data vendors. Once the principles of this book are understood, you will be prepared for foreign currency and OTC (Over the Counter) options, as well as for more advanced topics such as exotic options.

Because this book is designed to help US and UK investors, the examples chosen are from markets in both these countries. I have traded many products in the US and the UK; all the options strategies discussed in this book are identical, and only the nomenclature or jargon varies.

Part

1

Options
fundamentals

1 Options in everyday life

2 The basics of calls

3 The basics of puts

4 Pricing and behaviour

5 Volatility and pricing models

6 Risk assessment and the Greeks: Delta

7 Gamma and theta

8 Vega

Options in everyday life

Puts

We encounter options frequently in our daily lives, but we probably aren't aware of them. They occur in situations of uncertainty, and they are helpful in managing risk.

For example, most of us insure our home, our car and our health. We protect these, our assets, by taking out policies from insurance companies who agree to bear the cost of loss or damage to them. We periodically pay these companies a fee, or premium, which is based in part on the value of our assets and the duration of coverage. In essence, we establish contracts that transfer our risk to the companies.

If by accident our assets suffer damage and a consequent loss in value, our contract gives us the right to file a claim for compensation. Most often we exercise this right, but occasionally we may not, for example, if the damage to our car is small, it has been incurred by our teenage son, and filing a claim would produce an undesirable rise in our future premium level. Should we file a claim, however, our insurer has the obligation, under the terms of the contract, to pay us the amount of our loss.

Upon receipt of our payment we might say that the cost of our accident has been 'put to' the insurer by us. In effect, our insurance company had sold us a **put option** which we owned, and which we have exercised.

In the financial markets 'puts', as they are called, operate similarly. Pension funds, banks, corporations and private investors have assets in the form of stocks and bonds that they periodically protect against a decline in value. They do this by purchasing put options based on, or derived from, their stocks and bonds. These options give them the right to put the amount of an asset's decline onto the seller of the options. They transfer risk.

Subsequent chapters explain how this process of risk transfer works, but for now let's turn to another everyday use of options.

CALLS

Suppose we need to purchase a washing machine. In our local newspaper we see an advertisement for the machine that we want. It is 'on sale' at a 20 per cent discount from a local retailer until the end of the week. We know this retailer to be reputable and that no tricks or gimmicks are involved.

From our standpoint we have the right to buy this machine at the specified price for the specified time period. We may not exercise this right if we find the machine cheaper elsewhere. The retailer, however, has the obligation to sell the machine under the terms specified in the advertisement. In effect, he has entered into a contract with the general public.

If we decide to exercise our right, we simply visit the retailer and purchase our washing machine. We might say that we have 'called away' this machine from the retailer. He had given us a **call option** which we had accepted and which we have exercised. In this case our option is commonly known as a 'call'. It was given to us as part of the general public, free of charge. The retailer bore the cost of the call because he had a supply of washing machines that he wanted to sell.

Because, under the terms of the contract, the retailer is obligated to sell, he has also incurred a risk. Suppose we visit his store within the week and find that all washing machines have been sold. The retailer underestimated the demand that the advertisement generated, and he is now short of supply. He and his sales staff are anxious to meet the demand, and he has his good reputation to uphold. In the US, a consumer rights organization may threaten him with a charge of 'bait and switch', or false advertising, and certain customers are bound to become hysterical.

In the US then, our retailer will try to rush delivery from a distributor, even at additional cost to him. If no machines are available through the distribution network, he will give us a voucher for the purchase of our machine when more arrive.

This voucher is, again, a call option. It contains the right to buy at the sale price, but its duration has been extended. If in the meantime the factory or wholesale price of our machine rises, the retailer will still be obligated to sell it to us at the sale price. His profit margin will be cut, and he may even take a loss. The call option that he gave us may prove costly to him.

Suppose that we become enterprising with our voucher, or call option. Early the next week we are talking to our neighbor who expresses disappointment at having missed the sale on washing machines. The new supply has arrived, and the new price is above the old, pre-sale price. By missing the sale, he will need to pay considerably more than he would have paid. We, after reflection, decide that we can live with our old machine. We offer to sell him a new machine for an amount less than the new retail price but more than the old sale price. He accepts our offer. We then return to the retailer, exercise our option, purchase the machine, and resell it to our neighbour. He has a saving and we have a profit. We are now options traders.

Calls are a significant feature of commodity markets, where supply shortages often occur. Adverse weather, strikes, or distribution problems can result in unforeseen rises in the costs of basic goods. Petroleum manufacturers, transport companies, and grain distributors regularly purchase calls in order to ensure that they have the commodities necessary to meet output deadlines.

Conclusion

The trade in options contracts continues to grow because more and more companies and individuals need them to manage risk. Their needs are essentially very simple: the right to buy with **calls**, and the right to sell with **puts**. The next two chapters explain how these rights operate.

> The trade in options contracts continues to grow because more and more companies and individuals need them to manage risk.

The basics of calls

In the previous chapter we saw that options are used in association with a variety of everyday items from which they derive their worth. The value of our house determines, in part, the amount of our insurance premium. In the options business, each of these items is known as an underlying asset, or simply an 'underlying.' It may be a stock or share, a bond, or a commodity. Here, in order to get started, we will discuss an underlying with which we are all familiar, namely stock, bond, or commodity XYZ.

Owning a call

XYZ is currently trading at a price of 100. It may be 100 dollars, euros, or pounds sterling. Suppose you are given, free of charge, the right to buy XYZ at the current price of 100 for the next two months. If XYZ stays where it is or if it declines in price, you have no use for your right to buy; you can simply ignore it. But if XYZ rises to 105, you can exercise your right: you can buy XYZ for 100. As the new owner of XYZ, you can then sell it at 105 or hold it as an asset worth 105. In either case, you make a profit of 5.

What you do by exercising your right is to 'call XYZ away' from the previous owner. Your original right to buy is known as a **call option**, or simply a 'call.'

It is important, right from the start, to visualize profit and loss potential in graphic terms. Figure 2.1 is a profit/loss graph of your call, or call position, before you exercise your right.

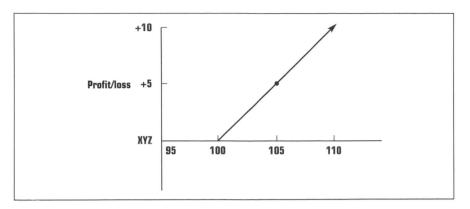

Fig 2.1 ■ Owning a call

Your profit is potentially unlimited.

If you choose, you can wait for XYZ to rise further before exercising your call. Your profit is potentially unlimited. If XYZ remains at 100 or declines in price, you have no loss because you have no obligation to buy.

Offering a call

Now let's consider the position of the investor who gave you the call. By giving you the right to buy, this person has assumed the obligation to sell. Consequently, this investor's profit/loss position is exactly the opposite of yours.

The risk for this investor is that XYZ will rise in price and that it will be 'called away' from him. He will relinquish all profit above 100. In this case, Figure 2.2 represents the amount that is given up.

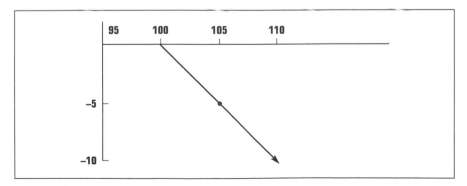

Fig 2.2 ■ Offering a call

On the other hand, this investor may not already own an XYZ to be called away. (Remember our retailer in Chapter 1 who was short of washing machines.) He may need to purchase XYZ from a third party in order to meet the obligation of the call contract. In this case, Figure 2.2 represents the amount this investor may need to pay for XYZ in order to transfer it to you. Your potential gain is his potential loss.

Buying a call

Obviously, then, the investor who offers a call also demands a fee, or premium. The buyer and the seller must agree on a price for their call contract. Suppose in this case the price agreed upon is 4. A correct profit/loss position for the buyer, when the call contract expires, would be graphed as in Figure 2.3.

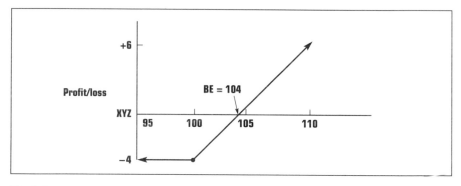

Fig 2.3 ■ Buying a call

By paying 4 for the call option, the buyer defers his profit until XYZ reaches 104. At 104 the call is paid for by the right to buy pay 100 for XYZ. Above 104 the profit from the call equals the amount gained by XYZ. Between 100 and 104 a partial loss results, equal to the difference between 4 and any gains in XYZ. Below 100 a total loss of 4 is realized. A corresponding table of this profit/loss position at expiration is shown in Table 2.1.

The first advantage of this position is that profit above 104 is potentially unlimited. The second advantage is that by buying the call instead of XYZ, the call buyer is not exposed to downside movement in XYZ. He has a potential savings. The disadvantage of this position is that the call buyer may lose the amount paid, 4.

XYZ	95	96	97	98	99	100	101	102	103	104	105	106	107	108	109	110
Cost of call	–4	–4	–4	–4	–4	–4	–4	–4	–4	–4	–4	–4	–4	–4	–4	–4
Value of call																
at expiration	0	0	0	0	0	0	1	2	3	4	5	6	7	8	9	10
Profit/loss	–4	–4	–4	–4	–4	–4	–3	–2	–1	0	1	2	3	4	5	6

Table 2.1 ■ Buying a call

All options contracts, like their underlying contracts, have contract multipliers. Both contracts usually have the same multiplier. If the multiplier for the above contracts is $100, then the actual cost of the call would be $400. The value of XYZ at 100 would actually be $1,000. In the options markets, prices quoted are without contract multipliers.

When trading options, it is important to know the **risk/return** potential at the outset. In this case, the potential **risk** of the call buyer is the amount paid for the option, 4 or $400. The call buyer's potential **return** is the unlimited profit as XYZ rises above 104. For a discussion of an actual risk/return scenario, see Question 3 (concerning Unilever) at the end of this chapter.

Calls can be traded at many different strike prices. For example, if XYZ were at 100, calls could probably be purchased at 105, 110 and 115. They would cost progressively less as their distance from the current price of XYZ increased. Many investors purchase these 'out-of-the-money' calls, as they are known, because of their lower cost, and because they believe that there is significant upside potential for the underlying.

Our 100 call, with XYZ at 100, is said to be 'at the money'.

In addition, if XYZ were at 100, calls could also be purchased at 95, 90 and 85. These 'in-the-money' calls, as they are known, cost progressively *more* as their distance from the underlying increases. Where the underlying is a stock, many investors purchase these calls because they approximate price movement of the stock, yet they are less expensive than a stock purchase. For both stocks and futures, the limited loss feature of these calls also acts as a built-in stop-loss order.

Out-of-the-money, in-the-money, and at-the-money calls will be discussed in later chapters, but for now let's return to the basics.

An example of a call purchase

Suppose IBM is trading at 149, and the November 150 calls are priced at $3\frac{3}{8}$. If you purchased one of these calls, the break-even level would be the strike price plus the price of the call, or $153\frac{3}{8}$. If IBM is above this level at expiration, you would profit one-to-one with the stock. Below 150, your call expires worthless. Between 150 and $153\frac{3}{8}$ you take a partial loss, equal to the stock price minus the strike price minus the cost of the call.

IBM	145	150	151	152	153	$153\frac{3}{8}$	154	155	156	157
Cost of call	$-3\frac{3}{8}$	-	-	-	-	-	-	-	-	-
Value of call at expiration	0	- - 0	1	2	3	$3\frac{3}{8}$	4	5	6	7
Profit/loss	$-3\frac{3}{8}$	$-3\frac{3}{8}$	$-2\frac{3}{8}$	$-1\frac{3}{8}$	$-\frac{3}{8}$	0	$+\frac{5}{8}$	$+1\frac{5}{8}$	$+2\frac{5}{8}$	$+3\frac{5}{8}$

Table 2.2 ■ IBM 150 call profit/loss

In graphic form, the expiration profit/loss is summarized in Figure 2.4.

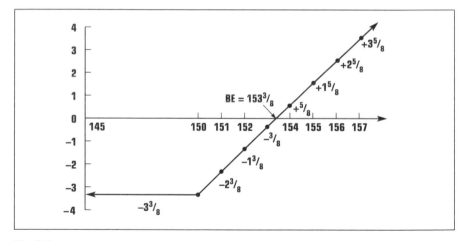

Fig 2.4 ■ Graph of IBM call profit/loss

The contract multiplier for IBM, and most stock options at the CBOE, is $100. Therefore, the cost of the November 150 call, and your maximum risk, would be $3\frac{3}{8}$ (3.375) × $100 = $337.50.

Selling a call

Now let's consider the profit/loss position of the investor who sold you the XYZ call for 4. Like the previous example, his position, when the contract expires, is exactly the opposite of yours.

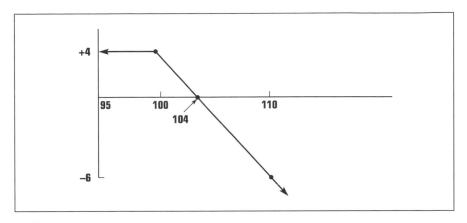

Fig 2.5 ■ Selling a call

In tabular form this position would be as shown in Table 2.3.

XYZ	95	96	97	98	99	100	101	102	103	104	105	106	107	108	109	110
Income from call	4	4	4	4	4	4	4	4	4	4	4	4	4	4	4	4
Value of call at expiration	0	0	0	0	0	0	–1	–2	–3	–4	–5	–6	–7	–8	–9	–10
Profit/loss	4	4	4	4	4	4	3	2	1	0	–1	–2	–3	–4	–5	–6

Table 2.3 ■ Selling a call

Consider also that the risk/return potential is opposite. The seller's potential return is the premium collected, 4. His potential risk is the profit given up, or the unlimited loss, if XYZ rises above 104.

The advantage for the call seller who owns XYZ is that by selling the call instead of XYZ, he retains ownership while earning income from the call sale. The disadvantage is that he may give up upside profit if his XYZ is called away. For the call seller who does not own XYZ, i.e., one who sells a call 'naked', the disadvantage is that he may need to purchase XYZ at increasingly higher levels in order to transfer it to you. His potential loss is unlimited. For this reason, *it is not advisable to sell a call without an additional covering contract, either a purchased call at another strike or a long underlying.*

Clearly, then, the greater risk lies with the seller. Through selling the right to buy, this investor incurs the potential obligation to sell XYZ at a loss-taking level. His loss is potentially unlimited. In order to assume this risk, he must receive a justifiable fee. The call seller must expect XYZ to be stable or slightly lower while the call position is outstanding or 'open'.

An example of a call sale

Again, suppose that IBM is trading at 149, and the November 155 calls are trading at $1\frac{1}{2}$. If you sold one of these calls, then at November expiration the break-even level would be the strike price plus the price of the call, or $156\frac{1}{2}$. Above $156\frac{1}{2}$ you would lose one to one with the stock. Below 155 you would collect $1\frac{1}{2}$. Between 155 and $156\frac{1}{2}$ you would have a profit equal to the strike price minus the stock price plus the call income. An expiration profit/loss table would be as in Table 2.4.

IBM	145	150	155	156	$156\frac{1}{2}$	157	158	159	160
Income from call	$1\frac{1}{2}$	-	-	-	-	-	-	-	-
Value of call at expiration	0	0	0	−1	$-1\frac{1}{2}$	−2	−3	−4	−5
Profit/loss	$1\frac{1}{2}$	$1\frac{1}{2}$	$1\frac{1}{2}$	$\frac{1}{2}$	0	$-\frac{1}{2}$	$-1\frac{1}{2}$	$-2\frac{1}{2}$	$-3\frac{1}{2}$

Table 2.4 ■ Sold IBM 155 call

An expiration graph of your profit/loss would be as in Figure 2.6.

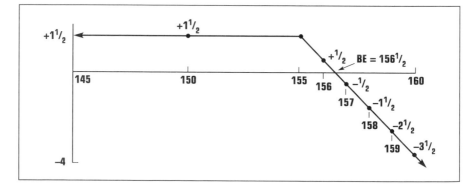

Fig 2.6 ■ Graph of sold IBM call

Again, the contract multiplier is $100, and therefore the maximum profit on the sold call would be $1\frac{1}{2}$, or 1.50 x $100 = $150.

Summary of the terms of the call contract:

A call option is the right to buy the underlying asset at a specified price for a specified time period. The call buyer has the right, but not the obligation, to buy the underlying. The call seller has the obligation to sell the underlying at the call buyer's discretion. These are the terms of the call contract.

Summary of the introduction to the call contract

A call is used primarily as a hedge for upside market movement. It is also used to hedge downside exposure as an alternative to buying the underlying. The buyer and the seller of a call contract have opposite views about the market's potential to move higher. The call buyer has the right to buy the underlying asset, while the call seller has the obligation to sell the underlying asset. Because the call seller incurs the potential for unlimited loss, he must demand a fee that justifies this risk. The call buyer can profit substantially from a sudden, unforeseen rise in the underlying. When exercised, the buyer's right becomes the seller's obligation.

By learning the basics of call options, you have also learned several characteristics of options in general. This will help you to understand the subject of the next chapter, puts.

Questions

Here are a few questions on call contracts. Don't expect to know all the answers. The answers are given, so you should treat the questions as additional examples from which to learn.

1   General Electric is currently trading at $87\frac{3}{16}$ and the August 90 calls are currently trading at $2\frac{1}{2}$
   a) If you sell one of these calls at the current market price, what is your break-even level?
   b) What is the maximum amount that you can gain?
   c) What is the maximum amount that you can lose?
   d) Answer questions a–c for a purchase of this call.

e) The multiplier for this options contract is $100, or 100 shares. What is the cash value of this call?

f) Write a profit/loss table for a sale of this call at expiration.

g) Draw a graph to show the expiration profit/loss for the call seller.

h) If General Electric is at 91 at expiration, what is the profit/loss for the call seller and the call buyer?

2 Coke is currently trading at $79\frac{13}{16}$, and the September 85 calls are trading at $1\frac{1}{2}$.

a) If you buy one of these calls at the current market price, what is your break-even level?

b) What is the maximum amount that you can gain?

c) What is the maximum amount that you can lose?

d) Answer questions a-c for a sale of this call.

e) Write a profit/loss table for a buy of this call at expiration.

f) Graph the profit/loss for a buy of this call at expiration.

g) If at September expiration, Coke closes at $88\frac{1}{8}$ what is the profit/loss for the call buyer and for the call seller?

3 This is a question to get you thinking about risk and return.

If counting in 8ths and 16ths is awkward then you might prefer to work with the following example from UK share options, which trade in decimals and halves at the LIFFE (London International Financial Futures and Options Exchange).

Unilever is currently trading at 553p (£5.53), and the March 550 calls are trading at 74p (£0.74). This year, Unilever shares have ranged from $346\frac{3}{4}$ to 741. You foresee a recession next year and you think that food producers will attract buying interest as defensive investments. You hesitate to risk an outright purchase of shares, and you would like to compare the risk of a call purchase.

a) If you buy one of these calls at the current market price, what is your break-even level?

b) What is the maximum amount that you can gain?

c) What is the maximum amount that you can lose?

d) Answer questions a-c for a sale of this call.

e) The multiplier for this options contract is £1,000, or 1,000 shares. What is the cash value of one of these calls?

f) If at March expiry Unilever closes at 650, what is the profit/loss for the call buyer, and for the call seller?

g) What is the amount of capital at risk for the call buyer versus the buyer of 1,000 shares? Calculate the difference.

h) If by March Unilever has retraced to its former low, what would be the amount lost on buying the shares versus buying the call?
Calculate the difference.
Calculate the risk/risk ratio.

i) If by March of next year Unilever has rallied to its former high, what would be the amount gained on buying the shares versus buying the call?
Calculate the difference.
Calculate the return/return ratio.

j) Looking at the above risk scenario h), and the above return scenario i), compare the risk/return ratios of the shares position versus the call position.
This is just one method of accessing risk/return. The point is that you do need to have a method.

4 Also in the UK, the FTSE-100 share index is currently trading at 5133, and the December 5300 call is trading at 253. Assume that you are a large unit trust, and if you miss a year-end rally, your investors will be disappointed. You could buy a basket of all the stocks in the index for a cost of £51,330, or you could take a long futures position with an exposure of £51,330. Lately the market has been volatile, however, and you don't want the downside risk.

a) If you buy one of these calls at the current market price, what is your break-even level?

b) What is the maximum amount that you can gain?

c) What is the maximum amount that you can lose?

d) Answer questions a-c for a sale of this call.

e) The multiplier for this options contract is £10. What is the cash value of one of these calls?

f) This year, the trading range of the FTSE-100 index has been 4648.7 to 6179. If the maket retraces part of its recent gains, at what level would the retracement equal the cost of the call?

g) Write a profit/loss table at expiry for a *sale* of this call with the FTSE in a range of 5000 to 6000 at intervals of 100.

h) Write a graph at expiry for a sale of this call with the FTSE in a range of 5000 to 6000 at intervals of 100.

5 March soybeans are currently trading at $573\frac{3}{4}$ and the March 575 calls are trading at $22\frac{3}{4}$.

a) If you buy one of these calls at the current market price, what is your break-even level?

b) What is the maximum amount that you can gain?

c) What is the maximum amount that you can lose?

d) Answer questions a-c for a sale of this call.

e) The multiplier for this options contract is $50. What is the cash value of one of these calls?

f) Write a profit/loss table for a buy of this call at expiration, which will be in February.

g) Graph the expiration profit/loss for a buy of this call.

h) If at March expiration, which is in February, the March futures contract settles at 590, what is the profit/loss for the call buyer and the call seller?

Answers

1 **a)** $92\frac{1}{2}$ **b)** $2\frac{1}{2}$

   c) unlimited   **d)** $92\frac{1}{2}$, unlimited, $2\frac{1}{2}$

   e) $2.50 \times \$100 = \$250$

   f)

General Electric	85	90	91	92	$92\frac{1}{2}$	93	94	95
Income from call	$2\frac{1}{2}$	- - -	- - -	- - -	- - -	- - -	- - -	- - -
Value of call at expiration	0	0	−1	−2	$−2\frac{1}{2}$	−3	−4	−5
Profit/loss	$2\frac{1}{2}$	$2\frac{1}{2}$	$1\frac{1}{2}$	$\frac{1}{2}$	0	$-\frac{1}{2}$	$−1\frac{1}{2}$	$−2\frac{1}{2}$

Answer 1.f ■

g)

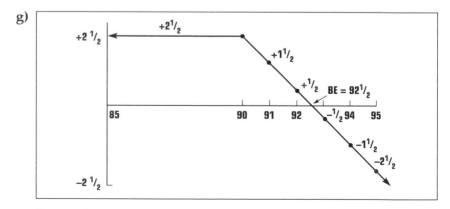

Answer 1g ■ Sale of General Electric call

h) Price of stock at expiration minus strike price, 91– 90 = 1, or expiration value of call.

Traded value of call minus expiration value of a call, $2\frac{1}{2} - 1 = 1\frac{1}{2}$

1.50 × $100 = $150 profit for seller, loss for buyer.

2 a) $86\frac{1}{2}$

b) unlimited

c) $1\frac{1}{2}$

d) $86\frac{1}{2}, 1\frac{1}{2}$, unlimited

e) See answer 2e on the next page.

f) See answer 2f on the next page.

g) Price of stock at expiration minus strike price, $88\frac{1}{8} - 85 = 3\frac{1}{8}$, or expiration value of call

$3\frac{1}{8}$ minus traded value of a call at $1\frac{1}{2} = 1\frac{5}{8}$

$1\frac{5}{8} = 1.625$

1.625 × contract multiplier of $100 = $162.50 profit for buyer, loss for seller

Coke	80	85	86	86½	87	88	89	90
Cost of call	$-1\frac{1}{2}$	- - -	- - -	- - -	- - -	- - -	- - -	- - -
Value of call at expiration	0	0	1	$1\frac{1}{2}$	2	3	4	5
Profit/loss	$-1\frac{1}{2}$	$-1\frac{1}{2}$	$-\frac{1}{2}$	0	$+\frac{1}{2}$	$+1\frac{1}{2}$	$+2\frac{1}{2}$	$+3\frac{1}{2}$

Answer 2e ■ Profit/loss Table

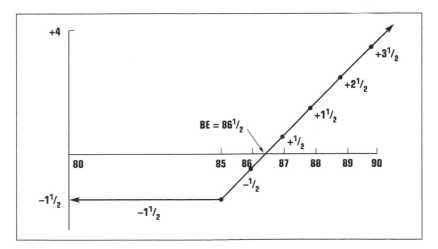

Answer 2f ■ Purchase of Coke call

3 a) 624

   b) unlimited

   c) 74

   d) 624, 74, unlimited

   e) £740

   f) Price of stock at expiration minus strike price, 650 − 550 = 100, or expiration value of call

   100 minus traded value of call at 74 = 26

   .26 × contract multiplier of £1,000 = £260 profit for buyer, loss for seller

   g) £740 versus £5,530, or a difference of £4,790

   h) $553 − 346\frac{3}{4} = 206\frac{1}{4}$ loss for the shares, versus 74 loss for the call
   $206\frac{1}{4} − 74 = 132\frac{1}{4}$ greater loss for the shares
   $206.25 ÷ 74 = 2.79$, or risk of 2.79 with shares purchase per 1.00 risk with call purchase

   i) 741 − 553 = 188 gain for the shares, versus 741 − 624 = 117 gain for the call
   188 − 117 = 71 greater gain for the shares
   188 ÷ 117 = 1.61 or return of 1.61 with shares per 1.00 return with call.

   j) Shares risk/return = 206.25 ÷ 188 = 1.10 = risk of 1.10 to return of 1.00. Call risk/return = 74 ÷ 117 = 0.63 to return of 1.00

4 a) 5553

   b) unlimited

   c) 253

   d) 5553, 253, unlimited

   e) £2,530

   f) 5133 − 253 = 4880

   g)

FTSE at expiry	5000	5100	5200	5300	5400	5500	5600	5700	5800	5900	6000
Income from call	253										
Value of call at expiry	0	0	0	0	−100	−200	−300	−400	−500	−600	−700
Profit/loss	253	253	253	253	153	53	−47	−147	−247	−347	−447

Answer 4g ■ **Sale of FTSE 5300 call at expiry**

   h) See answer 4h on the next page

5 a) 597 $\frac{3}{4}$

b) unlimited

c) 22 $\frac{3}{4}$

d) 597 $\frac{3}{4}$, 22 $\frac{3}{4}$, unlimited

e) $1,137.50

f) See answer 5f on the next page

g) See answer 5g on page 20.

h) Futures price at expiration minus strike price of call equals 590 − 575 = 15, or expiration value of call

Traded price of call minus expiration value of call, 22 $\frac{3}{4}$ − 15 = 7 $\frac{3}{4}$

7 $\frac{3}{4}$ × contact multiplier of $50 = $387.50 profit for seller, loss for buyer

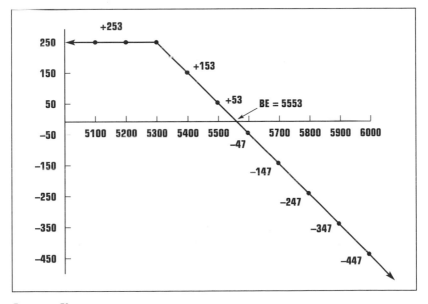

Answer 4h ■ Sale of FTSE 5300 call at expiry

Mar soybeans	550	575	600	625	650	675	700
Cost of call	−22 $\frac{3}{4}$	- - -	- - -	- - -	- - -	- - -	- - -
Value of call at expiration	0	0	25	50	75	100	125
Profit/loss	−22 $\frac{3}{4}$	−22 $\frac{3}{4}$	+2 $\frac{1}{4}$	+27 $\frac{1}{4}$	+52 $\frac{1}{4}$	+77 $\frac{1}{4}$	+102 $\frac{1}{4}$

Answer 5f ■ Purchase of March Soybeans 575 call at expiration

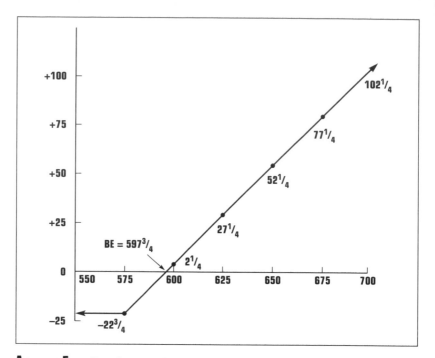

Answer 5g ■ **Purchase of Soybeans March 575 call at expiration**

The basics of puts

Put options operate in essentially the same manner as call options. The major difference is that they are designed to hedge downside market movement. Some common characteristics of puts and calls are as follows:

- The buyer purchases a right from the seller, who in turn incurs a potential obligation.
- A fee or premium is exchanged.
- A price for the underlying is established.
- The contract is for a limited time.
- The buyer and the seller have opposite profit/loss positions.
- The buyer and the seller have opposite risk-return potentials.

A put option hedges a decline in the value of an underlying asset by giving the put owner the right to sell the underlying at a specified price for a specified time period. The put owner has the right to 'put the underlying to' the opposing party. The other party, the put seller, consequently incurs the potential obligation to purchase the underlying.

> A put option hedges a decline in the value of an underlying asset by giving the put owner the right to sell the underlying at a specified price for a specified time period.

Buying puts

Suppose you own XYZ, and it is currently trading at a price of 100. You are concerned that XYZ may decline in value, and you want to receive a selling price of 100. In other words, you want to insure your XYZ for a value of 100. You do this by purchasing an XYZ 100 put for a cost of 4. If XYZ declines in price, you now have the right to sell it at 100.

First, let's consider the profit/loss position of the put itself. At expiration, this position would be graphed as shown in Figure 3.1.

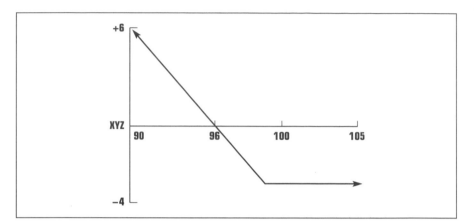

Fig 3.1 ■ Buying a put

This graph should appear similar to the graph for a call purchase, Figure 2.3. In fact, it is the identical profit/loss but with a reverse in market direction. Both graphs show the potential for a large profit at the expense of a small loss. Here, profit is made as the market moves downward rather than upward. In tabular form, this profit/loss position would be as shown in Table 3.1.

XYZ	90	91	92	93	94	95	96	97	98	99	100	101	102	103	104	105
Cost of put	-4	-4	-4	-4	-4	-4	-4	-4	-4	-4	-4	-4	-4	-4	-4	-4
Value of put at expiration	10	9	8	7	6	5	4	3	2	1	0	0	0	0	0	0
Profit/loss	6	5	4	3	2	1	0	-1	-2	-3	-4	-4	-4	-4	-4	-4

Table 3.1 ■ Buying a put

The break-even level of this position is 96. There, the cost of the put equals the profit gained by the right to sell XYZ at 100. Between 100 and 96 the cost of the put is partially offset by the decline in XYZ. Above 100, the premium paid is taken as a loss. Below 96 the profit on the put equals the decline in XYZ.

As the owner of XYZ, your loss is stopped at 96 by your put position. The cost of the put has effectively lowered your selling price to 96. But if XYZ falls sharply, you have a substantial saving because you are fully protected. In other words, you are insured. In the meantime, you still have the advantage of potential profit if XYZ gains in price.

The purchase of a put option can be profitable in itself. Suppose that you do not actually own XYZ, but you follow it regularly, and you believe that it is due for a decline. Just as you may have purchased a call to capture an upside move, you now may purchase a put to capture a downside move. [Your advantage, as an alternative to taking a short position in the underlying, is that you are not exposed to unlimited loss if XYZ moves upward.] The most you can lose is the premium paid. Figure 3.1 and the accompanying table (Table 3.1) illustrate the possible return from your put purchase.

Again, note the risk/return potential. With a put purchase the potential risk is the premium paid, 4. The potential return is the full amount that XYZ may decline below 96.

An example of a put purchase

Suppose Coke is trading at $67\frac{7}{16}$, and the November 65 puts are trading at $1\frac{3}{8}$. If you purchased one of these puts, the break-even level would be the strike price minus the price of the put, or $63\frac{5}{8}$. If Coke is below this level at expiration, you would profit one to one with the decline of the stock. Above 65, your put would expire worthless. Between 65 and $63\frac{5}{8}$, you would take a partial loss, equal to the strike price minus the stock price minus the cost of the put. A table of your expiration profit/loss would be as Table 3.2

Coke	60	61	62	63	$63\frac{5}{8}$	64	65	70
Cost of put	$-1\frac{3}{8}$							
Value of put at expiration	5	4	3	2	$1\frac{3}{8}$	1	0	0
Profit/loss	$3\frac{5}{8}$	$2\frac{5}{8}$	$1\frac{5}{8}$	$\frac{5}{8}$	0	$-\frac{3}{8}$	$-1\frac{3}{8}$	$-1\frac{3}{8}$

Table 3.2 ■ Purchased Coke November 65 put

In graphic form, your expiration profit/loss would be as in Figure 3.2.

The multiplier for stock options at the Chicago Board Options Exchange (CBOE) is $100, therefore the cost of the put, and your maximum risk, would be $1\frac{3}{8}$ (1.375) × $100 = $137.50.

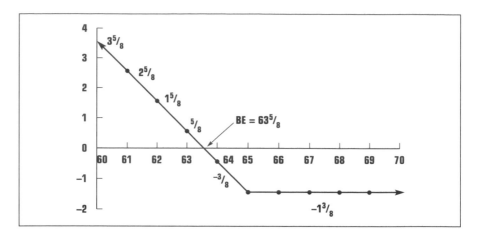

Fig 3.2 ■ **Graph of purchased November 65 Coke put**

Selling puts

Now let's consider the profit/loss position of the investor who sells the XYZ put. After all, you may decide that the put sale is the best strategy to pursue. Because the put buyer has the right to sell the underlying, the put seller, as a consequence, has the potential obligation to buy the underlying.

At expiration, the sale of the XYZ 100 put for 4 would be graphed as in Figure 3.3.

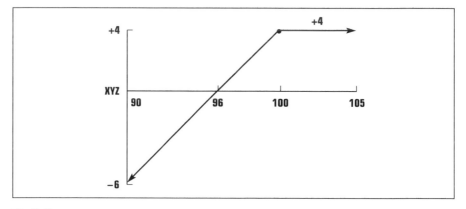

Fig 3.3 ■ **Selling a put**

This position should appear similar to that of the call sale, Figure 2.5. In fact, the profit/loss potential is exactly the same, but the market direction is opposite, or downward.

In tabular form, this profit/loss position would be as shown in Table 3.3.

XYZ	90	91	92	93	94	95	96	97	98	99	100	105
Income from put	4	4	4	4	4	4	4	4	4	4	4	4
Value of put at expiration	−10	−9	−8	−7	−6	−5	−4	−3	−2	−1	0	0
Profit/loss	−6	−5	−4	−3	−2	−1	0	1	2	3	4	4

Table 3.3 ■ **Selling a put**

The put seller's potential return is a maximum of 4 if XYZ remains at or above 100 when the contract expires. Between 100 and 96, a partial return is gained. 96 is the break-even level. Below 96, the put seller incurs a loss equal to the amount that XYZ may decline.

> The risk/return potential for the put seller is exactly opposite to the put buyer.

Again, the risk/return potential for the put seller is exactly opposite to the put buyer. The potential **return** of the put sale is the premium collected, 4. The potential **risk** is the full amount that XYZ may decline below 96.

[An investor may wish to purchase XYZ at a lower level than the current market price. As an alternative to an outright purchase, he may sell a put and thereby incur the potential obligation to purchase XYZ at the break-even level. The advantage is that he receives an income while awaiting a decline. The disadvantage is that XYZ may increase in price, and he will miss a buying opportunity, although he retains the income from the put sale. The other disadvantage is the same for all buyers of an underlying: XYZ may decline significantly below the purchase price, resulting in an effective loss.

For the investor who has a short position in XYZ, the sale of a put gives him the advantage of an income while he maintains his short position. The disadvantage is that he may give up downside profit if he must close his short position through an obligation to buy XYZ.

Practically speaking, there are few investors who adopt the latter strategy, although many market makers do, simply because they supply the demand for puts.]

Clearly then, as with calls, the greater risk of trading puts lies with the seller. He may be obligated to buy XYZ in a declining market. The put seller must therefore expect XYZ to remain stable or slightly higher. He must demand a fee that justifies the downside risk.

An example and a strategy

Suppose that Coke is, as before, trading at $67\frac{7}{16}$, and the December 60 puts are trading at $1\frac{1}{4}$. If you are decidedly bullish, you could sell one December 60 put. At expiration your break-even level would be the strike price minus the price of the put, or $58\frac{3}{4}$. Above 60, you would collect the premium. Below 60, you would be obligated to buy the stock, and your profit/loss is the closing price of the stock minus the strike price plus the premium income. A table of the expiration profit/loss would be as Table 3.4.

Coke	55	56	57	58	$58\frac{3}{4}$	59	60	65
Income from put	$1\frac{1}{4}$	-	-	-	-	-	-	-
Value of put at expiration	-5	-4	-3	-2	$-1\frac{1}{4}$	-1	0	0
Profit/loss	$-3\frac{3}{4}$	$-2\frac{3}{4}$	$-1\frac{3}{4}$	$-\frac{3}{4}$	0	$+\frac{1}{4}$	$+1\frac{1}{4}$	$+1\frac{1}{4}$

Table 3.4 ■ Expiration profit/loss for sold Coke December 60 put

In graphic form, the expiration profit/loss would be as shown in Figure 3.4.

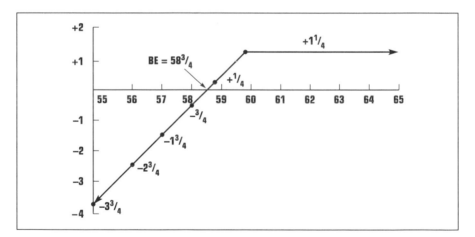

Fig 3.4 ■ Graph of sold December 60 Coke put

Remember that if Coke declines significantly, you are still obligated to purchase it at an effective price of $58\frac{3}{4}$. Be mindful that all markets can drop suddenly, leaving the investor virtually no opportunity to take corrective action. For this reason, *selling naked puts,* as this strategy is called, contains a high degree of risk. A preferred strategy is the *short put spread*, which is discussed in Part Two.

On the other hand, suppose you think that stock in Coke would be a good investment. If the stock is currently trading at $67\frac{7}{16}$, you may, quite reasonably, think that an effective purchase price of $58\frac{3}{4}$ represents good value. After all, this would represent a decline of almost 13 per cent. You may decide to sell the December 60 put as an alternative to buying the stock. If the stock remains above 60, then you are content to collect the $1\frac{1}{4}$ premium. You may even decide on a combined strategy of an outright stock purchase with put sales, i.e., you might purchase a number of shares at $67\frac{7}{16}$ and sell a number of December 60 puts, therefore averaging down the purchase price.

In order to apply the above strategy you must be convinced that the stock is good value at the level of the effective purchase price. In fact, it is not advisable to sell naked puts if you do not wish to own the stock or other underlying. Should you, as a result of employing this strategy, eventually purchase the stock, and should the stock, as it often does, decline below the purchase price, you must be secure in the knowledge that buying stock at the lowest point of a move is a matter only of luck. Few investors in 1932 bought the stocks in the DJIA when it was at 41.22.

Summary of the terms of the put contract

A put option is the right to sell the underlying asset at a specified price for a specified time period. The put buyer has the right, but not the obligation, to sell the underlying. The put seller has the obligation to buy the underlying at the put buyer's discretion. These are the terms of the put contract.

> **A put option is the right to sell the underlying asset at a specified price for a specified time period.**

A comparison of calls and puts

Now that you've learned how calls and puts operate, it will be constructive to compare them.

The **call buyer** has the right to **buy** the underlying, consequently the **call seller** may have the obligation to **sell** the underlying.

The **put buyer** has the right to **sell** the underlying, consequently the **put seller** may have the obligation to **buy** the underlying.

If the underlying is a futures contract, the above terms are modified.

The **call buyer** has the right to take a **long position** in the underlying, consequently the **call seller** may have the obligation to take a **short position** in the underlying.

The **put buyer** has the right to take a **short position** in the underlying, consequently the **put seller** may have the obligation to take a **long position** in the underlying.

If these statements seem confusing, bear in mind that they are related to each other by simple logic: if one is true, then the others must be true. It may be helpful to review the graphs and tables presented. As you work through the examples in the next few chapters, familiarity will help comprehension.

Conclusion

Markets can be bullish, bearish, or range-bound, and different options strategies are suitable to each. Any particular strategy cannot be said to be better than any other. These strategies, and those that follow, vary in terms of their risk/return potential. They accommodate the degree of risk that each investor thinks is appropriate. It is this flexible and limiting approach to risk that makes options trading appropriate to many different kinds of investors.

Questions

Here are some questions on puts, and on the difference between calls and puts. Again, don't expect to know all the answers.

1 What is the similarity and difference between:
   a) a long call and a short put?
   b) a long put and a short call?

2 A long call provides downside protection, while a long put provides upside protection. True or false? why or why not?

3 Boeing is currently trading at 36, and the May 35 puts are trading at $3\frac{1}{8}$.
   a) If you buy one of these puts at the current market price, what is your break-even level?
   b) What is the maximum amount that you can gain?
   c) What is the maximum amount that you can lose?
   d) Answer questions a–c for a sale of this put.

e) If you sell one of these puts at the current market price, what is the potential effective purchase price of the stock at expiration?

f) The multiplier for this options contract is $100. What is the cash value of one of these puts?

g) If at May expiration Boeing closes at 30, what is the profit for the put buyer, and what is the loss for the put seller?

h) Write a profit/loss table for a sale of this put at expiration.

i) Draw a graph of the expiration profit/loss for a sale this put.

4   IBM is trading at 149, and the November 145 puts are trading at $3\frac{1}{4}$.

a) If you buy one of these puts at the current market price, what is your break-even level?

b) What is the maximum amount that you can gain?

c) What is the maximum amount that you can lose?

d) Answer questions a-c for a sale of this put.

e) If you sell one of these puts at the current market price, what is the potential effective purchase price of the stock at expiration?

f) The multiplier for this options contract is $100. What is the cash value of one of these puts?

g) If at November expiration IBM closes at 135, what is the profit for the put buyer, and what is the loss for the put seller?

h) Write an expiration profit/loss table for a buy of this put.

i) Draw a graph of the expiration profit/loss for a buy of this put.

5   The Options Exchange Index (OEX) is currently priced at 531.97, and the January 500 puts are currently trading at $17\frac{3}{8}$. The stock market has recently rallied from its lows for the year, and you, as a pension fund manager, think that all the good news is in the market. You would like to protect a portion of your stock portfolio from a year-end downside retracement.

a) If you buy one of these puts at the current market price, what is your break-even level?

b) What is the maximum amount that you can gain?

c) What is the maximum amount that you can lose?

d) Answer questions a-c for a sale of this put.

e) If you sell one of these puts at the current market price, what is the potential effective purchase price of the index at expiration?

f) The multiplier for this options contract is $100. What is the cash value of one of these puts?

g) If at January expiration the OEX settles 10 per cent below its current price, what is the profit for the put buyer, and what is the loss for the put seller?

h) Write a profit/loss table at expiration for a buy of this put with the OEX from 460 to 510 in intervals of 10 points.

i) Draw a graph of the expiration profit/loss for a buy of this put.

6   At the LIFFE, British Airways is currently trading at 434p (£4.34), and the January 420 puts are trading at 39p (£ 0.39).

a) If you buy one of these puts at the current market price, what is your break-even level?

b) What is the maximum amount that you can gain?

c) What is the maximum amount that you can lose?

d) Answer questions a-c for a sale of this put.

e) If you sell one of these puts at the current market price, what is the potential effective purchase price of the shares at expiry?

f) The multiplier for this options contract is £1,000. What is the cash value of one of these puts?

g) If at January expiry British Airways closes at 400, what is the profit for the put seller, and what is the loss for the put buyer?

h) Write a profit/loss table at expiry for a sale of this put at 10-point intervals from 370 to 430.

i) Draw a graph of the expiration profit/loss for a sale of this put

7   This question involves put options on the Chicago Board of Trade (CBOT) Treasury Bond futures contract. The futures contract trades in ticks of 32 per full futures point, i.e. $1.00 = \frac{32}{32}$. The options contract, however, trades in ticks of 64 per full futures point, i.e. $1.00 = \frac{64}{64}$. An options tick is simply half the value of a futures tick. Both contracts have a multiplier of $1,000, therefore $\frac{1}{32} = \$31.25$, and of course, $\frac{1}{64} = \$15.625$.

December Bonds are currently trading at 129.26 ($129\frac{26}{32}$), and the December 129 puts are currently trading at .58 ($\frac{58}{64}$). (A 129 price for bonds is possible during a flight to quality.)

a) What is the value of the December 129 put?

b) If you buy one of these puts at the current market price, what is your break-even level?

[The formula is the same for all put options, i.e., break-even = strike price minus price of put. Here, you must first convert the futures strike price from a decimal listing into the equivalent number of options ticks. Next you subtract the put price from the converted strike price. Then you reconvert the break-even level into a decimal listing. The process is tedious but not difficult.]

c) What is the maximum amount that you can gain?

d) What is the maximum amount that you can lose?

e) Answer questions a-c for a sale of this put.

f) If you sell one of these puts at the current market price, what is the potential effective purchase price of the December futures contract at expiration?

8 At the LIFFE, Shell Transport is currently trading at $356\frac{1}{2}$p (£3.56$\frac{1}{2}$), and the April 330 puts are trading at $28\frac{1}{2}$p (£0.28$\frac{1}{2}$). This year's range for Shell Transport is 312 to 499$\frac{1}{2}$. The oil sector is currently under pressure because the global ecomomy is sluggish and the price of oil is approximately $13 per barrel. You think that Shell Transport would be a good long-term investment, however, and you want to compare a purchase of shares to a sale of the April put.

a) If you sell the put, what is your potential purchase price?

b) If you bought the shares at $356\frac{1}{2}$, at what level would an increase in their price by April equal the income from the put?

c) Suppose you sell the put instead of buying the shares. What is the potential savings from a purchase of shares if assigned on the put compared to the potential opportunity cost of not buying the shares, should Shell Transport regain its former high by April expiry?

d) Suppose you sell the put and place a stop order to buy the shares at 385. Shell rallies to 385 and you are filled on your stop order at that price. Shell then remains above 330 through April expiry and your put expires worthless. What is the effective purchase price of the shares?

e) If you buy 1,000 shares at the current market price of $356\frac{1}{2}$ and you sell one April 330 put at $28\frac{1}{2}$, what is your average cost if the shares decline and you are assigned on the put?

Puts are often a confusing subject to those new to the options markets. But once you get used to them, they becomes as easy as tying your necktie with a mirror.

Answers

1 **a)** Both are a potential purchase or a potential long position. The long call has the right, while the short put has the obligation.

   b) Both are a potential sale or a potential short position. The long put has the right, while the short call has the obligation.

2 True, because a long call is a limited risk alternative to the purchase of an undelying, while a long put is a limited risk alternative to the sale of an underlying.

3 **a)** $31\frac{7}{8}$

   b) $31\frac{7}{8}$

   c) $3\frac{1}{8}$

   d) $31\frac{7}{8}, 3\frac{1}{8}, 31\frac{7}{8}$

   e) Obligation to buy stock at strike price minus income from put, or $35 - 3\frac{1}{8} = 31\frac{7}{8}$.

   f) $312.50

   g) Strike price minus price of stock at expiration. $35 - 30 = 5$, or expiration value of put.

   5 minus traded value of put at $3\frac{1}{8} = 1\frac{7}{8}$

   $1\frac{7}{8} = 1.875$

   $1.875 \times$ contract multiplier of $100 = $187.50 profit for buyer, loss for seller

   h)

Boeing	25	30	31	$31\frac{7}{8}$	32	33	34	35	40
Income from put	$3\frac{1}{8}$	-	-	-	-	-	-	-	-
Value of put at expiration	–10	–5	–4	$3\frac{1}{8}$	–3	–2	–1	0	0
Profit/loss	$-6\frac{7}{8}$	$-1\frac{7}{8}$	$-\frac{7}{8}$	0	$+\frac{1}{8}$	$+1\frac{1}{8}$	$+2\frac{1}{8}$	$+3\frac{1}{8}$	$+3\frac{1}{8}$

   Answer 3h ■ Sale of Boeing May 35 put

   i) See next page.

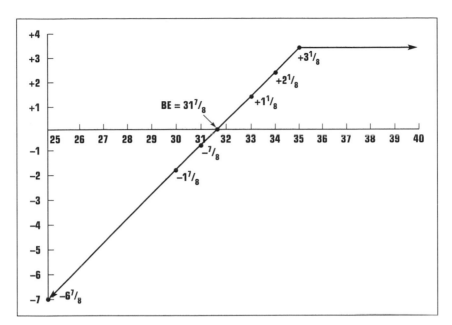

Answer 3i ■ Sale of Boeing May 35 put

4 a) $141\frac{3}{4}$

   b) $141\frac{3}{4}$

   c) $3\frac{1}{4}$

   d) $141\frac{3}{4}, 3\frac{1}{4}, 141\frac{3}{4}$

   e) Obligation to buy stock at strike price minus income from put, or
      $145 - 3\frac{1}{4} = 141\frac{3}{4}$.

   f) $325

   g) Strike price minus price of stock at expiration. $145 - 135 = 10$, or
      expiration value of put.
      10 minus traded value of put at $3\frac{1}{4} = 6\frac{3}{4}$
      $6\frac{3}{4} = 6.75$
      $6.75 \times$ contract multiplier of $100 = $675 profit for buyer, loss for seller

   h)

IBM	135	140	141	$141\frac{3}{4}$	142	143	144	145	150
Traded value of put	$-3\frac{1}{4}$	- - -	- - -	- - -	- - -	- - -	- - -	- - -	- - -
Expiration value of put	10	5	4	$3\frac{1}{4}$	3	2	1	0	0
Profit/loss	$6\frac{3}{4}$	$1\frac{3}{4}$	$\frac{3}{4}$	0	$-\frac{1}{4}$	$-1\frac{1}{4}$	$-2\frac{1}{4}$	$-3\frac{1}{4}$	$-3\frac{1}{4}$

Answer 4h ■ Purchase of IBM November 145 put

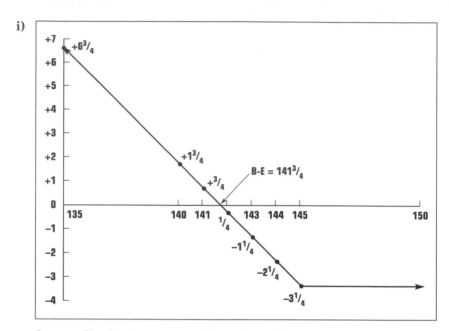

Answer 4i ■ **Purchase of IBM November 145 put**

5   **a)** $482\frac{5}{8}$ or 482.625

    b) 482.625

    c) $17\frac{3}{8}$

    d) 482.625, $17\frac{3}{8}$, 482.625

    e) Obligation to buy index at strike price minus income from put, or $500 - 17\frac{3}{8} = 482\frac{5}{8}$

    f) $100 \times 17.375 = \$1737.50$

    g) $531.97 - 53.20 = 478.77$, or index level with 10 per cent retracement

        Strike price minus price of index at expiration. $500 - 478.77 = 21.23$, or expiration value of put.

        21.23 minus traded value of put at 17.375 = 3.86

        3.86 × contract multiplier of $100 = \$386$ profit for buyer, loss for seller

    h) See next page.

    i) See next page.

6   **a)** 381

    b) 381

    c) 39

    d) 381, 39, 381

5 h)

OEX	460	470	480	482 5/8	490	500	510
Cost of put	−17 3/8						
Expiration value of put	40	30	20	17 3/8	10	0	0
Profit/loss	22 5/8	12 5/8	2 5/8	0	−7 3/8	−17 3/8	−17 3/8

Answer 5h ■ Purchase of OEX January 500 put

5 i)

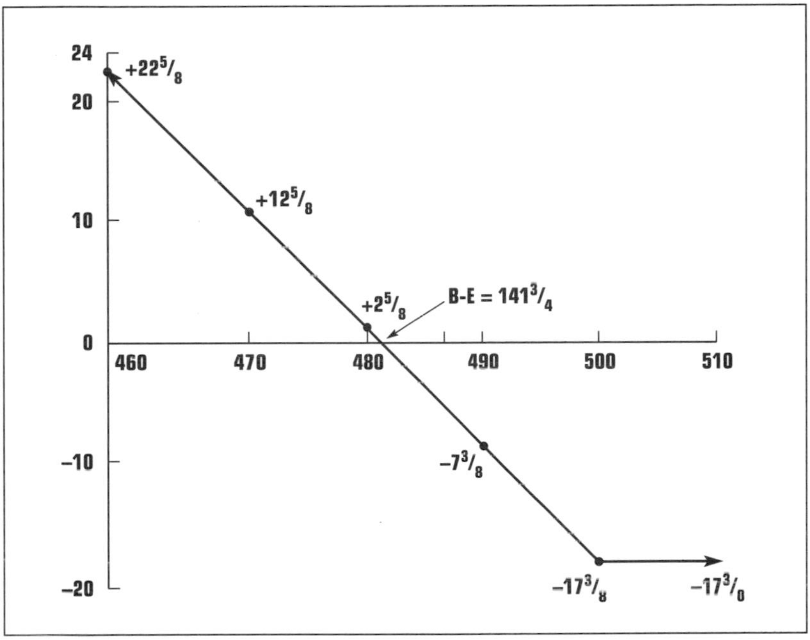

Answer 5i ■ Purchase of OEX January 500 put

6 e) Obligation to buy shares at strike price minus income from put, or 420 – 39 = 381.

f) £390

g) Strike price minus price of shares at expiration. 420 – 400 = 20, or expiration value of put.

Income from put minus cost to redeem, or buy back put, 39 – 20 = 19 0.19 × contract multiplier of £1,000 = £190 profit for seller, loss for buyer.

h)

British Airways	370	380	381	390	400	410	420	430
Cost of put	−39							
Expiration value of put	−50	−40	−39	−30	−20	−10	0	0
Profit/loss	−11	−1	0	+9	+19	+29	+39	+39

Answer 6h ■ Sale of British Airways January 420 put

i)

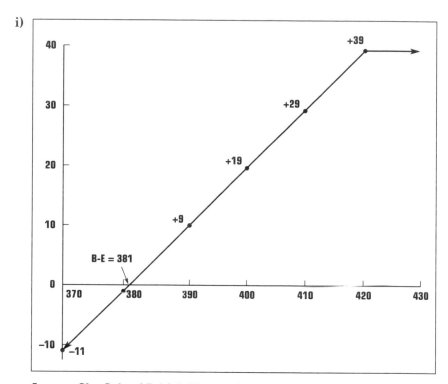

Answer 6i ■ Sale of British Airways January 420 put

7) a) $\frac{58}{64} \times \$1,000 = \$906.25$

b) $129.00 = 128\frac{32}{32} = 128\frac{64}{64}$, or strike price in options ticks

$128\frac{64}{64} - \frac{58}{64}, = 128\frac{6}{64} = 128\frac{3}{32} = 128.03$, or break-even level

c) 128.03

d) .58

e) 128.03, .58, 128.03

f) Obligation to buy futures contract at strike price minus income from put, or $129.00 - .58 = 128\frac{6}{64} = 128.03$ futures price.

8 **a)** Strike price minus income from put. $330 - 28\frac{1}{2} = 301\frac{1}{2}$.

b) Shares purchase price plus income from put. $356\frac{1}{2} + 28\frac{1}{2} = 385$

c) $356\frac{1}{2} - 301\frac{1}{2} = 55$ potential savings. $499\frac{1}{2} - 385 = 114\frac{1}{2}$ potential opportunity cost.

d) Cost of shares minus income from put: $385 - 28\frac{1}{2} = 356\frac{1}{2}$. Remember that before expiry your put contract is still outstanding, and if Shell retraces to below 330, you will be obligated to buy 1,000 shares. If you don't want to make an additional purchase, then buy back your put at the current market price. This will raise the effective purchase price of your shares.

e) Cost of purchase via put is strike price minus income from put, or $330 - 28\frac{1}{2} = 301\frac{1}{2}$. Average cost of shares is $(301\frac{1}{2} + 356\frac{1}{2}) \div 2 = 329$p, or £3.29.

Pricing and behaviour

Now that you understand the nature of calls and puts, you need to know how they are priced and how they behave. In this chapter you will learn that options are both dependent on, and independent of, their underlying

Options are both dependent on, and independent of, their underlying asset.

asset. They have lives of their own because they are traded separately as hedges. They indicate market sentiment, or the outlook for price changes in the underlying.

Price levels

We will begin with a straightforward options contract. Its underlying is the short-term cost of money in the US. Table 4.1 is the Eurodollar futures contract, traded at the Chicago Mercantile Exchange, the CME.

Strike price	93.50	93.75	94.00	94.25	94.50	94.75	95.00
Call value	$.80\frac{1}{2}$	.56	.32	.12	.04	.02	.01
Put value	—	.01	.02	$.06\frac{1}{2}$	.23	.46	.70

Table 4.1 ■ December Eurodollar Options

On this day the December futures contract settled at $94.30\frac{1}{2}$, or an equivalent interest rate of 5.695 per cent. As the interest rate falls, the futures contract increases; as the interest rate rises, the price of the futures contract decreases. An investor wishing to hedge a rise in the interest rate to 6 per cent could pay .02 for the 94.00 put. An investor wishing to hedge a fall in the interest rate to 5.5 per cent could pay .04 for the 94.50 call. The contract multiplier is $25, which means that the 94.50 call has a value of 4 × $25, or $100. There are 132 days until the options contracts expire on December 14.

The number of different options contracts listed is designed to accommodate investors with different levels of interest rate exposure. Each listed price level is known as a **strike price**, e.g., 94.00, 94.25, 94.50, etc.

When an option is closest to the underlying, it is termed **at-the-money** (ATM). Here, both the 94.25 call and the 94.25 put are at-the-money. When a call is above the underlying, it is termed **out-of-the-money** (OTM), e.g., all the calls at 94.50, 94.75 and 95.00. When a put is below the underlying, it is also out-of-the-money, e.g., the puts at 93.75 and 94.00.

When a call is below the underlying, it is termed **in-the-money** (ITM), e.g., the calls at 93.75 and 94.00. When a put is above the underlying, it is also in-the-money, e.g. all the puts at 94.50, 94.75 and 95.00.

Generally speaking, the options most traded are those at-the-money or out-of-the-money. If an upside hedge is needed, then at-the-money, or out-of-the money calls will work, and they are less costly than in-the-money calls. For a downside hedge, the same reasoning applies to puts.

> Generally speaking, the options most traded are those at-the-money or out-of-the-money.

Aspects of premium

The premium of an option corresponds to its probability of expiring in the money. The 94.75 call and the 94.00 put are each worth only .02 because most likely the underlying will not reach these levels before expiration. More specifically, the .02 value of each of these is termed the **time premium**.

The premium of an in-the-money option consists of two components. The first of these is the amount equal to the difference between the strike price and the price of the underlying, and it is termed the **intrinsic value**. The second component is the **time premium**. The 94.00 call, with the underlying at $94.30\frac{1}{2}$, is worth .32; it has an intrinsic value of $.30\frac{1}{2}$ and contains a time premium of $.01\frac{1}{2}$.

When an option is deeply in the money, it will trade as a proxy for the underlying, and its premium will consist of intrinsic value only. This kind of option is said to be **at parity** with the underlying. The 93.50 call, with a value of $.80\frac{1}{2}$, is at parity with the underlying at $94.30\frac{1}{2}$.

An at-the-money option will contain the most time premium because there the two advantages to owning an option are equal and greatest. A call that is exactly at-the-money, whose strike price equals the price of the underlying, can profit fully from upside market movement, less the cost of the call. As an alternative to purchasing the underlying, it can also save the call buyer the full amount that the underlying may decline, less the cost of the call. With an at-the-money call, the potential profit theoretically equals the potential savings. An at-the-money put has the same **profit/ savings potential**.

Duration and time decay

Another aspect that determines the amount of an option's premium is, quite reasonably, the time till expiration. A long-term hedge will cost more than a short-term hedge. Time decay, however, is not linear. Figure 4.1 illustrates that an option loses its value at an accelerating rate as it approaches expiration.

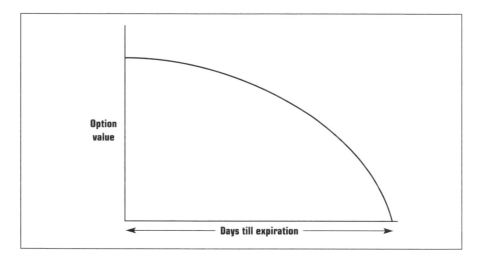

Fig 4.1 ■ Value of option with respect to time

Another way of stating this is that the proportion of an option's daily time decay to its value increases toward expiration. Using two options based on Corn futures, Table 4.2 illustrates this in percentage terms.

Note that the out-of the-money option enters its accelerated time decay period much earlier than the at-the-money option. This is true for in-the-money options as well.

To the trader this means that the risk/return potential also accelerates with time. Because near-term options cost less, they have the potential to profit more from an unexpected, large move in the underlying. However, their time decay can be severe. The risk of time decay is great, but the return of substantial savings or large profit is also great.

Options with accelerated time decay are best utilized by professionals who are certain of their outlook for the underlying at expiration. The

December Corn at $2.20 Implied volatility at 20 per cent				
Days until expiration (DTE)	120 DTE	90 DTE	60 DTE	30 DTE
Price of December 220 call with multiplier included	493.75	431.25	350.00	250.00
Cost of time decay per day	1.97	2.31	2.88	4.13
Daily time decay as percentage of option's value or theta/price ratio	0.40%	0.54%	0.82%	1.65%
Price of December 250 call with multiplier included	87.50	56.25	25.00	0
Cost of time decay per day	1.16	1.10	.90	–
Daily time decay as percentage of option's value or theta/price ratio	1.33%	1.96%	3.60%	–

Table 4.2 ■ **December Corn calls**

Data courtesy of FutureSource – Bridge; the percentage calculations are the author's.

risks can be reduced by spreading, but for most investors a straight long call or put position with 2 per cent time decay should either be closed or 'rolled' to a later contract month. Trading time decay is discussed further in Part Three.

Interest rates, dividends, and margin versus cash payment

It is best to check with the exchange where you wish to trade in order to determine whether margin or cash payment applies. The following are general guidelines for interest rate and dividend pricing characteristics. Except under special circumstances, interest rate and dividend pricing components are outweighed by the volatility component of options.

> It is best to check with the exchange where you wish to trade in order to determine whether margin or cash payment applies.

Futures options

On most exchanges a purchased option on a futures contract must be paid for in full at the outset. Accordingly, its price will be discounted by the cost of carry on the option until expiration. Given the low (in late 1999), or historically average, rates of interest, this discount is minor when compared to other pricing components. This discount becomes greater, however, with deep in-the-money options.

The LIFFE, however, charges margin for purchased options on futures contracts, and therefore the interest on the cash or bonds held by the clearing firm is retained by the options buyer.

All sold or short options on most exchanges have margin requirements because their potential risks are greater than bought or long options.

Stock options

The situation is different for options on stocks. Because a call is an alternative to buying stock, the call holder has the use of the cash that he would otherwise use to purchase the stock. The cost of a call is therefore increased by the cost of carry on the stock via the strike price of the option, until the option's expiration.

Because the holder of a call on stocks does not receive dividends, the cost of the call is discounted by the amount of dividends for the duration of the call contract.

For example, suppose DuPont pays a dividend of $.35 on 14 December. The current short-term interest rate is 5 per cent as determined by the December Eurodollar futures contract at 95.00. There are 60 days until the DuPont options expire on the third Friday of January. The interest rate and dividend components of the DuPont January 55 call can be estimated as follows. A more accurate calculation is obtained with an options model.

a) $55 \times \frac{60}{360} \times .05 = \$ .46$ interest added to call price

b) $ .35 dividend subtracted from call price

c) $ .46 – .35 = \$ .11$, total added to call price, approximately $\frac{1}{8}$

Note that the price of the stock is not a factor in this calculation. In fact, DuPont was trading at 57 at the time of this example. There is a difference of opinion, however. Some traders think that the current price of the stock is a more accurate basis from which to calculate the interest rate component of the option. Practically speaking, the difference between these two methods is not significant unless the options are far out-of-the-money with many days till expiration. Again, an options model accounts for this. More important would be a change in the dividend or the interest rate until expiration. Also note that unless special circumstances occur with respect to dividends and interest rates, these pricing components are far less significant than the volatility component.

Puts on stocks have the opposite pricing characteristics to calls with respect to cost of carry and dividends. Purchased calls and puts on stocks are paid for in cash up-front on most exchanges. Sold or short options, however, are margined because short calls incur potentially unlimited risk, and short puts incur extreme risk.

Options on stock indexes

A stock index is a proxy for all the stocks that comprise it. Calls and puts on a stock index are priced according to the cost of carry of the index, and the amount of dividends contained in the index. The costs of carry and dividends are added and discounted in the same manner as options on individual stocks. These options are also paid for in cash.

Long and short options positions

In practice, once a call or put is bought, it is considered to be a **long options position**. 'I'm long 10, June 550 puts,' you might say. Conversely, a call or put sold is considered to be a **short options position**. 'I'm too short for my own good,' means that you have sold too many calls or puts, or both, for your peace of mind.

It may be helpful to think that when the terms 'long' and 'short' are applied to options, they designate **ownership**. The same terms applied to a position in the underlying designate exposure to **market direction**. To be short puts is to be long the market, i.e. you want the market to move upward. The following chapter on deltas clarifies this.

Exercise and assignment

In practice, most options are not held through expiration. They are closed beforehand because the holders of options do not want to take delivery

> **In practice, most options are not held through expiration.**

of the underlyings. The exceptions are options on stock indexes and options on short-term interest rate contracts such as Eurodollars. In these contracts, no delivery of an underlying is involved.

Long and short options positions that are in the money at expiration will be converted into underlying positions through **exercise** and **assignment**, respectively. The clearing firms manage this procedure. The resulting positions are similar to those stated at the end of Chapter 3 under *a comparison of calls and puts* (pages 27–28). There are slight differences for each type of contract.

Stocks

Through exercise, the holder of a long call will buy, at the strike price, the number of shares in the underlying contract. Through assignment, the holder of a short call will sell the shares. If the short call holder does not own stock to sell, he will be assigned a short stock position.

Through exercise, the holder of a long put will sell, at the strike price, the number of shares in the underlying contract. If the long put holder does not own shares to sell, he will be assigned a short stock position. Through assignment, the holder of a short put will buy the shares.

Futures

Through exercise, the holder of a long call will acquire, at the strike price, a long futures position in the underlying. Through assignment, the holder of a short call will acquire a short futures position at the strike price. On many futures exchanges, an options contract expires one month before its underlying futures contract.

For example, expiration for options on November soybeans at the Chicago Board of Trade (CBOT) normally occurs on the third Friday in October. If on the day of expiration the November futures contract settles at 552, then the holder of a long November 550 call will exercise to a long November futures position at the price of 550. The holder of a short November 550 call will be assigned a short November futures position at a price of 550. In this case the former long call holder obviously has a credit of 2, but he may have originally paid more or less than that for his November 550 call.

Through exercise, the holder of a long put will acquire, at the strike price, a short futures position in the underlying. Through assignment, the holder of a short put will acquire a long futures position at the strike price.

For example, if on the day of expiration the November soybeans futures contract settles at 552, then the holder of a long November 575 put exercises to a short November futures position at a price of 575. The holder of a short November 575 put is assigned a long November futures position at 575. The 23 credit for the former long put holder is no indication of the price at which he originally traded the option.

Cash settled contracts: stock indexes and short-term interest rate contracts

Through exercise, the holder of a long call will receive the cash differential between the price of the index or underlying and the strike price of the call. Through assignment, the holder of a short call will pay the cash differential.

For example, if at expiration the OEX settles at 527.00, the holder of an expiring long 525 call position receives 2.00, while the holder of an expiring short 525 call position pays 2.00. The contract multiplier for the OEX is $100, so in this case $200 changes hands.

Through exercise, the holder of a long put will receive the cash differential between the strike price of the put and the price of the index or underlying. Through assignment, the holder of a short put will pay the cash differential.

For example, if at expiration the OEX settles at 527.00, the holder of an expiring long 530 put position receives 3.00, while the holder of an expiring short 530 put position pays 3.00.

The same procedures apply to short-term interest rate contracts such as Eurodollars and Short Sterling. For example, in either of these contracts if an option settles one tick in the money, then the long is credited with one tick times the contract multiplier, and the short is debited one tick times the contract multiplier. The multiplier for Eurodollars is $25, and the multiplier for Short Sterling is £12.50.

Pin risk

Pin risk is rare, but it is important to know about. Occasionally, options expire exactly at-the-money, i.e. the underlying equals the strike price at the time of expiration. We say that these options, both the call and the put, are **pinned**. This causes a problem for options on stocks and options on futures contracts, but not for options on stock indexes and short-term interest rate futures contracts.

While there is no immediate profit to be made from exercising these options, those who hold them may have a short-term directional outlook for the underlying that warrants exercising them.

For example, if the expiration price of XYZ is 100, the owner of a 100 call may exercise because he thinks that XYZ will increase in price during the next trading session, or he may simply want to own it while risking a short-term decline. The owner of a 100 put may exercise for the opposite reasons.

The problem lies with the holder of a short position in either of these options. He may or may not be assigned a position in XYZ. The assignment process is carried out on a random basis by the clearing firms. If the short option holder is assigned, he will be notified by the opening of the next trading session. If as usual he does not want to keep a position in XYZ, he will need to make an offsetting buy/sell transaction at the opening. If the market opens against him, he will cover his position at a loss.

There is no pin risk with cash settled index options such as the OEX and the FTSE-100 because with these contracts there is no underlying futures contract or quantity of shares to be assigned, or to exercise to. The same is true of most short-term interest rate contracts such as Eurodollars and Short Sterling.

How to manage pin risk

If you are short an option that is close to the underlying with a week until expiration, it is advisable to buy it back rather than ring the last amount of time decay from it and risk an unwanted position in the underlying. If you wait until the morning of expiration, you may find that you are joined by others with the same position, and you may be forced to pay up to get out.

European versus American style

An option is **European style** if it cannot be exercised before expiration. The only way to close this style of option before expiration is to make the opposing buy/sell transaction. One example is the SPX options on the Standard and Poor's 500 Index (S&P 500) traded at the Chicago Board Options Exchange (CBOE). Another example is the ESX options (at the 25 and 75 strikes) on the Financial Times 100 Index (FTSE 100) traded at the London International Financial Futures and Options Exchange (LIFFE)

More prevalent is the **American-style** option, which can be exercised at any time before expiration. If such an option becomes so deeply in-the-money that it trades at parity with the underlying, then it has served its purpose and represents cash tied up. As a result, it can be sold, or it can be exercised to a position in the underlying stock or futures contract. In the case of a stock index, such as the OEX, it can be exercised for the cash differential. Most stock options and futures options are American style.

Black-Scholes model

The Black-Scholes options pricing model assumes that the option is held until expiration. This model is therefore appropriate for European-style options, but it is less appropriate for American-style options. For index options subject to early exercise, it must be modified significantly.

Early exercise premium

Because American-style options can be exercised before expiration, those in-the-money will often contain an additional early exercise premium. This is not a significant amount for most options on futures contracts. It is more significant for puts on individual stocks because they can be exercised to sell stock and as a result, interest is earned on the cash.

Early exercise premium is a highly significant amount for in-the-money index options such as the OEX options on the S&P 100 traded at the CBOE, and the SEI options (at the 00 and 50 strikes) on the FTSE-100 traded at the LIFFE. The reason is that at the end of each trading session, both of these contracts close at different times from their respective, underlying indexes. Their in-the-money options, especially their puts, can be driven to parity with the cash index, and can then become an exercise. To be assigned in this manner often results in a loss. It is advisable not to sell, or have a short position in, the in-the-money options of these two contracts.

Conversely, because of the potential for early exercise, long out-of-the-money or at-the-money positions in the above two contracts can profit significantly. As these options become in the money, their early exercise premium increases drastically. Holders of these options then profit twofold.

This brings to mind a story concerning risk and early exercise premium.

I have a personal rule with American styled index options, and that is always to cover a short position when it becomes .50 delta. I made this rule after one or two incidents when I was short FTSE-100 options and they went deep in-the-money on me. Their early exercise premium mounted, and I became reluctant to pay up in order to buy them back. I lost more sleep than usual, and then eventually, a few days or weeks later, they became an exercise at the close. As a result, I lost my hedge, i.e., I was no longer delta neutral, which is what all market makers strive to be. The next morning at the opening, the market moved against me and I took a loss.

One or two incidents such as this are not serious, but I could see the potential for serious damage in a highly volatile market. It was then that I decided on my rule. Subsequently, I paid up whenever I had a short position that went to .50 deltas. This wasn't often, but it seemed as if it was because it always cost me. Anyway, that was the price of a good night's sleep, or just a better night's sleep.

A year or so later, during mid-1997, the emerging market crisis started to develop. At first, the US seemed to ignore it, and that held London up. Still, I thought it was time to buy a little extra premium in case the US changed its mind. The extra premium cost me in time decay, especially because the FTSE implied was around 20 per cent. In the back of my mind was, and always is, October 19, 1987.

In October 1997 the UK market started to weaken because of its exposure to Hong Kong, and one day towards the close, I found myself short a number of 4800 puts which were at-the-money, or .50 deltas. A rule is a rule, I said, which was some consolation for the amount I paid up to buy them back. I was now longer premium than I generally like to be, and because we were at the close, I knew I was going to bear the cost of the time decay.

That night the US cracked. The next morning, the BBC news was calling for serious losses in London, and I knew there were going to be casualties at the opening. I arrived early at the office, and I had my clerks do an extensive risk analysis, though I knew, as all market makers do, that at a time like this, options theory takes a back seat. I went to the floor and wedged my way into the crowd, and I waited, knowing that I was covered.

The bell sounded and the shouting began, and after a few brief stops the FTSE landed at 4400. The traders who were short options were screaming to buy them back, paying any price from those willing to sell. The implied leaped to 70 per cent before settling down to a cool 50 per cent after the opening. I made few trades that day, but they were the ones I wanted to make. I had my best day ever.

One lesson from this is obvious. Make a plan to cover your risk and stick to it. Your goal here is not to make money but to avoid taking a serious loss. Had I not covered my short options over the course of a year or more, I would have been one of the casualties. My profit on that day more than offset all my days of paying up.

> Make a plan to cover your risk and stick to it.

Another lesson is that by covering risk, you leave your mind clear to deal with the circumstance at hand. You can make reasonable trading decisions. This is equally true for an extraordinary event or for a more routine trading day.

Questions on pricing

1   If IBM is trading at 150, the 130 puts and the 180 calls are both out-of-the-money? True or false?

2   Microsoft is trading at $104\frac{5}{8}$. The August 100 calls are quoted at 7, and the August 100 puts are quoted at $1\frac{1}{4}$. What are the intrinsic and time values of the options?

3 At the LIFFE, Prudential is trading at $741\frac{1}{2}$. The November 750 calls are quoted at 39, and the November 750 puts are quoted at 45. What are the intrinsic and time values of the options?

4 Parity options contain approximately equal amounts of intrinsic and time premiums? True or false?

5 Why do at-the-money options contain the most time premium?

6 Which option or options have the most accelerated time decay as they approach expiration?

   a) In-the-money option

   b) At-the-money option

   c) Out-of-the-money option

7 Which options always require margin?

   a) Long puts

   b) Short calls

   c) Short puts

   d) Long calls

8 Concerning options on stocks or shares, which of these statements are true?

   a) The short-term interest rate is added to the price of a call.

   b) The dividends until expiration are added to the price of a call.

   c) The dividends until expiration are subtracted from the price of a put.

   d) The short-term interest rate is subtracted from the price of a put.

9 Which positions are potentially long the underlying, and which positions are potentially short the underlying?

   a) Long calls

   b) Short puts

   c) Long puts

   d) Short calls

10 You are short one IBM 140 put at expiration, and IBM has closed at 138. Do you exercise, or will you be assigned? What is your resulting position and at what price?

11 At the LIFFE, you are long one Glaxo 1800 call at expiration, and Glaxo has closed at $1825\frac{1}{2}$. Do you exercise, or will you be assigned? What is your resulting position and at what price?

12 It is the third week in November, and the December Corn options contracts have expired. You are short one December 280 Corn call, and the December futures contract has settled at $284\frac{1}{4}$. Do you exercise, or will you be assigned? What is your resulting position, if any, and at what price?

13 You are long one OEX 520 call at expiration and the closing index price is 529.45. Do you exercise, or will you be assigned? What is your resulting position, if any, and at what price?

14 At the LIFFE, you are short one FTSE 5550 put at expiration and the closing index price is 5479.6. Do you exercise, or will you be assigned? What is your resulting position, if any, and at what price?

15 You have previously sold one Texas Instruments November 65 call at $4\frac{1}{2}$. It is now three weeks until expiration and the call is worth $1\frac{7}{8}$. The stock is at $63\frac{5}{8}$, and it has been ranging from 62 to 66 in the last two weeks, and you expect it to continue to do so for the foreseeable future. You would like to continue to collect time decay. What do you do?

16 A European styled call can only be exercised when it is in-the-money? True or false?

17 Early exercise premium is a major component of all in-the-money American styled put options? True or false?

Answers

1 True.

2 Call intrinsic, $104\frac{5}{8} - 100 = 4\frac{5}{8}$; call time, $7 - 4\frac{5}{8} = 2\frac{3}{8}$. Put time value = $1\frac{1}{4}$; no put intrinsic value.

3 Call, no intrinsic; time value is 39
Put intrinsic is $750 - 741\frac{1}{2} = 8\frac{1}{2}$; time value is $45 - 8\frac{1}{2} = 36\frac{1}{2}$.

4 False; parity options contain only intrinsic value or premium.

5 Because they are the only options that hedge the underlying for equal amounts of upside and downside movement.

6 All have accelerated time decay.

7 b and c, all short options require margin.

8 **a)** True.

   b) False.

   c) False.

   d) True.

9 **a)** Long.

   b) Long.

   c) Short.

   d) Short.

10 You will be assigned a purchase of 100 shares at 140.

11 You exercise, and you will then purchase 1,000 shares at 1800p [£18.00].

12 You will be assigned one short December futures contract at 280.

13 You exercise, and you will receive the cash differential between the index price and the strike price of the option. 529.45 – 520 = 9.45. You have no remaining position. Remember the contract multiplier is $100, therefore you receive $945.

14 You will be assigned, and you will pay the cash differential between the strike price and the index price. 5550 – 5479.6 = 70.4. You have no remaining position. Remember that the multiplier is £10, therefore you pay £704.

15 You have a profit. You don't want the risk of a large, unforeseen move by the stock to the upside, which could result in a loss and an unwanted assignment to a short stock position. You also want to avoid pin risk. You should soon buy this call back. If you want to continue with a short call position, you could sell the November-December or November-January time spread, thereby rolling your short call position to a more distant month.

16 False; there is no early exercise possible for European options.

17 False; stock and stock index puts have significantly greater early exercise premium than puts on futures contracts because they can be exercised to gain cash and, therefore, interest.

Volatility and pricing models

The most sophisticated and the most significant aspect of options pricing is that of volatility.

The most sophisticated and the most significant aspect of options pricing is that of volatility. After all, the primary purpose of options is to hedge exposure to market volatility. Increased market volatility leads to increased options premiums, while decreased market volatility has the opposite effect. Although a thorough review of volatility involves a study of statistics, a layman's explanation is practical and sufficient for the purpose of trading options.

Volatility is generally described in terms of normal price distribution. On most days, an underlying settles at a price that is not very different from the previous day's settlement. Occasionally, there occurs a large price change from one day to the next. One can safely say that the greater the price change, the less frequent its occurrence will be.

A typical set of price changes for an underlying can be graphed with a bell curve. *See* Figure 5.1.

The bell curve places each day's closing price at the centre, and plots the next closing day's price to the right or left, depending on whether the next day's price is upward or downward, respectively. The x-axis denotes the magnitude of the price changes, and the y-axis denotes their frequency.

Some underlying contracts routinely have greater daily price changes than others. They are said to be more volatile. In these cases their bell curves indicate greater price distribution by exibiting a lower, flatter curve. A particular contract may also undergo periods of higher volatility. In both cases the bell curve becomes more like the example shown in Figure 5.2.

The bell curve is a helpful way of visualizing the concept of volatility. It illustrates the need for higher options prices due to higher volatility.

Normal price distribution is similar to waiting for public transport. In normal circumstances, the bus appears shortly before or after you arrive

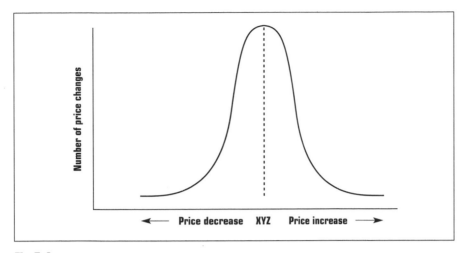

Fig 5.1 ■ **Low volatility**

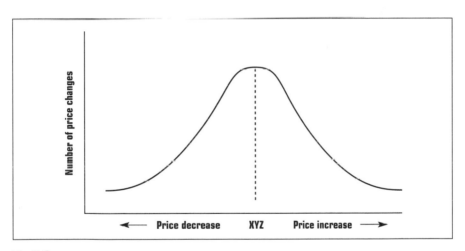

Fig 5.2 ■ **High volatility**

at the bus stop. Occasionally, the previous bus has already departed some time ago, and the next bus arrives at the stop just as you do. At other times, you just miss the bus, and you need to wait longer than usual.

Unfortunately, normal circumstances like normal markets are themselves unusual. Arrivals and departures are subject to a variety of traffic, weather, and professional complications, making it difficult to anticipate bus movements. Sometimes, the street is bumper to bumper with buses. At other times, you may wait for 20 or more minutes in the rain, and then find yourself passed by a bus with a sign that says 'Out of Service'. At these times you are at the ends of the bell curve.

There are two types of volatility used in the options markets: the **historical volatility** of the underlying, and the **implied volatility** of the options on the underlying.

Historical volatility

The historical volatility describes the range of price movement of the underlying over a given time period.

The historical volatility describes the range of price movement of the underlying over a given time period. If, for a certain time period, an underlying's daily settlement prices are three to five points above or below its previous daily settlement prices, then it will have a greater historical volatility than if its settlement prices are one to two points above or below. Historical volatility is concerned with price movement, not with price direction.

Properly speaking, volatility itself is calculated as a one-day, one standard deviation move, annualized. The annualized figure is used in computing historical volatility. For example, a stock, bond, or commodity with a volatility of 20 per cent has a 68 per cent probability of being within a 20 per cent range of its present price one year from now; and it has a 95 per cent probability of being within a 40 per cent range of its present price one year from now. If XYZ is currently at 100 and the current historical volatility is 20 per cent, then we can be 68 per cent certain that it will be between 80 and 120 one year from now. We can be 95 per cent certain that XYZ will be between 60 and 140 one year from now.

Most trading firms have mathematical models to calculate volatility, but for most underlyings there is a simplified way to calculate an annualized volatility based on a day's price movement.

An annualized volatility for an underlying can be computed by multiplying the day's percentage price change by 16 (*see footnote*[1]). For example, if XYZ settles at 100, and the next day it settles at 102: $\frac{2}{100}$ = 2%. 2% × 16 = 32% annualized volatility. Note that if on the following day XYZ retraces to 100: $\frac{2}{102}$ = 1.96%. 1.96% × 16 = 31.36% annualized volatility.

This way of calculating volatility is, as mentioned before, simplified, but it will provide insight into how price changes and the value of the underlying affect the volatility calculation. The above formula is insufficient for short-term interest rate contracts such as Eurodollars, where the volatility calculation should be based on the change in the yield or interest rate, and not on the change in the underlying futures contract.

---

[1] 16 is the approximate square root of 250, the approximate number of trading days in a year.

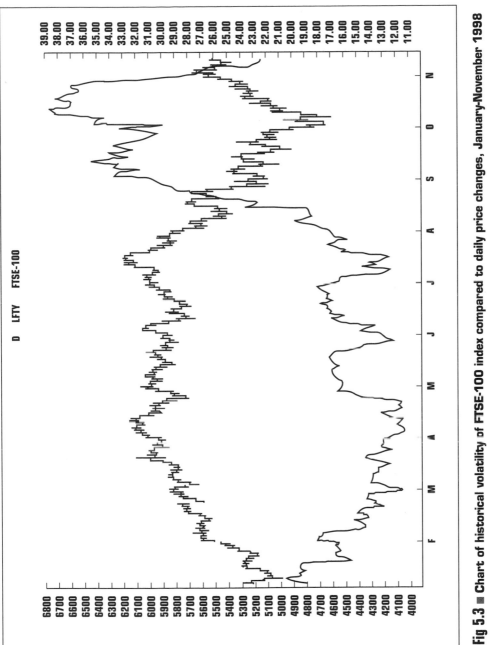

Fig 5.3 ■ Chart of historical volatility of FTSE-100 index compared to daily price changes, January–November 1998

Chart courtesy of FutureSource – Bridge

Volatility fluctuates from day to day, but over a time period it often trends up or down, or remains in a range. In order to put daily volatility fluctuations in perspective, they are averaged into time intervals of 10, 20, 30 days or more. This process of averaging creates a useful historical volatility. It is similar to the more familiar moving average of daily settlement prices.

Because markets frequently change their volatility levels, and because options are short-term investments, many traders use a 20-day average in order to compute their historical volatility. For longer-term options it is beneficial to examine the 20-day historical volatility over longer time periods, perhaps a year or more. In markets that are undergoing a sudden change of volatility, a 5-day average or less may be used for near-term contracts. It is particularly useful to know what a contract's historical volatility can be under extraordinary circumstances, both active and quiet. See Figure 5.3 for an example.

Pricing models

Once the historical volatility is known, it becomes an input for an options pricing model.

Once the historical volatility is known, it becomes an input for an options pricing model. The primary model used in the options industry is the Black-Scholes model; almost all other models used are variations of it. This model has been revised over the past 25 years or so in order to price options on different underlyings, but it remains the foundation of the business[2].

The other pricing inputs are those already discussed:

1 Strike price of the option

2 Price of the underlying

3 Time until expiration

4 Short-term interest rate

5 Dividends

6 Volatility, historical or implied

With these inputs the model yields an option price which can become a basis from which to trade. If we compare this option price to its current market price, however, we will probably find a discrepancy. The reason for this is simply a difference between theory and practice.

---

[2] There are many books that discuss the differences between options models. Needless to say this topic requires an extensive maths background. See the bibliography for recommended readings.

Implied volatility

Although a theoretical value for an option can be determined by the historical volatility, an option's market price is determined by supply and demand. An options market accounts for past price movement, but it also tries to anticipate future price movement. The market price of an option, then, implies a range of expected price movements for the underlying through expiration.

If we insert the market price of the option into the pricing model, and if we delete the former historical volatility, the model substitutes another volatility number, the implied volatility of the option.

This implied volatility can then be used as *the* implied volatility to calculate market prices of options at other strike prices within the same contract month. As a result, market prices of options spreads can also be calculated.

For example, if the December Corn futures contract is at 220, and the December 220 calls, with 60 days till expiration, are priced at 7 ($350), an options model can calculate that these calls have an implied volatility of 20 per cent. If the demand for these options bids up their price to $10\frac{1}{2}$ ($525), while at the same time the price of the underlying and the days till expiration remain constant, the model will calculate that they have an implied volatility of 30 per cent.

If demand has bid up the 220 calls, then the 240 calls are also worth more because they are a hedge for underlying price movement as well. The last traded price of the 240 calls may have been $1\frac{3}{8}$, but that was before the 220 calls became bid up. Suppose we want to estimate the new theoretical value for the 240 calls.

If we know that the 220 calls have increased their implied to 30 per cent, we can assume that the implied for all the options, including the 240 calls, has increased to 30 per cent[3]. We can assume this because the market is implying a new volatility for the underlying through expiration, and all the options will be priced to account for it.

We then insert the 30 per cent implied into the options model, and it yields a price of $3\frac{3}{8}$ ($193.75) for the December 240 calls. (*Figures courtesy of FutureSource.*)

You can experiment with the effect of implied volatility changes on options prices by using an options calculator. Several options' websites, including numa.com, offer one of these. In fact, anyone who seriously

---

[3] This assumption becomes modified with respect to volatility skews, which are discussed in Part Three.

wants to learn about the effects of all the options variables on options prices should spend a minimum of several hours with this device.

Comparing historical and implied volatility

Historical and implied volatility move in tandem; they seldom coincide. Figure 5.4 compares the historical and implied volatilities for January Crude Oil, traded at the New York Mercantile Exchange (NYMEX).

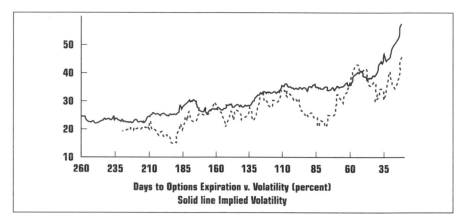

Fig 5.4 ■ **Historical and implied volatilities, January Crude Oil 1998**
Courtesy of pmpublishing.com

Here, the dotted line is the historical volatility and the solid line is the implied volatility.

This chart can be interpreted in at least two ways. Because it is an indicator of expected price movement for the underlying, the implied volatility can be seen as the leader of historical volatility. Conversely, the historical volatility can be seen as the trend volatility of the underlying, to which movements in the implied volatility eventually return. Again, this kind of analysis is similar to that associated with moving averages and trendlines. The study of volatility is a form of technical analysis.

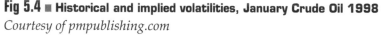

The study of volatility is a form of technical analysis.

Conventional usage

Although it is confusing, in the options markets the term 'volatility' can refer to the daily, historical, or implied volatility. But when an options trader says 'Exxon's at 20 per cent,' he is referring to the implied volatility of the front-month, at-the-money call and put.

Risk/Return

By now, it should be apparent that volatility can be traded in its own right, independently of market direction. There are many approaches to this, and several are discussed in later chapters. For now, bear in mind that if the volatility of an underlying contract increases or decreases, the volatility component of an option will likely increase or decrease respectively.

Because volatility can trend, there is a **risk/return** potential associated with volatility direction. Like more conventional kinds of directional trading, an options trader can take a position that follows the volatility trend, or not. The options buyer is actually a volatility buyer, while the options seller is the opposite.

For the volatility buyer, the potential return is the increased volatility component, or time premium, of the option as the underlying becomes more active. He can profit significantly if the underlying makes an unexpected, large move. The volatility buyer's major risk is that the underlying may suddenly come to a halt, and that options premiums collapse.

For the volatility seller, the potential return is the decreased volatility component of the option as the underlying becomes less active. He can profit significantly if the underlying quickly settles into a range. The volatility seller's major risk (and nightmare) is that an unexpected event will cause the underlying to move sharply while options premiums explode.

The main problem for options traders is to anticipate changes in volatility. It is comparable to the problem of price direction for stock or commodity traders.

Conclusion

The volatility calculation is based on statistical analysis of asset price movement. It has the benefit of a great deal of data, but like any other form of analysis, it cannot predict the future. Ultimately, it is the most comprehensive means of determining the value of an option.

A thorough understanding of volatility requires research and experience, but even a basic understanding can be profitable for the options trader. You may wish to reread this chapter as you work through this book.

Questions on volatility

1 What is the difference between the historical and the implied volatility?

2 Suppose that the S&P 500 index has just made a 5 per cent downside correction. If the implied volatility of the near-term at-the-money put has increased, then the implied volatility of the near-term at-the-money call has decreased. True or false?

3 The implied volatility always adjusts to the 20-day historical volatility within several days. True or false?

4 a) A 5-day historical volatility gives a more accurate indication of an underlying contract's volatility than a 30-day historical volatility. True or false?

   b) What do these different readings tell you?

5 The December US 30-Year Treasury Bond Futures contract is currently trading at 129.01. The December 129.00 calls, with 60 days till expiration, are trading at 1.43 with an implied volatility of 8 per cent. Bonds suddenly break to 128.00 on the monthly employment report, but gradually retrace throughout the day to settle at 129.01. The settlement price of the December 129 calls is 1.49.

   What has happened to the implied volatility, and what does this tell you about the historical volatility? What market explanation could you give for this?

6 Referring to question 5, above, if an options trader expects the implied volatility trend to continue, he will most likely do which of the following? Why?

   a) Buy calls and sell puts.

   b) Buy puts.

   c) Sell calls and buy puts.

   d) Buy calls and buy puts.

7 The S&P 500 index has closed at 1085.93, up 17.84. What is a layman's estimate for the day's annualized volatility of the index?

8 You note that the daily volatility in question 4, above, is about average for the past five days. You also note that the current, at-the-money implied volatility is 35 per cent. What are these figures telling you?

9 During the course of several weeks, the average day-to-day price range of Shell Transport has been increasing. Is the 10-day historical volatility of Shell Transport increasing or decreasing?

10 Last night the FTSE-100 index settled at 4800, and this morning, after an overnight fall in the US market, it has opened at 4400. The front-month at-the-money options are bid with an implied volatility of 70 per cent. (October 1997) Are you a seller? *(Hint: First, estimate the volatility of the index at the opening, then compare it to the implied volatility of the options.)*

Answers

1 The historical volatility is an average of a set of daily annualized volatilities of the underlying, while the implied volatility is an indication, by the price of an option, of the historical volatility expected through expiration.

2 False. Both implieds have increased the same amount because they are at the same strike price. Both options hedge the same expected range of underlying price movement.

3 False. The two volatilities can differ for months at at time.

4 a) False. the five-day volatility only gives a more recent indication. A 30-day volatility gives a better indication of the volatility trend.

   b) The five-day can lead the 30-day if the short-term trend continues. But if the five-day is a short-term aberration based on a special event that has no long-term consequences, then the volatility will revert to the 30-day.

5 The implied has increased [to 8.25 per cent], which indicates that the near-term historical volatility is expected to increase. The options market may indicate that there are components in the employment report that will continue to unsettle the futures market.

6 The trader is likely to do b or d, i.e., any combination of buying calls and puts. He is buying the volatility trend, which is increasing. This is comparable to a trader in the stock market who buys stocks because his outlook is for increased prices.

7 1085.93 – 17.84 = 1068.09 was yesterday's closing price.
17.84/1068.09 = .0167, or 1.67%.
1.67 × 16 = 26.72% estimate of day's annualized volatility.

8 One possibility is that the options have yet to account for a decrease in the historical volatility, and that they may be over valued. Another possibility is that the options are anticipating a near-term increase in the historical volatility, and if so, they are correctly valued.

9 Ten-day historical volatility is increasing.

10 4800 – 4400 = 400 points change at opening.
400/4800 = .0833, or 8.33% price change.
8.33% × 16 = 133% volatility of index.
The options, at 70 per cent, are extremely undervalued. On the other hand, the implied volatility is at an exceptionally high level and it may average down during the next few days. You may not want to buy these options because of their high cost, but you certainly wouldn't go short them unless you are well capitalized.

6 The Greeks and risk assessment: delta

Because there are several components that contribute to the price of an option, it is essential to understand how each of these components can be affected by changes in the market. Short-term interest rates and dividends, especially with respect to a stock index, are fairly predictable. The three major variables that affect an option's price are:

- a change in the underlying
- the passage of time
- a change in the implied volatility.

Options theory is able to quantify exposure to these variables. The terms that are applied to the calculations are borrowed from other mathematical fields, and they are Greek:

- **delta** and **gamma** express exposure to a change in the underlying
- **theta** expresses exposure to the passage of time
- **vega** expresses exposure to a change in the implied volatility.

'The Greeks,' as they are called, are invaluable aides in determining the risk/return potential of an

> 'The Greeks,' as they are called, are invaluable aides in determining the risk/return potential of an options position.

options position. They are the fundamental parameters of risk assessment.

Delta

Delta is the amount that an option changes with respect to a small change in the underlying.

If an option is so deeply in-the-money that it is at parity with the underlying, its price will change one for one with the underlying. Its delta is therefore 1.00. Traders often say that this option has a one-hundred delta because it has a 100 per cent correlation with the underlying.

An option that is at-the-money changes price at half the rate of the underlying, and therefore has a delta of .50. Traders often say that this option has a fifty delta.

In an extreme case, an option may be so far out-of-the-money that it is virtually worthless. Practically any change in the underlying can not affect its price. Its delta is therefore 0.00.

Table 6.1 gives a typical example of a set of options with their deltas for one contract month.

	December Corn at 220			
Strike	**Call value**	**Call delta**	**Put value**	**Put delta**
190	$30\frac{1}{8}$	.92	$\frac{5}{8}$	.06
200	$21\frac{1}{2}$	.83	$1\frac{7}{8}$	.15
210	$14\frac{1}{4}$	.69	$4\frac{3}{8}$	.30
220	$8\frac{5}{8}$	.51	$8\frac{5}{8}$	.47
230	$4\frac{3}{4}$	.34	$14\frac{5}{8}$	.65
240	$2\frac{3}{8}$	.20	$22\frac{1}{8}$	.78
250	$1\frac{1}{8}$	.11	$30\frac{5}{8}$	.88

Table 6.1 ■ December corn options 90 DTE implied volatility at 20%
The tables in this chapter are courtesy of FutureSource – Bridge

If the December futures contract moves up by one point, then the 220 call moves up by $\frac{1}{2}$ point, to $9\frac{1}{8}$; the 220 put then moves down by $\frac{1}{2}$ point, to $8\frac{1}{8}$. If the December futures contract moves down by one point, then the 220 call moves to $8\frac{1}{8}$ and the 220 put moves to $9\frac{1}{8}$. You may note that out-of-the-money calls and puts that are equidistant from the underlying have different values and deltas. Also, the at-the-money call and put have deltas that are not equal, and that approximate .50. These anomalies are due to refinements in the options model which need not concern us at this point.

As an underlying changes, the delta itself changes. A large move in the underlying can change an option's status from in-the-money to at-the-money or out-of-the-money, or vice versa. The option's delta will change too radically for the purpose of price assessment. The delta calculation therefore only applies to a small change in the underlying.

Delta and time decay

The delta of an out-of-the-money option decreases with time. This is because the probability of the underlying reaching its strike price also decreases with time. The delta of an in-the-money option increases with time. This is because the probability of its strike price remaining in the money also increases with time. The delta of an at-the-money option remains at .50. Table 6.2 is another set of options contracts on the above underlying; it is the same contract month with fewer days until expiration.

Strike	December Corn at 220			
	Call value	Call delta	Put value	Put delta
190	29$\frac{7}{8}$	.99	0	0
200	20$\frac{1}{8}$	.95	$\frac{1}{4}$	.05
210	11$\frac{3}{8}$	.80	1$\frac{1}{2}$	.20
220	5	.51	5	.49
230	1$\frac{5}{8}$	.23	11$\frac{1}{2}$	.77
240	$\frac{3}{8}$	.07	20$\frac{1}{4}$	.93
250	0	0	29$\frac{7}{8}$	.98

Table 6.2 ■ **December Corn options 30 DTE, Implied at 20%**

A comparison of each strike price from Table 6.1 to Table 6.2 demonstrates the effect of time decay on deltas.

Delta position: equivalence to underlying

A delta position corresponds to a long or short position in the underlying. For example, a long call has a long delta position which corresponds to a long underlying position. All the **delta correspondences** are summarized below:

- ■ long call = long delta = long underlying
- ■ short call = short delta = short underlying
- ■ long put = short delta = short underlying
- ■ short put = long delta = long underlying

A consequence of these correspondences is that a delta becomes **equivalent to a percentage of the underlying contract**. One short, at-the-money call with a .50 delta equals half of a short underlying contract. Four such calls equal two short underlyings, and so on.

All the deltas in an options position can then be summarized into a net delta position. Table 6.3 is an example of a small position.

Long	Short	Call/ Put	Month/Strike	Delta per Option	Deltas per position at strike (+/-)
	5	P	December 200	.15	+.75
10		P	December 220	.47	– 4.70
10		C	December 220	.51	+5.10
	10	C	December 240	.20	– 2.00
	10	C	December 250	.11	– 1.10
Net delta position...					– 1.95

Table 6.3 ■ Sample options position, December Corn, 90 DTE, implied at 20 %

Here, an equivalent long underlying position is given a plus sign (+), and an equivalent short underlying position is given a minus sign (–). The net delta position of – 1.95 is equivalent to an underlying position that is short approximately two contracts. Remember that this equivalency only applies to a small move in the underlying.[4]

Hedge ratio

Because a net delta position is an equivalent futures position, it can indicate exposure to an unwanted move by the underlying. This exposure would be hedged simply by buying or selling the number of underlying contracts needed to create a delta neutral position. As a **hedge ratio**, the delta indicates the number of contracts to buy or sell.

For example, an option with a .50 delta is hedged by half the amount of underlying contracts. A position of 10 long, .50 delta calls is equivalent to a position of long five underlying contracts. This position is exposed to downward move by the underlying, and so may be hedged by selling, or going short, five underlying contracts. The total delta position is then zero, or, as we say, the position is *delta neutral*. For a small move by the underlying in either direction, the profit/loss of the total position changes little, if at all.

The hedge ratio is especially useful to risk managers with large options portfolios. They regularly adjust their exposure to market direction with off-setting transactions in the underlying contracts. Suppose you are a risk manager with the position given in Table 6.3. How do you hedge this position?

> The hedge ratio is especially useful to risk managers with large options portfolios.

---

[4] Occasionally in the options business, the plus sign (+) is used to refer to a call delta, and the minus sign (–) is used to refer to a put delta. This practice confuses the process of calculating a net delta position; it is not used in this book.

Delta and probability

A useful way to think of delta is that it indicates the probability of an option expiring in-the-money. An option that is at-the-money, with a .50 delta, has an even chance of expiring in-the-money. By associating delta with probability, we can determine the market's assessment of the range of the underlying until expiration. This can help us decide how much risk lies in an options position.

For example, the above December 250 call, with an .11 delta, has an 11 per cent probability of expiring in-the-money, and might be considered a low-risk sale. The return on the sale of this call would also be low, but this is a justifiable risk/return scenario for some investors.

On the other hand, an 11 per cent probability of December Corn moving to 250 by expiration may be the point at which another investor wishes to cover a short position in the underlying. Although the market currently indicates that such a move is unlikely, this investor is willing to pay the small premium that would enable him to retain his short position.

As an indicator of probability, a delta is only as good as the current market assessment of price movement until expiration. This assessment is continually subject to new information, and as a result it is continually revised. **Profitable options trading** is often a matter of anticipating, or being one of the first to discern, changes in probability.

Summary of delta

There are four ways to think of delta; the first is the definition, and the following three are the uses:

■ the rate of change of the option with respect to a small change in the underlying

■ a percentage of an underlying contract

■ a hedge ratio

■ the probability of an option expiring in the money

Delta is discussed further in Part Three.

Questions on delta

1   State whether the following positions are equivalent to a long or short underlying position.

   a) short call

   b) long put

   c) short put

   d) long call

2   A .20 delta put decreases at 80 per cent of the underlying if the underlying moves up. True or false?

3   For a small upward move in the underlying a .50 delta call changes more than a .50 delta put, but for a small downward move in the underlying a .50 delta put changes more than a .50 delta call. True or false? Why or why not?

4   Given the following set of options with their deltas, what is the new price of each option if the underlying moves *up* by one point?

Underlying	Option	Price	Delta	New price
BP Amoco	July 950 call	$74\frac{1}{2}$	.51	
BP Amoco	July 650 call	296	.98	
December Corn	December 230 call	$1\frac{5}{8}$	.23	
December Corn	December 220 put	5	.49	

5   Given the following set of options with their deltas, what is the new price of each option if the underlying moves *down* by one point?

Underlying	Option	Price	Delta	New price
FTSE-100	March 6200 put	$199\frac{1}{2}$	.48	
FTSE-100	March 5275 call	935	.98	
Microsoft	January 120 call	$2\frac{1}{2}$	.25	
Microsoft	January 90 put	1	.12	

6   A .50 delta option has the same correlation with the underlying from 50 to 10 days till expiration. True or false? Why or why not?

7   Five long .20 delta calls have the same delta equivalence as five (long or short?) .20 delta puts.

8   A delta neutral hedge can be created with 20 short, .30 delta calls and how many long or short underlying contracts?

9   As time passes, the deltas of out-of-the-money calls and in-the-money puts both decrease. True or false?

10 Given the following position in March US Treasury Bond options, calculate the total delta for the position. (*Figures courtesy of pmpublishing.com*)

Long	Short	Option	Delta per option	Deltas per strike
5		March 128 call	.51	
	2	March 124 call	.75	
	10	March 132 call	.27	
10		March 120 put	.14	

Total delta position

a) What is the equivalent futures position?

b) How would you create a delta neutral hedge for the above options position?

11 For the above example in US T-Bond options, the March futures contract is currently at 128.01 with 87 days until expiration. Suppose you are short 2, March 124 calls. What is the probability of your being assigned two short futures contracts at expiration?

Answers

1   a) short underlying
    b) short underlying
    c) long underlying
    d) long underlying

2   False, a .20 delta put decreases in price by 20 per cent for a small upwards move in the underlying.

3   False, they both change the same amount in either case. If the underlying moves up, the .50 delta call increases in value at half the rate of the underlying, while the .50 delta put decreases in value at half the rate of the underlying. If the underlying moves down, the call decreases while the put increases.

4   New price
    75
    297
    $1\frac{7}{8}$
    $4\frac{1}{2}$

5   New price
    200
    934
    $2\frac{1}{4}$
    $1\frac{1}{8}$

6   True, a .50 delta, at-the-money option correlates the same with the underlying because its delta is not affected by time.

7   Short

8   False. A delta neutral hedge is here created with six long underlying contracts assuming, as in most cases, that the options contract and the underlying contract have the same multiplier.

9   False. As time passes, the deltas of out-of-the-money calls decrease because they have less probability of becoming in-the-money, while the deltas of in-the-money puts increase because they have more probability of staying in-the-money.

10 Deltas per strike
    +2.55
    -1.50
    -2.70
    $\underline{-1.40}$
    -3.05 Total delta position.

    a) Short three futures contracts.

    b) Buy, or go long, three futures contracts.

11 75 per cent.

Gamma and theta

It should be apparent after reading the previous chapter that delta is an indispensable tool for understanding an option's behaviour. But because an option's delta changes continually with the underlying, we need to be able to assess its own rate of change. **Gamma** quantifies the rate of change of the delta with respect to a change in the underlying.

> Gamma quantifies the rate of change of the delta with respect to a change in the underlying.

To understand gamma is to understand how quickly or slowly a delta can change. Suppose XYZ is trading at a price of 100, and there are just two hours until the front-month options contract expires. The typical daily range of XYZ is two points, so we expect it to be between 99 and 101 at the time of expiration.

Now suppose that XYZ starts to move erratically, and for the next two hours it trades between 99 and 101. During this time, what is the delta of the expiring 100 call? If XYZ settles below 100, the 100 call will expire worthless, with a delta of zero. If XYZ settles above 100, the call will close at parity, with a delta of 1.00.

During these last two hours it would have been pointless to calculate the delta because it is changing so rapidly. This rapid and most extreme change of delta, however, is an example of the highest possible gamma that an option can have.

If we consider the out-of-the-money options in the same contract month, such as the 105 calls and the 95 puts, we can be almost certain that they will expire worthless. Their deltas are zero and will not change. They have no gamma. Likewise in-the-money, parity options such as the 90 calls and the 110 puts have no gamma because their deltas will remain at 1.00 through expiration.

The first situation above occasionally occurs, but most options contracts expire well out-of or in-the-money. Nevertheless, several points about gamma are illustrated. In any contract month, gamma is the highest with the at-the-money options, and it decreases as the strike prices become more distant from the money, whether they are in-the-money or out-of-the-money.

As a contract month approaches expiration, the gammas of both the at-the-money options, and the options near-the-money, increase. The effect of time decay, however, causes the gammas of the far out-of-the-money and far in-the-money options to approach zero. Generally speaking, however, time decay least affects the gammas of options in the .10 and .90 delta ranges. This all becomes complicated, of course, by the fact that deltas change with time. You should simply remember that as time passes, the nearer an option is to the underlying, the more its gamma increases.

Table 7.1 is a typical example of a set of options with deltas and gammas in one contract month.

Strike	Call value	December Corn at 220 Call delta	Put value	Put delta	Gamma
190	$30\frac{1}{8}$	.92	$\frac{5}{8}$	.06	.006
200	$21\frac{1}{2}$	.83	$1\frac{7}{8}$	.15	.011
210	$14\frac{1}{4}$	.69	$4\frac{3}{8}$	.30	.016
220	$8\frac{5}{8}$	.51	$8\frac{5}{8}$	.47	.018
230	$4\frac{3}{4}$	.34	$14\frac{5}{8}$	.65	.017
240	$2\frac{3}{8}$	.20	$22\frac{1}{8}$	.78	.013
250	$1\frac{1}{8}$	.11	$30\frac{5}{8}$	.88	.008

Table 7.1 ■ December Corn options 90 DTE implied volatility at 20 per cent
The tables in this chapter are courtesy of FutureSource – Bridge

The gamma-delta calculation is a matter of simple addition or subtraction. Here, the December 230 call with a .34 delta has a gamma of .017 . This means that if the December futures contract moves up one point, from 220 to 221, the delta of the call will increase to .357, rounded to .36. If the futures contract moves down one point, the delta of the same call will decrease to .323, rounded to .32. Accordingly, if the futures contract moves up 10 points, then the delta of the 230 call will increase by .17, to .51, the equivalent delta of the 220 call at present.

If the December futures contract moves down by one point, then the delta of the December 200 put will increase by its gamma of .011, from .15 to .16; if the futures contract moves up by one point, the delta will decrease by .011.

Note that gamma describes the absolute change in delta, whether increased or decreased.

An option's gamma, like its delta, changes as the underlying changes. If you calculate the new theoretical delta for the December 200 put over a decrease of 10 points in the futures contract, the result will be .26. You might expect the new delta to be equivalent to that of the present December 210 put at .30. This discrepancy is due to the fact that the gamma is increasing from .011 to .016 as the futures contract moves down. The gamma-delta calculation is therefore best applied to a small change in the delta.

Table 7.2 lists the same set of options but with less time until expiration. If we compare it with Table 7.1, the points previously made about gamma become evident. With the passage of time, the deep in-the-money and far out-of-the-money options have gammas that are unchanged to decreased, while at-the-money and near-the-money options have increased gammas.

| Strike | Call value | December Corn at 220 | | Put delta | Gamma |
		Call delta	Put value		
190	29 $\frac{7}{8}$	.99	0	0	0
200	20 $\frac{1}{8}$	.95	$\frac{1}{4}$	.05	.008
210	11 $\frac{3}{8}$	.80	1 $\frac{1}{2}$	.20	.022
220	5	.51	5	.49	.031
230	1 $\frac{5}{8}$	.23	11 $\frac{1}{2}$	.77	.024
240	$\frac{3}{8}$	.07	20 $\frac{1}{4}$	.93	.010
250	0	0	29 $\frac{7}{8}$	.98	0

Table 7.2 ■ December Corn options, 30 DTE, implied volatility at 20 per cent

Gamma can be though of as the heat of an option. It tells us how fast our option's delta, or our equivalent underlying position, is changing.

Positive and negative gamma

Because gamma determines the absolute change in delta, and delta determines the absolute change in an option's price, gamma helps us determine our exposure to absolute underlying movement.

> Gamma helps us determine our exposure to absolute underlying movement.

Remember that a long call is an alternative to a purchase of the underlying. It is a hedge for underlying movement in either direction: it gains price appreciation on the upside, and it offers price protection on the downside. A long call yields a benefit when the market moves; its value has a positive correlation with market movement.

The same is true for a long put as an alternative to a sale or short position in the underlying. If you buy a put instead of selling your stock, you'll be very content if the stock makes a large move in either direction.

Positive correlation with market movement is commonly known as **positive gamma**. Just as a long at-the-money option has the most profit/savings potential, a long at-the-money option has the most positive gamma.

Conversely, negative correlation with market movement is known as **negative gamma**. If you sell an at-the-money call instead of selling your stock, you'll be disappointed if the stock moves above or below the amount of the call sale. If you sell an at-the-money put instead of buying stock, you may curse your luck if the stock moves outside the range of the sale price. Should this be unclear, imagine yourself with a potential XYZ position at 100 and with a potential 100 call or put priced at 4.

The following discussion becomes somewhat more advanced. You may return to it later, or have a glance now.

Gamma and volatility trading

The gamma calculation is particularly useful to those who trade volatility, i.e., absolute price movement or price movement in either direction.

Long options can be combined in order to profit from absolute market movement, and short options can be combined to profit from a static market.

If we use the set of options in Table 7.2, a position of long 1 December 220 call plus long 1 December 220 put will have a total positive gamma of +.031 × 2, or +.062 . This position is known as a **long straddle**, and it will profit from an underlying move in either direction greater that the purchase price of 5 + 5 = 10. It has two break-even levels, at 210 and 230.

Because this position is long both a call and a put, the gamma figure tells us that its combined delta *increases* by .062 for each 1 point increase in the underlying: the call increases its delta by .031, and the put decreases its delta by .031. The gamma figure also tells us that for each 1 point decrease in the underlying, the combined delta *decreases* by .062: the put increases its delta by .031, and the call decreases its delta by .031.

In other words, as the underlying rallies, this position becomes longer, and as the underlying breaks, this position becomes shorter. As confirmed by the break-even levels, the long straddle profits from increased volatility, or absolute price movement.

Conversely, the opposite position, a *short straddle*, will have a negative gamma position of −.062 , and will profit if December Corn remains between 210 and 230. These two positions are discussed further in the chapter on straddles (Chapter 12).

The gamma calculation is useful to market makers who carry large positions on their books. The above gamma reading of +/− .062 indicates more exposure to market movement than, for example, +/− .018, which would be obtained by buying or selling both the December 240 call and the December 200 put. Here, the break-even levels are $240\frac{5}{8}$ and $199\frac{3}{8}$. This position is known as the **strangle**, and it is also discussed in Chapter 12.

Positive and negative gamma help to quantify the risk/return potential of a position with respect to absolute market movement.

Theta

Compared to gamma and delta, theta is a straightforward concept. The **theta** of an option is the amount that the option decays in one day. A short options position receives income from time decay and therefore has **positive theta**. A long options position incurs an

> The theta of an option is the amount that the option decays in one day.

expense from time decay and therefore has **negative theta**.

Tables 7.3 and 7.4 are similar to the previous Tables 7.1 and 7.2, but they include the daily theta numbers for all the contracts listed. Here, the theta figures are expressed in actual dollars and cents. (They can also be expressed in options ticks.)

| | | | December Corn at 220 Theta in $/day | | | | |
Strike	Call value	Call delta	Call Theta	Put value	Put delta	Put Theta	Gamma
190	$30\frac{1}{8}$	.92	.50	$\frac{5}{8}$	.06	.74	.006
200	$21\frac{1}{2}$	.83	1.26	$1\frac{7}{8}$	.15	1.42	.011
210	$14\frac{1}{4}$	.69	1.97	$4\frac{3}{8}$	.30	2.05	.016
220	$8\frac{5}{8}$	.51	2.31	$8\frac{5}{8}$	.47	2.31	.018
230	$4\frac{3}{4}$	.34	2.17	$14\frac{5}{8}$	.65	2.09	.017
240	$2\frac{3}{8}$	.20	1.68	$22\frac{1}{4}$	.78	1.52	.013
250	$1\frac{1}{8}$	.11	1.10	$30\frac{5}{8}$	.88	.86	.008

Table 7.3 ■ December Corn options 90 DTE implied volatility at 20 per cent

			December Corn at 220 Theta in $/day				
Strike	Call value	Call delta	Call Theta	Put value	Put delta	Put Theta	Gamma
190	$29\frac{7}{8}$	.99	0	0	0	0	0
200	$20\frac{1}{8}$	.95	.83	$\frac{1}{4}$	.05	1.00	.008
210	$11\frac{3}{8}$	.80	2.84	$1\frac{1}{2}$	.20	2.92	.022
220	5	.51	4.13	5	.49	4.13	.031
230	$1\frac{5}{8}$	.23	3.14	$11\frac{1}{2}$	.77	3.06	.024
240	$\frac{3}{8}$	.07	1.37	$20\frac{1}{4}$	.93	1.21	.010
250	0	0	0	$29\frac{7}{8}$	.98	.13	0

Table 7.4 ■ **December Corn options 30 DTE, implied at 20 per cent**

As we said in Chapter 4, all options lose their value at an accelerated rate as they approach expiration. The at-the-money options, the 220s, have the most increase in theta because they contain the most time premium. Those nearest the money, the 210s and the 230s, also have increased theta. The far out-of-the-money and deep in-the-money options can have decreased theta, but this is because they contain only a small amount of time premium with 30 DTE.

Use and abuse of theta

Theta quantifies the expense of owning or the income from selling an option for a day of the option's life. You may have an outlook for movement in a particular underlying. What is the cost of a long options position for the duration of your outlook? If your outlook is for a stable market, what is your expected return from a short options position during this time period?

The subject of theta gives rise to a few words of caution. It is tempting to sell options simply to collect money from time decay. This strategy contains a hidden risk. It can become habitual because it often works on a short- and medium-term basis. In the long term, however, it usually fails. The reason is that it ignores the basis of options theory: that **time premium is a fair exchange for volatility coverage**. Many traders have gone bust by ignoring this basic principle. To sell options in such a manner is to ignore probability, and to hope that you are out of the market when it eventually moves.

The following story tells what can go wrong with a short options position, but also how trouble can be avoided.

A few years ago I worked for one of the more prominent traders in index options in Chicago. His strategy was to sell index calls and hedge them with long S&P 500 futures contracts. We were in a bear market. Stocks and the index implied volatility were both in a downtrend. The trader I worked for, Bobby, routinely leaned short, i.e., his overall delta position was negative from day to day. He had made substantial profits in this way.

I did then as I do now, follow a number of technical indicators. One of them was the 200-day moving average. The S&P 500 was holding at this level after an extensive decline, and I became worried that Bobby's strategy, which had worked so well for many months, might have run its course, at least for the time being. Because I was new to the business, Bobby would have none of my beginner's advice. After all, he was my boss, and he had recently made a substantial amount of money. He had also substantially increased the size of his positions.

A week or two later, I was on the floor early for a government economic indicator. The report was bullish, bonds were up, and so was the call for stocks. I phoned in my report, and Bobby greeted the news with dead silence. A few minutes later, he joined me in the pit, and the stock market gapped open higher with no chance to cover his position. We stood there for about half an hour just watching the order flow and the indexes amid frenetic trading. Then things started to quiet down. The indexes downticked a little, but they weren't picking up momentum.

Bobby made his first trades, big ones – he sold calls. I tapped him on the shoulder and tried to say, 'Bobby, they're not going down', but he cut me off by saying 'Shut up and gimme the count', meaning calculate his position. Several minutes later, the market made its second move, fast and higher. Again, there was no chance to cover. It leveled off at about half again the distance of the first move. Bobby then covered as best as he could by buying in calls, which were well bid, and by buying futures. He left the pit without saying a word, and I stayed on to tally his position.

A half hour later, I joined him upstairs in his office to give him my report. He was sitting in his chair, staring through his trading screen. He didn't hear a word I was saying; he was speechless and catatonic. He had lost a great deal of money. I knew his position was safe for the moment, so I left the office.

There are a few lessons to be learned from this story. One is to know why your strategy is working. Of course you're talented, astute, and you work hard, but is your style of trading or your strategy particularly suited to a certain kind of market? What happens if the market changes its character?

Another lesson is the converse. Perhaps the strategies that you're most comfortable with aren't the ones that profit in the current market. Can you adapt? If you don't feel comfortable with a different style or strategy, then by all means take a break from the market.

Finally, remember that options are derivatives. Once you're in the business a while, it becomes easy to lose touch with the fundamental and technical analyses of underlying contracts. Lack of awareness sooner or later proves costly.

The trader I worked for eventually worked his way back into the market, and has done very well in recent years. We've still never discussed the 200-day moving average.

Questions on gamma and theta

1   .50 delta options in the same contract month have more gamma and theta than .80 delta options. True or false? Why?

2   Given the following options with their deltas and gammas, what is the approximate new delta if the underlying moves up by one point?

Underlying	Option	Delta	Gamma	New delta
CBOT US T-Bonds	January 128 call	.51	.15	
CBOT US T-Bonds	January 125 put	.14	.08	
NYMEX Crude oil	April 15.00 call	.29	.12	
NYMEX Crude oil	April 16.50 put	.83	.09	

Figures courtesy of pmpublishing.com

3   Given the following options with their deltas and gammas, what is the approximate new delta if the underlying moves *down* by one point?

Underlying	Option	Delta	Gamma	New delta
CBOT Corn	December 210 call	.69	.016	
CBOT Corn	December 220 put	.47	.018	
NYMEX Crude oil	June 12.00 call	.73	.10	
NYMEX Crude oil	June 13.00 put	.37	.12	

Figures courtesy of FutureSource – Bridge and pmpublishing .com

4   Given the following options, which are expressed in ticks and whose multiplier is $50, and given their thetas expressed in dollars and cents, calculate the approximate new value of the options after 7 days' time decay. Both options have 90 DTE.

Underlying	Option	Value	Theta	New value
CBOT Corn	December 220 call	$8\frac{5}{8}$	2.31	
CBOT Corn	December 250 call	$1\frac{1}{8}$	1.10	

5   High theta options have a greater probability of making a profit than low theta options. True or false? Why?

6   Referring to Tables 7.3 and 7.4, what is the percentage increase in gamma of the December 220 call from 90 to 30 DTE?

   a)   What is the percentage increase in theta for this option over the same time period?

7   What is the correlation between gamma and theta?

8   Is it possible to have positive gamma and positive theta? Why is this?

Answers

1   True, because at-the-money options always have the largest gamma and theta in any contract month.

2   New delta
   .66
   .06
   .41
   .74

3   New delta
   .67
   .49
   .63
   .49

4   New value
   $415.08, or appx. $8\frac{1}{4}$
   $48.55, or appx. 1

   For the 220 call: $8\frac{5}{8}$ = 8.625; 8.625 × $50 = $431.25; $2.31 × 7 = $16.17; $431.25 – $16.17 = $415.08; 415.08/50 = 8.30, or appx. $8\frac{1}{4}$

   For the 250 call: $1\frac{1}{8}$ = 1.125; 1.125 × $50 = $56.25; $1.10 × 7 = $7.70; $56.25 – $7.70 = $48.55; 48.55/50 = .97, or appx 1.

5 False, because there is no correlation between theta and profit/loss. High theta options, those with .50 deltas are more likely to expire in-the-money than low theta options with .20 deltas, but their greater time premium, and therefore their greater theta, is a fair exchange for this.

6 .031 − .018 = .013, .013/.018 = 72%

   a) 4.13 − 2.31 = 1.82, 1.82/2.31 = 78%

7 Increased gamma correlates to increased theta.

8 Not possible, because positive gamma indicates that the options position profits from market movement, while positive theta indicates that the options position profits from market stasis.

Vega

Often in an options market circumstances arise that cause the volatility of the underlying to increase or decrease suddenly. This may be the result of the inception or conclusion of an unforseen market event. During such circumstances the implied volatility of each options contract month reacts to a different degree, and this in turn affects the price of each option of each contract month to a different degree. Under these as well as more usual circumstances there is a need to quantify the effect of a change in implied

> **Vega is the amount that an option changes if the implied volatility changes by one percentage point.**

volatility on the price of a particular option. **Vega** is the amount that an option changes if the implied volatility changes by one percentage point.

Vega itself can be expressed in either options ticks or in an actual currency amount. Table 8.1 shows a set of options with their vegas for one contract month. The vegas are expressed in dollars and then rounded into ticks.

Strike	Call value	Call delta	Call theta	Put value	Put delta	Put theta	Gamma	Vega ($)	Vega (ticks)
				December Corn at 220 Theta in $/day					
190	$29\frac{7}{8}$	.99	0	0	0	0	0	0	0
200	$20\frac{1}{8}$	.95	.83	$\frac{1}{4}$	.05	1.00	.008	3.00	0
210	$11\frac{3}{8}$	.80	2.84	$1\frac{1}{2}$	.20	2.92	.022	8.80	$\frac{1}{8}$
220	5	.51	4.13	5	.49	4.13	.031	12.51	$\frac{1}{4}$
230	$1\frac{5}{8}$	.23	3.14	$11\frac{1}{2}$	.77	3.06	.024	9.47	$\frac{1}{4}$
240	$\frac{3}{8}$	.07	1.37	$20\frac{1}{4}$	.93	1.21	.010	4.13	$\frac{1}{8}$
250	0	0	0	$29\frac{7}{8}$	.98	.13	0	0	0

Table 8.1 ■ December Corn options, 30 DTE, implied at 20 per cent

The tables in this chapter are courtesy of FutureSource – Bridge

An increase in implied volatility leads to an increase in options premiums, while a decrease in implied volatility has the opposite effect. If the current implied volatility increases from 20 per cent to 21 per cent, the value of the December 220 call increases from 5 to $5\frac{1}{4}$. If the implied volatility decreases from 20 per cent to 19 per cent, the value of the December 220 call decreases from 5 to $4\frac{3}{4}$.

Note that the vega, or the number of options ticks, is multiplied by the number of percentage points that the implied volatility changes. The above implied may increase 3 per cent (commonly meaning three percentage points), from 20 per cent to 23 per cent. The new value of the December 220 call will then be $5\frac{3}{4}$.

For out-of-, and in-the-money options, the vega itself increases as the implied increases, and it decreases as the implied decreases. Therefore with these options the vega calculation is most accurate for a small change in the implied. For at-the-money options, the vega remains constant through changes in the implied.

At-the-money options have larger vegas than out-of- and in-the-money options. This is because a change in volatility increases or decreases their range of coverage more than out-of- and in-the-money options. Their value becomes increased or decreased accordingly.

Table 8.2 shows a set of longer-term options, with their vegas, on the same underlying.

December Corn at 220, options multiplier at $50									
				Theta in $/day					
Strike	Call value	Call delta	Call theta	Put value	Put delta	Put theta	Gamma	Vega ($)	Vega (ticks)
190	$30\frac{1}{8}$	.92	.50	$\frac{5}{8}$	.06	.74	.006	6.70	$\frac{1}{8}$
200	$21\frac{1}{2}$	.83	1.26	$1\frac{7}{8}$	.15	1.42	.011	12.90	$\frac{1}{4}$
210	$14\frac{1}{4}$	.69	1.97	$4\frac{3}{8}$	.30	2.05	.016	18.77	$\frac{3}{8}$
220	$8\frac{5}{8}$	.51	2.31	$8\frac{5}{8}$	.47	2.31	.018	21.44	$\frac{3}{8}$
230	$4\frac{3}{4}$	.34	2.17	$14\frac{5}{8}$	.65	2.09	.017	19.84	$\frac{3}{8}$
240	$2\frac{3}{8}$	.20	1.68	$22\frac{1}{8}$	.78	1.52	.013	15.26	$\frac{1}{4}$
250	$1\frac{1}{8}$	.11	1.10	$30\frac{5}{8}$	.88	.86	.008	9.98	$\frac{1}{4}$

Table 8.2 ■ December Corn options, 90 DTE, Implied volitality at 20 per cent

The vega of an option increases with the time until expiration. This is because an increase in implied volatility over a longer term necessitates a greater increase in the options premiums. Consequently, if the implied volatility increases equally for both a near and a long-term contract, the options in the latter will increase more.

A long options position profits from an increase in implied volatility, and therefore it has a **positive vega**. A short options position profits from a decrease in implied volatility, and therefore it has a **negative vega**.

Vega and implied volatility trends

Practically speaking, the implied volatility of long-term contracts is more stable than those of near-term contracts. Front-month implied volatility is the most reactive to current events, or current non-events.

In quiet markets, the the front-month implied can trend lower and lower for months in anticipation of continued conditions. Each point that the implied decreases in turn multiplies, by the vega, the number of options ticks that the options' values decrease. The frustration of and the risk to the premium holders becomes almost unbearable as their accounts diminish, while the premium sellers nonchalantly collect their time decay.

If an unexpected event shocks the market, the front-month implied can leap five, ten, 30 or more percentage points within minutes. As the vegas become multiplied by the increase in the implied volatility, even small positions take on almost unmanageable proportions. The premium holders become vindicated, while the premium sellers see months of profits eliminated.

Risk/return of vega

Because at-the-money options have the largest vegas, they are the most exposed to a change in implied volatility. All options, of course, face this exposure. In quiet markets, a short options position can profit not only from time decay, but also from a decline in the implied. In active markets, a long options position can profit from an increase in the implied that more than offsets the cost of time decay.

It is important to know how much the vegas of options on a particular contract can be affected by changes in volatility, and for that, you need to research the past historical and implied volatility ranges. Most data vendors, the exchanges, and many websites have this information. For example, if you want to know how the crash of '87 and the grinding retracement of '88 affected OEX implieds, how in turn the implieds multiplied the vegas, and how in turn the vegas affected the options prices, consult the CBOE.

Questions on vega

1 A short call position has negative vega, and therefore it takes a loss from an increase in the implied volatility. True or false?

2 Given the following OEX options, which have a contract multiplier of $100, what is their new value both in dollars and rounded into ticks if the implied increases by 3 percentage points? The December OEX is currently at 590.00, and the January OEX is currently at 592.75.

Option	Option value	DTE	Implied	Vega	New value
December 590 call	$10\frac{1}{2}$ (10.50)	23	17.82	.59	
December 610 call	$2\frac{3}{8}$ (2.375)	23	15.12	.41	
January 590 call	$19\frac{1}{8}$ (19.125)	51	20.21	.87	
January 610 call	$8\frac{3}{4}$ (8.75)	51	17.80	.81	

a) If the implied increases by three percentage points, which of the above options gains the most in percentage terms?

3 Increased implied volatility leads to increased vegas. True or false? Why?

4 In the example in question 2, the January at-the-money implied volatility is 20 per cent, and the range of the OEX implied volatility during the past year is 18 per cent to 25 per cent.

In dollar terms, what is the vega risk/return ratio for a position that is short ten of the January 590 calls if the implied remains within its range during the next week?

Answers

1 True for both short calls and puts, because negative vega profits from decreased implied volatilities, while positive vega profits from increased implieds.

2 New value
12.27, $1227, $12\frac{1}{4}$
3.605, $360.50, $3\frac{5}{8}$
21.735, $2173.50, $21\frac{3}{4}$
11.18, $1118, $11\frac{1}{8}$

a) December 610 call increases .41 × 3 / 2.375 = 52 per cent

3 False, because only vegas of out-of- and in-the-money options increase with an increase in the implied. At-the-money options vegas remain practically unchanged.

4 The simple answer is a vega risk of $\frac{5}{2} = 2.5$. An answer than better communicates the amount at risk is as follows: Vega equals .87, or $87; 2 × $87 = $174 reduction in one option's value if the implied decreases from 20 per cent to 18 per cent; 10 × $174 = $1740 total potential vega return. 5 × $87 = $435 increase in one option's value if the implied increases from 20 per cent to 25 per cent; 10 × $435 = $4,350 total potential vega risk. R/R = $4350 / $1740 = $2.50 potential risk for each potential return of $1.

Part

2

Options spreads

Introduction

9 Call spreads and put spreads, or one by one directional spreads

10 One by two directional spreads

11 Combos and hybrid spreads for market direction

12 Volatility spreads

13 Iron butterflies and iron condors: combining straddles and strangles for reduced risk

14 Butterflies and condors: combining call spreads and put spreads

15 The covered write, the calendar spread and the diagonal spread

Introduction

Spreading risk

'I'm bullish, what do I do?' Occasionally I am asked this question, and I usually begin my response with another question: 'How much risk do you want to take?' In the options business there are many ways of taking a position, and they all have varying degrees of risk. As with all other kinds of investments, there is a risk/return trade-off. High risk corresponds to high return, while low risk corresponds to low return. The advantage of options spreads is that each investor can take the amount of risk that he or she is able to justify and manage. This section outlines the major strategies that spread risk. These strategies can be traded on all the exchanges, and with few exceptions, they can be traded in one transaction.

At the outset, It Is Important to know what risks you want to spread. Premiums may be too high to justify an outright options purchase. The potential for unlimited risk from a short call or put position may be unjustified, even though premiums are at a high and declining level. Your outlook may call for a directional move, but it may be uncertain of the extent. The market may be due for a large move but the direction may be difficult to assess. Implied volatilities may be decreasing but they may be subject to frequent, upward spikes. You may want to buy a short-term option, but its cost in terms of time decay may be too great. These are just a few of the reasons for spreading risk.

> **At the outset, it is important to know what risks you want to spread.**

Most options spreads can be classified as either directional or volatility spreads. Directional spreads are those that profit from either bullish or bearish market movement. Volatility spreads profit from either increased or decreased *absolute* market movement, regardless of direction. Any spread has the opposite risk and return potential depending on whether it is bought or sold.

On the next page is an index of the major spreads. It will serve as a quick reference in selecting strategies. In a few cases the terms that are applied to these spreads vary, but these will be noted. If you are first starting to trade, or if this is your first reading, focus on the spreads marked with an asterisk (*), because they have the least and most manageable risk.

Index of spreads

Bull spreads

* long call spread 94
* short put spread 99
  long 1 × 2 call spread 111
  long call ladder 117
  long call, short put combo 127
* long OTM call butterfly 165
* long OTM call condor 168
* long diagonal call spread 188

Bear spreads

* short call spread 96
* long put spread 97
  long 1 × 2 put spread 114
  long put ladder 119
  long put, short call combo 129
* long OTM put butterfly 167
* long OTM put condor 171
* long diagonal put spread 188

Volatile market spreads

  long straddle 137
  long strangle 142
* long iron butterfly 148
  short ATM butterfly, call or put 164
* long iron condor 154
* short ATM put condor 173
* short ATM call condor 175

Stationary market spreads

  short straddle 140
  short strangle 144
* short iron butterfly 151
* long ATM butterfly, call or put 159, 162
* short iron condor 152
* long ATM put condor 172
* long ATM call condor 170
  covered write 181
  long calendar spread 185

Terms to use when placing spread orders

Whenever you place an order for one of these spreads, omit the jargon.

Whenever you place an order for one of these spreads, **omit the jargon.** It is most important to know the price at which you want to trade the spread. Then, you must know the approximate prices of the individual options that you want to trade.

When you ring your broker, state that you are placing an order for an options spread, and state the stock or other underlying. Next, specify the following: buy or sell, quantity, month, strike price, and call(s) or put(s). Do this for each options strike. Next, specify the net debit or credit for *one* spread quantity. Then, specify the total debit or credit for the trade. Make sure your broker repeats all the specifications to you. Last of all, use the jargon, but only if you and your broker have previously agreed on the terms. Your conversation with your broker should sound like the following:

You: *Hi, I want to place an options spread order in Microsoft.*
Broker: *Go ahead.*
You: *On a spread buy 5 January 115 calls, and sell 5 January 120 calls for a net debit of 1¾ times 5. Total debit is 8 ¾.' [You should know that 8¾ equals $875.00.]*
Broker: *Checking, in Microsoft options you are buying 5 January 115 calls, and selling 5 January 120 calls as a spread, for a debit of 1¾ times 5. Your total debit is 8¾.*
You: *Yes, that's correct.*
Broker: *Working, I'll call you back.*

When your broker calls you back to confirm he or she should specify all of the above plus the prices of each option.

Broker: *Hi, you're filled on your spread.*
You: *Good, read it off.*
Broker: *On a spread in Microsoft you bought 5 January 115 calls, and sold 5 January 120 calls for a debit of 1¾ times 5. Your total debit is 8 ¾. You paid 5 for 5 of the January 115 calls, and you sold 5 of the January 120 calls at 3 ¼.*
You: *Yes, that's correct.*
Broker: *Checking, you paid 1¾ for 5 January 115 – 120 call spreads.*
You: *Yes, I paid 1¾ to go long (to buy) 5 January 115 – 120 call spreads.*
Broker: *Can you confirm that again?*
You: *Have a nice day, wise guy.*

Note that when reporting the prices of the options, your broker should use the following terms:

when buying: price *for* quantity
when selling: quantity *at* price

These terms avoid confusion, and they have been used for many years on most of the major exchanges, including the CBOT and the LIFFE. Learn to use them.

Advice for beginners

Before we begin our discussion of spreading, here are two pieces of advice:

■ The first is not to change your risk/return profile in order to reduce your premium outlay or to pay less commissions. Trade an options position because your outlook tells you it is the best position to take under the current market conditions. Specifically, selling extra options may reduce the cost of your spread, or failing to buy protective options may reduce the amount of your brokerage bill, but in both cases, you incur added and unjustifiable risk.

■ Second, if you are new to trading options, do not take a position that is net short an option or options. There are many ways to trade from the short side without taking unlimited, or practically unlimited, risk. They all involve the purchase of one or more risk limiting options. Each *short* option should be covered by a long option.

> **Each short option should be covered by a long option.**

It is helpful to discuss the profit/loss potential of spreads in terms of their value at expiration. Practically spreaking, however, you will most often close a spread before expiration because you will not want to exercise or be assigned to an underlying contract. You also do not want pin risk.

Call spreads and put spreads, or one by one directional spreads

Investors with a directional outlook often find the risks of a straight long or short options position to be undesirable. A stock index may be at a historically high level, and therefore an investor may want to sell calls or buy puts in order to profit from a decline. But perhaps the market is still too strong to sell 'naked' calls, i.e., short calls without a hedge. If premium levels are high, then the investor may not want to risk investing in a straight put purchase. A sensible alternative is to spread the risk of a straight options position by taking the opposite long or short position at a strike price that is more distant from the underlying.

> Spread the risk of a straight options position by taking the opposite long or short position at a strike price that is more distant from the underlying.

For example, if XYZ is trading at 100, we may buy the 95 put and simultaneously sell the 90 put, thereby creating a **long put spread,** a bearish strategy. If instead we are bullish, we may sell the 95 put and buy the 90 put, creating a **short put spread.**

Another bullish strategy is to buy the 105 call while selling the 110 call, creating a **long call spread.** If instead we sell the 105 call while buying the 110 call, we create a **short call spread,** an alternative bearish strategy. These four spreads are also known as **vertical spreads**.

In practice, both strikes of the call or put spread are usually placed out of the money. The key to all these spreads is the option that is at, or nearest to, the underlying. We will discuss each of them.

The profit/loss calculations that form the basis of these spreads can be applied to any underlying in stocks, bonds, or commodities. For the purpose of illustration, a set of options on a stock is given in Table 9.1.

Microsoft at $111\frac{3}{4}$

60 days until January expiration

Contract multiplier of $100

Strike	90	95	100	105	110	115	120	125	130
January calls				$10\frac{7}{8}$	$7\frac{5}{8}$	5	$3\frac{1}{4}$	2	$1\frac{1}{8}$
January puts	$\frac{15}{16}$	$1\frac{1}{8}$	$1\frac{7}{8}$	$3\frac{1}{8}$	$4\frac{7}{8}$	$7\frac{1}{4}$			

Table 9.1 ■ **Microsoft January options**

*Long call spread (adjacent strikes)

Bullish strategy

Microsoft is currently trading at $111\frac{3}{4}$. You may wish to purchase the 115 call to profit from an upside move. It's close to expiration, time decay is costly, and the implied volatility is higher than it has been recently, so an expenditure of 5 × $100, or $500 may seem too large. You could sell the 120 call for $3\frac{1}{4}$ at the same time as you buy the 115 call, for a total debit of $1\frac{3}{4}$. Your short call then effectively finances the purchase of your long call, and mimimizes your exposure to the Greeks.

With this spread, you have a potential buy at 115 and a potential sell at 120, for which you pay a premium. Your analysis may indicate that the near-term price gain for Microsoft is expected to be 120. You are willing to trade unlimited upside potential for a reduced risk in your premium exposure.

This position is known as the **long call spread** because it is similar to a long call.[5] In order to assess the profit/loss potential of the spread at expiration, first the price of the spread is considered as a unit, $1\frac{3}{4}$.

The maximum profit is gained if the stock is at or above the higher strike, or 120, at expiration. This is calculated as the difference between the strike prices minus the cost of the spread, or $(120 - 115) - 1\frac{3}{4} = 3\frac{1}{4}$.

The maximum loss of the spread is equal to its cost, or $1\frac{3}{4}$. This loss is incurred if the stock is at or below the lower strike, or 115, at expiration.

The break-even level is the level at which an increase in the stock pays for the spread. This is calculated as the lower strike price plus the cost of the spread, or $115 + 1\frac{1}{4} = 116\frac{3}{4}$. Here is a summary of this spread's profit/loss at expiration:

---

[5] This spread is also known as the **bull call spread**, and the **long vertical call spread**.

Debit from long January 115 call: -5
Credit from short January 120 call: $3\frac{1}{4}$
Total debit: $-1\frac{3}{4}$

Maximum profit: Difference between strikes – cost of spread: $(120 - 115) -$
$1\frac{3}{4} = 3\frac{1}{4}$
Maximum loss: Cost of spread: $1\frac{3}{4}$
Break-even level: Lower strike + cost of spread: $115 + 1\frac{3}{4} = 116\frac{3}{4}$

The risk/return potential of this spread is maximum loss ÷ maximum profit, or $1\frac{3}{4} \div 3\frac{1}{4}$. A risk of .54 has a potential gain of 1.00.

Table 9.2 shows the expiration profit/loss for this spread.

Microsoft	110	115	116	116$\frac{3}{4}$	117	118	119	120	125
Spread debit	$-1\frac{3}{4}$	- - -	- - -	- - -	- - -	- - -	- - -	- - -	- - -
Value of spread at expiration	0	0	1	$1\frac{3}{4}$	2	3	4	5	5
Profit/loss	$-1\frac{3}{4}$	$-1\frac{3}{4}$	$-\frac{3}{4}$	0	$\frac{1}{4}$	$1\frac{1}{4}$	$2\frac{1}{4}$	$3\frac{1}{4}$	$3\frac{1}{4}$

Table 9.2 ■ Long Microsoft January 115–120 call spread

In graphic terms, the expiration profit/loss can be illustrated as shown in Figure 9.1:

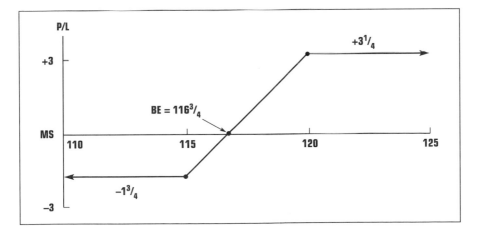

Fig 9.1 ■ Long Microsoft January 115–120 call spread

*Short call spread (adjacent strikes)

Neutral to bearish strategy

Suppose you are neutral to bearish on Microsoft. With 60 days till expiration, January time decay is beginning to accelerate. You would like to collect premium if the stock stays in its current range or if it declines, but you don't want to risk the unlimited loss from a short call. You may then sell the January 115 call at 5, and in the same transaction pay $3\frac{1}{4}$ for the January 120 call, for a net credit of $1\frac{3}{4}$. Your position is known as the **short call spread** because it is similar to a short call.[6]

The advantage of your spread is that it has a built-in stop-loss cover at the higher strike, or 120. You may think of this spread as a potential sale of the stock at 115, and a potential buy of the stock at 120. For this risk, you collect a premium.

The expiration profit/loss of this spread is opposite to the above long call spread, but the break-even level is the same. Here, the maximum profit is the credit received from the spread, or $1\frac{3}{4}$. This profit is earned if the stock is at or below the lower strike, or 115.

The maximum loss occurs if the stock is at or above the higher strike. This is calculated as the difference between strike prices minus the income from the spread, or $(120 - 115) - 1\frac{3}{4} = 3\frac{1}{4}$.

The break-even level is the same as the long call spread. This is the level at which a loss due to an increase in the stock price matches the income from the spread. The calculation is the lower strike price plus the price of the spread, or $115 + 1\frac{3}{4} = 116\frac{3}{4}$. Following is a summary of this spread's expiration profit/loss:

Credit from short January 115 call:	5
Debit from long January 120 call:	$-3\frac{1}{4}$
Total credit:	$1\frac{3}{4}$

Maximum profit: credit from spread: $1\frac{3}{4}$
Maximum loss: (difference between strikes) – credit from spread: $(120 - 115) - 1\frac{3}{4} = 3\frac{1}{4}$.
Break-even level: lower strike + credit from spread: $115 + 1\frac{3}{4} = 116\frac{3}{4}$

The risk/return potential from this spread is also opposite to the long call spread, or maximum loss ÷ maximum return at $3\frac{1}{4} ÷ 1\frac{3}{4}$. Here, a risk of each $1.86 offers a potential return of $1.00.

---

[6] This spread is also known as the **bear call spread**, and the **short vertical call spread.**

In tabular form, the expiration profit/loss for this short call spread is as follows:

Microsoft	110	115	116	116¾	117	118	119	120	125
Spread credit	1¾	–	–	–	–	–	–	–	–
Value of spread at expiration	0	0	−1	−1¾	−2	−3	−4	−5	−5
Profit/loss	1¾	1¾	¾	0	−¼	−1¼	−2¼	−3¼	−3¼

Table 9.3 ■ Short Microsoft January 115–120 call spread

The expiration profit/loss for this spread is graphed as shown in Figure 9.2:

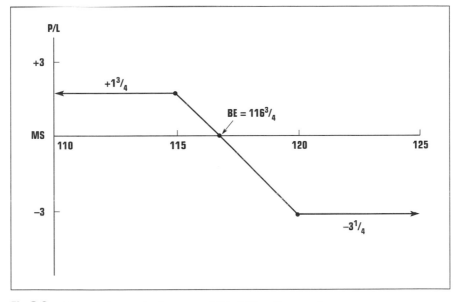

Fig 9.2 ■ Short Microsoft January 115–120 call spread

*Long put spread (adjacent strikes)

Bearish strategy

Microsoft is currently trading at 111¾, and you are bearish, short term, on the stock. You may wish to purchase the January 110 put to profit from a downside move. With 60 days till expiration time decay is accelerating and the implied volatility is higher than it has been recently, so an expenditure of 4⅞, or $487.50, may seem too great.

Instead, you could sell the January 105 put at $3\frac{1}{8}$, and in the same transaction pay $4\frac{7}{8}$ for the January 110 put, for a total debit of $1\frac{3}{4}$. Your short put then effectively finances the purchase of your long put, and mimimizes your exposure to the Greeks.

The trade-off is that your downside profit is limited by the 105 put, but at that point you have probably captured the best part of the move. Your analysis may tell you that Microsoft is supported below 105, in which case your 105 put would effectively be the level at which you take the profit from your 110 put.

In this case, you are buying the January 110 – 105 put spread. This position is known as the **long put spread** because it is similar to a long put.[7] You may simply think of this spread as a potential sale of the stock at 110, and a potential buy of the stock at 105. For this profit potential you pay a premium.

In order to assess the profit/loss potential of the spread at expiration, first the price of the spread is considered as a unit: $1\frac{3}{4}$.

At expiration, the maximum profit is gained if the stock is at or below the lower strike, or 105. This is calculated as the difference between strike prices minus the cost of the spread, or $(110 - 105) - 1\frac{3}{4} = 3\frac{1}{4}$.

The maximum loss is taken if the stock is at or above the higher strike, or 110, at expiration. This is calculated simply as the cost of the spread, or $1\frac{3}{4}$.

The break-even level is the level at which a decline in the stock pays for the cost of the spread. This is calculated as the higher strike minus the cost of the spread, or $110 - 1\frac{3}{4} = 108\frac{1}{4}$. The expiration profit/loss is summarized as follows:

Debit from long January 110 put:	$-4\frac{7}{8}$
Credit from short January 105 put:	$3\frac{1}{8}$
Total debit:	$-1\frac{3}{4}$

Maximum profit: Difference between strikes – cost of spread: $(110 - 105) - 1\frac{3}{4} = 3\frac{1}{4}$

Maximum loss: cost of spread: $1\frac{3}{4}$

Break-even level: higher strike – cost of spread: $110 - 1\frac{3}{4} = 108\frac{1}{4}$

The risk/return potential of this spread is maximum loss ÷ maximum profit, or $1\frac{3}{4} \div 3\frac{1}{4}$. In other words you are risking $ .54 for each potential profit of $1.00.

In tabular form the expiration, profit/loss is as in Table 9.4:

---

[7] This spread is also known as the **bear put spread** and the **long vertical put spread**.

Microsoft	100	105	106	107	108	$108\frac{1}{4}$	109	110	115
Spread debit	$-1\frac{3}{4}$								
Value of spread at expiration	5	5	4	3	2	$1\frac{3}{4}$	1	0	0
Profit/loss	$3\frac{1}{4}$	$3\frac{1}{4}$	$2\frac{1}{4}$	$1\frac{1}{4}$	$\frac{1}{4}$	0	$-\frac{3}{4}$	$-1\frac{3}{4}$	$-1\frac{3}{4}$

Table 9.4 ■ Long Microsoft January 110–105 put spread

In graphic terms, the profit/loss of this spread is illustrated in Figure 9.3:

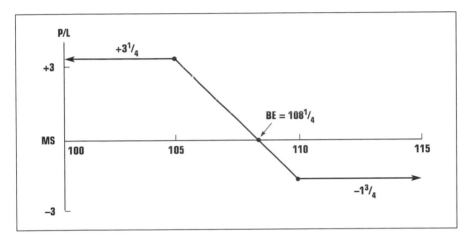

Fig 9.3 ■ Long Microsoft January 110–105 put spread

*Short put spread (adjacent strikes)

Neutral to bullish strategy

On the other hand, suppose that you are neutral to bullish on Microsoft. Your analysis tells you that it is oversold, or that its earnings prospects are better than expected. You would like to sell a put in order to profit either from time decay if the stock stabilizes, or from a decline in the put's value if the stock rallies. At the same time, you do not want the exposure of a naked short put.

You may then sell the January 110 put at $4\frac{7}{8}$, and in the same transaction pay $3\frac{1}{8}$ for the January 105 put, for a net credit of $1\frac{3}{4}$. This position is known as the **short put spread** because it is similar to a short put.[8] The advantage of this spread is that if the stock declines, a possible loss is cut

---

[8] This spread is also known as the **bull put spread** and the **short vertical put spread**.

at the lower strike, or 105. You may think of this spread as a potential buy of the stock at the higher strike, or 110, and a potential sale of the stock at the lower strike, or 105. For this potential risk you collect a premium.

The expiration profit/loss of this short put spread is exactly opposite to the former long put spread. The maximum profit is earned if the stock is at or above the higher strike, or 110. This amount is simply the premium collected for the spread, or $1\frac{3}{4}$.

The maximum loss occurs if the stock is at or below the lower strike, or 105. This is calculated as the difference between the strike prices minus the income from the spread: $(110 - 105) - 1\frac{3}{4} = 3\frac{1}{4}$.

The break-even level is the level at which a decline in the stock matches the spread income. This is calculated as the higher strike minus the price of the spread, or $110 - 1\frac{3}{4} = 108\frac{1}{4}$.

The profit/loss at expiration is summarized as follows:

Credit from short January 110 put: $4\frac{7}{8}$
Debit from long January 105 put: $-3\frac{1}{8}$
Total credit from spread: $1\frac{3}{4}$

Maximum profit: credit from spread: $1\frac{3}{4}$
Maximum loss: difference between strikes – credit from spread:
$$(110 - 105) - 1\frac{3}{4} = 3\frac{1}{4}$$
Break-even level: higher strike – credit from spread: $110 - 1\frac{3}{4} = 108\frac{1}{4}$

The risk/return potential for this spread is also opposite to the long put spread, at maximum loss ÷ maximum profit, or $3\frac{1}{4}$ ÷ $1\frac{3}{4}$. Here, you risk 1.86 to make 1.00.

In tabular form the expiration profit/loss is shown in Table 9.5.

Microsoft	100	105	106	107	108	108 $\frac{1}{4}$	109	110	115
Spread credit	$1\frac{3}{4}$	- - -	- - -	- - -	- - -	- - -	- - -	- - -	- - -
Value of spread at expiration	-5	-5	-4	-3	-2	$-1\frac{3}{4}$	-1	0	0
Profit/loss	$-3\frac{1}{4}$	$-3\frac{1}{4}$	$-2\frac{1}{4}$	$-1\frac{1}{4}$	$-\frac{1}{4}$	0	$\frac{3}{4}$	$1\frac{3}{4}$	$1\frac{3}{4}$

Table 9.5 ■ Short Microsoft January 110–105 put spread

The graph of the profit/loss position at expiration is shown in Figure 9.4.

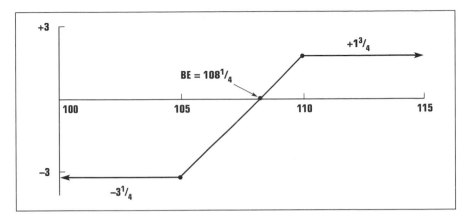

Fig 9.4 ■ **Short Microsoft January 110–105 put spread**

Long versus short call and put spreads

So far we have seen that both a long call spread and a short put spread profit from an upside move. Likewise both a long put spread and a short call spread profit from a downside move. The

> **Both a long put spread and a short call spread profit from a downside move.**

question may arise as to which one is preferable. The basic difference is that of buying or selling premium, and the trade-offs are similar to straight long or short positions in calls or puts.

Compare the above Microsoft long January 115–120 call spread to the short January 110–105 put spread. Both spreads are valued at $1\frac{1}{4}$, and both spreads are equidistant from the underlying.[9]

If a long and a short spread are both out-of-the-money and equidistant from the underlying, the maximum profit of the long spread is greater than the maximum profit of the short spread, but the short spread has the greater probability to profit.

The probability of either spread expiring in the money can be approximated by the delta of the strike that is nearest the underlying. In the above example, both the 115 call and the 110 put have a delta that is approximately .45. If the stock has a 45 per cent probability of moving to a strike in either direction, then the direction which is short has a 55 per cent probability of collecting its premum.The maximum loss, however, is greater with the short spread. The maximum profit, of course, favours the long spread, and this is a fair return for an outcome that is less probable.

---

[9] In fact, the options prices indicate that Microsoft is trading at $112\frac{3}{4}$. This is the synthetic price of the stock for January delivery, as explained in Part 4.

The difference between a spread and a straight call or put is that the spread's maximum profit/loss can be quantified at the outset. Spreads do not remove the need for sound trading decisions, however. In the end, you must be the judge of foreseeable market activity. Spreads will, however, reduce your risk, and as any professional knows, this is the key to staying in business.

Often in the stock or bond markets, the out-of-the-money put spread costs less than the equidistant out-of-the-money call spread. This is because the lower strike put is priced higher than the higher strike call, although they are the same distance from the underlying. This is a function of what are known as volatility skews, which are discussed in Part 3.

Call spreads and put spreads with non-adjacent strikes

Call spreads and put spreads can be created with any two strikes. Again using Microsoft as an example, you could pay 5 for the January 115 call, and sell the January 125 call at 2, for a net debit of 3. You would then be long the January 115 – 125 call spread. You have a potential buy of the stock at 115 and a potential sale of the stock at 125. The formula for calculating the expiration profit/loss is the same as with adjacent strikes.

> Call spreads and put spreads can be created with any two strikes.

At expiration, the maximum profit is earned if the stock settles at the higher strike. This profit is calculated as the difference between the strike prices minus the cost of the spread, or $(125 - 115) - 3 = 7$.

The maximum loss is the cost of the spread, or 3. This loss occurs if the stock is at or below the lower strike, or 115, at expiration.

The break-even level is the level at which an increase in the stock pays for the spread. This is calculated as the lower strike plus the cost of the spread, or $115 + 3 = 118$.

This expiration profit/loss is as follows:

Debit from long January 115 call: –5
Credit from short January 125 call: 2
Total debit: –3

Maximum profit: (difference between strikes) minus cost of spread:
$$(125 - 115) - 3 = 7$$
Maximum loss: cost of spread: 3
Break-even level: lower strike plus cost of spread: $115 + 3 = 118$

The risk/return ratio for this spread is maximum loss ÷ maximum profit, or 3 ÷ 7. Here, $ .43 is risked for each $1.00 of potential gain.

In tabular form, the expiration profit/loss for this January 115–125 call spread is as shown in Table 9.6.

Microsoft	110	115	116	117	118	119	120	121	122	123	124	125	130
Spread debit	-3												
Value of spread at expiration	0	0	1	2	3	4	5	6	7	8	9	10	10
Profit/loss	-3	-3	-2	-1	0	1	2	3	4	5	6	7	7

Table 9.6 ■ Microsoft long January 115–125 call spread

The expiration profit/loss is graphed as in Figure 9.5.

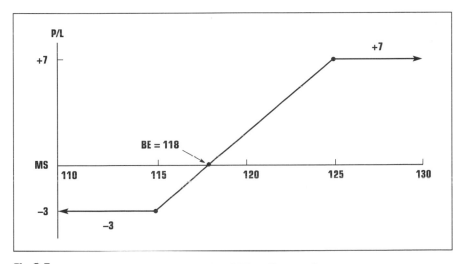

Fig 9.5 ■ Microsoft long January 115–125 call spread

A short of this spread has the opposite profit/loss characteristics with the same break-even level. A non-adjacent put spread with Microsoft is given at the conclusion of this chapter in the questions section.

With a non-adjacent strike call or put spread, the greater the distance between the strikes, the greater is the debit or credit from the spread, and the greater is the degree of market movement covered by the spread. For the longs, this means greater cost with greater potential return. For the shorts, this means greater income with greater potential risk.

A call or put spread with non-adjacent strikes behaves less like a spread and more like the option closer to the underlying, with increased exposure to that option's delta, gamma, theta, and vega. Generally speaking, this exposure is not significant unless the strikes are far apart, and/or until the spread has 30 days or less till expiration. In any case, it does not affect the expiration profit/loss. Many investors are willing to assume the added risk from spreading with non-adjacent strikes because the risk is still less than with a straight call or put position.

Call spreads and put spreads at different distances from the underlying

Call spreads and put spreads can be any distance from the underlying.

Call spreads and put spreads can be any distance from the underlying. The trade-offs are similar to those between straight out-of-the-money and at-the-money calls or puts. The farther a spread is from the underlying, the less cost or income it has, and the less probability it has of becoming in-the-money.

For example, in Microsoft you could sell the January 105 put at $3\frac{1}{8}$, and in the same transaction pay $1\frac{7}{8}$ for the January 100 put, for a net credit of $1\frac{1}{4}$.

At expiration, the maximum profit of the short January 105 – 100 put spread is the income from the spread, or $1\frac{1}{4}$. This profit occurs if the stock closes above the higher strike, or 105.

The maximum loss occurs of the stock closes below the lower strike. This is calculated as the difference between the strikes minus the income from the spread, or $(105-100) - 1\frac{1}{4} = 3\frac{3}{4}$.

The break-even level is the level at which the decline of the stock equals the price of the spread. This is calculated as the higher strike minus the income from the spread, or $105 - 1\frac{1}{4} = 103\frac{3}{4}$. The expiration profit/loss is summarized below:

Maximum profit: income from spread: $1\frac{1}{4}$
Maximum loss: difference between strikes minus income from spread: $(105 - 100) - 1\frac{1}{4} = 3\frac{3}{4}$
Break-even level: higher strike minus income from spread: $105 - 1\frac{1}{4} = 103\frac{3}{4}$
The risk/return of this trade is maximum loss ÷ maximum profit, or $3\frac{3}{4} ÷ 1\frac{1}{4}$. For each risk of $3.00 the potential return is $1.

In tabular form the expiration prfoit/loss for this spread is as in Table 9.7.

Microsoft	95	100	101	102	103	103¾	104	105	110
Credit from Spread	1¼	- - - -	- - - -	- - - -	- - - -	- - - -	- - - -	- - - -	- - - -
Value of spread at expiration	-5	-5	-4	-3	-2	-1¼	-1	0	0
Profit/loss	-3¾	-3¾	-2¾	-1¾	-¾	0	¼	1¼	1¼

Table 9.7 ■ **Microsoft short January 105–100 put spread**

The profit/loss graph at expiration is as in Figure 9.6.

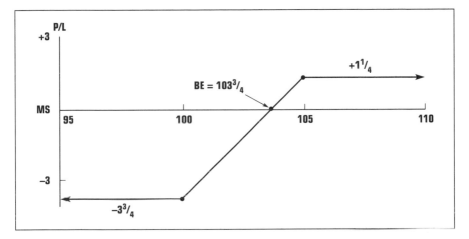

Fig 9.6 ■ **Microsoft short January 105–100 put spread**

Premium sellers often short out-of-the-money spreads that are at a safe distance from the underlying because these spreads have limited risk. Premium buyers, however, can afford to place their position closer to the underlying because the cost of the spread is less than the cost of a straight call or put.

Conclusion

Call spreads and put spreads have the advantage of known risk at the outset. For the longs, the cost of the spread is the maximum loss, and if the trader is good with technicals, he can pick his levels. For the shorts, these spreads allow for premium selling with a built-in stop-loss order.

On a risk/return basis they can be recommended to everyone, especially beginners.

Questions on call spreads and put spreads

1   Refer again to the Microsoft options prices in Table 9.1. Suppose you are bearish on the stock for the short term, and you wish to buy the January 105 – 95 put spread.

   a) What is the net debit in ticks and in dollars for this spread?

   b) What is the maximum profit?

   c) What is the maximum loss?

   d) What is the break-even level?

   e) What is the risk/return ratio?

   f) Microsoft is currently at $111\frac{3}{4}$. In percentage terms, how much would the stock need to retrace in order for the spread to break even?

   g) Write a table and draw a graph of the expiration profit/loss.

2   At the LIFFE, where most options and shares sensibly trade in decimals with only one fraction, the half, British Telecom is currently priced at $834\frac{1}{2}$p (£8.34$\frac{1}{2}$). The February 850 calls are priced at $65\frac{1}{2}$, and the February 900 calls are priced at 47. Remember that the contract multiplier here is £1,000, so the value of the February 850 calls are .655 × £1,000 = £655, and the February 900 calls are .47 × £1,000, or £470.

   a) What is the cost of a going long one February 850 – 900 call spread?

   b) What is the break-even level of the spread?

   c) What is the maximum profit?

   d) What is the maximum loss?

   e) What is the risk/return ratio?

   f) Write a table and draw a graph of the profit/loss at expiry.

3   General Electric is currently trading at $92\frac{1}{16}$. The yearly high for the stock is $96\frac{7}{8}$. You think that within the next 30 days GE is unlikely to make a new high, and most likely it will be stable through the year end. The December 95 calls are priced at $1\frac{7}{8}$, and the December 100 calls are priced at $\frac{1}{2}$.

   a) What is the net credit from a sale of the December 95 – 100 call spread?

b) What is the break-even level?

c) What is the maximum loss?

d) What is the risk/return ratio?

e) What is the loss if GE reaches its old high?

4 In London, the FTSE-100 index is currently trading at 5422. Suppose you're bearish for the next several weeks, with a target of 5300 by December expiration. You would like to buy one December 5400 put, but the cost of 193p (£1,930) is too great, especially with accelerated time decay. You note that the 5300 puts are priced at 154p, and you decide to buy this put spread. The contract multiplier is £1,000.

a) What is the cost of buying this spread, in ticks and in actual pounds sterling?

b) What is the break-even level?

c) What is the maximum profit?

d) What is the maximum loss?

e) What is the risk/return ratio?

5 The following options on the Dow Jones Industrial Average trade at CBOE. Here, the value of the Dow Jones Index is divided by 100 in order to give the value of the index, known as DJX, on which the options are based. For example, if the Dow closes at 9056, the DJX settles at 90.56. You may think of the index as a stock with a price of 90.56, etc. Your only problem then is to transfer fractions into decimals. The options contract multiplier is $100, so the December 91 call at $1\frac{15}{16}$ is worth $1.9375 \times \$100$, or $193.75.

DJX at 90.56
30 days until December expiration

Strike	87	88	89	90	91	92	93	94
December calls			$3\frac{1}{4}$	$2\frac{5}{8}$	$1\frac{15}{16}$	$1\frac{3}{8}$	$1\frac{1}{8}$	$\frac{5}{8}$
December puts	1	$1\frac{1}{8}$	$1\frac{1}{2}$	$1\frac{13}{16}$	$2\frac{1}{4}$			

a) What is the break-even level for a purchase of one straight December 91 call?
What value of the Dow would this break-even level correspond to?
What is the break-even level for a purchase of one straight December 90 put?
What value of the Dow would this break-even level correspond to?

b-i) Suppose you think that the Dow has topped out for the time being, and you anticipate a Christmas break, i.e., a correction of 3 per cent by December expiration. What index level would this correspond to?

b-ii) Which out-of-the-money put spread would completely cover this range?

b-iii) If you buy, or go long, this spread, what is your net debit in options ticks?

b-iv) What is your maximum profit?
What is your maximum loss?
What is your break-even level
What is your risk return ratio?

c-i) Suppose you believe in the Christmas rally. Your chart analysis, however, tells you that there is resistance at 9300 in the Dow. What out-of-the-money call spread could you buy?

c-ii) What is your debit for this spread?
What is the maximum profit?
What is the break-even level?
What is the maximum loss?
What is the risk/return ratio?

Answers

1 **a)** $3\frac{1}{8} - 1\frac{1}{8} = 2$ ticks; $2 \times \$100 = \$200$

   b) $[105 - 95] - 2 = 8$

   c) 2

   d) $105 - 2 = 103$

   e) $\frac{2}{8} = \$.25$ at risk for each potential return of $1.00

   f) $111\frac{3}{4} - 103 = 8\frac{3}{4}$; $8.75 \div 111.75 = 7.8\%$

   g)

Microsoft	90	95	96	97	98	99	100	101	102	103	104	105	110
Spread debit	−2	-	-	-	-	-	-	-	-	-	-	-	-
Value of spread at expiration	10	10	9	8	7	6	5	4	3	2	1	0	0
Profit/loss	8	8	7	6	5	4	3	2	1	0	−1	−2	−2

See next page for graph.

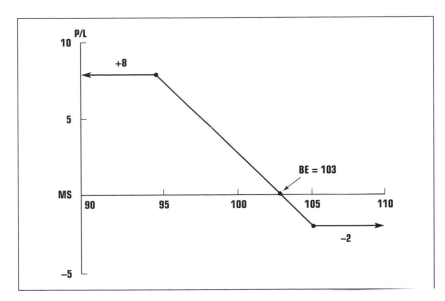

Answer 1g ■ Microsoft long January 105–95 put spread

2   a) $65\frac{1}{2} - 47 = 18\frac{1}{2}$; $.185 \times £1,000 = £185$

   b) $850 + 18\frac{1}{2} = 868\frac{1}{2}$

   c) $[900 - 850] - 18\frac{1}{2} = 31\frac{1}{2}$

   d) $18\frac{1}{2}$

   e) $18.5 \div 31.5 = 59p$ risk for each £1 of potential return

   f) see next page

3   a) $1\frac{7}{8} - \frac{1}{2} = 1\frac{3}{8}$

   b) $95 + 1\frac{3}{8} = 96\frac{3}{8}$

   c) $[100 - 95] - 1\frac{3}{8} = 3\frac{5}{8}$

   d) $3\frac{5}{8} \div 1\frac{3}{8} = 2.63$ to 1

   e) $96\frac{7}{8} - 96\frac{3}{8} = \frac{1}{2}$

4   a) $193 - 154 = 39$ ticks; $.39 \times £1,000 = £390$

   b) $5400 - 39 = 5361$

   c) $[5400 - 5300] - 39 = 61$

   d) 39

   e) $39 \div 61 = 64p$ at risk for each potential return of £1

5   a) $91 + 1.9375 = 92.9375$
       9293.75
       $90 - 1.8125 = 88.1875$
       8818.75

BT	800	850	860	868 ½	870	880	890	900	950
Spread debit	–18 ½								
Value of spread at expiry	0	0	10	18 ½	20	30	40	50	50
Profit/loss	–18 ½	–18 ½	–8 ½	0	1 ½	11 ½	21 ½	31 ½	31 ½

Answer 2f ■ British Telecom long February 850–900 call spread

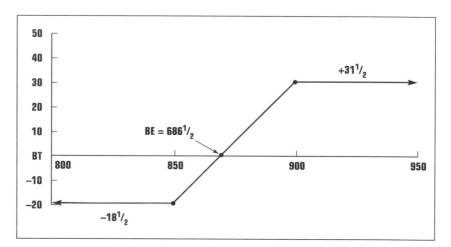

Answer 2f ■ British Telecom long February 850–900 call spread

5 **a) b-i)** $90.56 \times .03 = 2.72; 90.56 - 2.72 = 87.84$

    b-ii) Long December 90 – 87 put spread

    b-iii) $1 \frac{13}{16} - 1 = \frac{13}{16}$

    b-iv) $3 - \frac{13}{16} = 2 \frac{3}{16} = 2.1875 = \$218.75$

          $\frac{13}{16} = \$81.25$

          $90 - \frac{13}{16} = 89 \frac{3}{16} = 89.1875$

          $81.25 \div 218.75 = .37$ for 1

    c-i) December 91 – 93 call spread

    c-ii) $1 \frac{15}{16} - 1 \frac{1}{8} = \frac{13}{16} = \$81.25$

          $2 - \frac{13}{16} = 1 \frac{3}{16} = \$118.75$

          $91 + \frac{13}{16} = 91 \frac{13}{16} = 91.8125$

          $\frac{13}{16} = \$81.25$

          $81.25 \div 118.75 = .68$ for 1

10 One by two directional spreads

There are other ways of financing the purchase of a directional position. Those that we will discuss in this chapter are variations of the long call and put spreads. Again, they involve buying an option to take advantage of a chosen market direction. But instead of selling one, they sell two options at the strike price that is more distant from the underlying.

The spreads in this chapter are suitable for slowly trending markets, and they are unsuitable for markets that are trending rapidly higher or lower, or volatile markets that are subject to sudden shifts in direction.

Long one by two call spread

Bullish strategy

The **long one by two call spread** is a long call spread with an additional short call at the higher strike. If XYZ is at 100, you could buy one 105 call and sell two 115 calls in the same transaction. This spread is also known as the one by two ratio call spread or the one by two vertical call spread.

In order to trade this spread, your outlook should call for the underlying to increase to a level that is near, but not substantially above, the higher strike. This spread, like the long call spread, has its maximum profit if the underlying is at the higher strike at expiration. It is less costly than the long call spread because it is financed by an extra short call. But because of the extra short call, this spread has the potential for unlimited loss if the underlying rallies substantially. The extra short call includes added exposure to the Greeks. Let's take our examples from the preceding chapter.

Microsoft at $111\frac{3}{4}$

60 days until January expiration

Contract multiplier of $100

Strike	90	95	100	105	110	115	120	125	130
January calls				$10\frac{7}{8}$	$7\frac{5}{8}$	5	$3\frac{1}{4}$	2	$1\frac{1}{8}$
January puts	$\frac{15}{16}$	$1\frac{1}{8}$	$1\frac{7}{8}$	$3\frac{1}{8}$	$4\frac{7}{8}$	$7\frac{1}{4}$			

Table 10.1 ■ **Microsoft January options**

Here, you could pay 5 for one January 115 call and sell two January 125 calls at 2 for a net debit of 1. At expiration, the maximum profit occurs if the stock closes at the higher strike; this is the same level as with a long call spread at the same strike. This profit is calculated as the difference between the strike prices less the cost of the spread, or $(125 - 115) - 1 = 9$.

Because of the extra short call there are two break-even levels. The lower break-even level is, like the long call spread, the lower strike price plus the cost of the spread, or $115 + 1 = 116$.

The upper break-even level is the maximum profit plus the higher strike price, or $9 + 125 = 134$.

Above the upper break-even level this spread takes a loss equivalent to the amount that the stock increases. A summary of the profit/loss at expiration is as follows.

Debit from January 115 call:	–5
Credit from two January 125 calls: 2 × 2 =	4
Total debit:	–1

Maximum profit: (Difference between strikes) minus cost of spread:
$$(125 - 115) - 1 = 9$$
Lower break-even level: lower strike plus cost of spread: $115 + 1 = 116$
Upper break-even level: maximum profit plus higher strike: $9 + 125 = 134$
Maximum loss: unlimited

In order to evaluate the risk/return potential of this spread, you must consider the upside potential of the stock or underlying. Remember that the maximum loss is potentially unlimited.

In tabular form, the expiration profit/loss is as shown in Table 10.2.

Microsoft	110	115	116	120	125	130	134	135	140	(above)
Spread debit	-1--	---	---	---	---	---	---	---	---	---
Value of one by one spread at expiration	0	0	1	5	10	10	10	10	10	10
Value of extra short call at expiration	0	0	0	0	0	-5	-9	-10	-15	unlimited
Profit/loss	-1	-1	0	4	9	4	0	-1	-6	unlimited

Table 10.2 ■ Microsoft long January 115–125 one by two call spread

In graphic form, the expiration profit/loss of this spread is as shown in Figure 10.1.

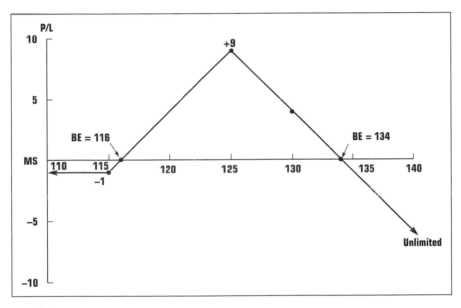

Fig 10.1 ■ Microsoft long January 115–125 one by two call spread

Long one by two call spread for a credit

Bearish to slightly bullish strategy

With adjacent strikes, or strikes that are close to each other, the long one by two call spread can often be done for a credit. Effectively, then, there is no lower break-even level, and the spread will profit from a downside market move. The upper break-even level, however, becomes much closer to the underlying. There is a hidden danger in this spread, however.

For example, using the above strikes, you could pay 5 for one January 115 call and sell two January 120 calls at $3\frac{1}{4}$ for a net credit of $1\frac{1}{2}$ on the spread.

At expiration, the maximum profit occurs if the stock closes at the higher strike price. This profit is calculated as the difference between strikes *plus* the credit from the spread, or $(120 - 115) + 1\frac{1}{2} = 6\frac{1}{2}$.

Between the strikes, the spread profits the amount that the stock closes above the lower strike price plus the income from the spread. For example, if Microsoft closes at 117, then the profit on the spread is $(117 - 115) + 1\frac{1}{2} = 3\frac{1}{2}$.

If the stock declines below the lower strike price, or 115, then the spread profits the amount of the credit, or $1\frac{1}{2}$.

The upper break-even level is calculated as the higher strike plus the maximum profit, or $120 + 6\frac{1}{2} = 126\frac{1}{2}$.

Above the upper break-even level, the spread has the potential for unlimited loss. Note that that in this case, the upper break-even level is much closer to the underlying than the 134 level of the January 115–125, one by two call spread, above.

This spread may look like easy money, but *don't be misled*. If the one by two call (or put) spread can be done for a credit, it means that the underlying is sufficiently volatile to be above the upper break-even level at expiration. Perhaps for this reason, the one by two spread for a credit is not often traded. If, after considering these factors, your outlook still calls for the stock to remain below the upper break-even level through expiration, then the long one by two call spread for a credit is a justifiable strategy. This is not recomended for beginners.

Long one by two put spread

Bearish strategy

The **long one by two put spread** is a long put spread with an extra short put at the lower strike. It is also known as the one by two ratio put spread or the one by two vertical put spread. If XYZ is at 100, you could by one 95 put and sell two 85 puts in the same transaction.

> The long one by two put spread is a long put spread with an extra short put at the lower strike.

In order to trade this spread, your outlook should call for the underlying to decline to a level that is near, but not substantially below, the lower strike. At expiration the maximum profit is earned if the stock closes at the lower strike, but because of the extra short put, the maximum downside loss is potentially great. The extra short put includes added exposure to the Greeks. This spread is less costly than the long put spread because it is financed by the extra short put.

Using the previous set of Microsoft options, you could pay $3\frac{1}{8}$ for one January 105 put and sell two January 95 puts at $1\frac{1}{8}$ for a net debit of $\frac{7}{8}$. At expiration, the maximum profit occurs if the stock closes at 95. This profit is calculated as the difference between strikes minus the cost of the spread, or $(105 - 95) - \frac{7}{8} = 9\frac{1}{8}$.

Like the long one by two call spread, there are two break-even levels. The upper break-even level is calculated as the higher strike minus the cost of the spread, or $105 - \frac{7}{8} = 104\frac{1}{8}$. The lower break-even level is calculated as the lower strike minus the maximum profit, or $95 - 9\frac{1}{8} = 85\frac{7}{8}$.

Below the lower break-even level the spread loses point for point with the decline of the stock.

A summary of the expiration profit/loss is as follows.

Debit from long January 105 put:	$-3\frac{1}{8}$
Credit from two short January 95 puts: $2 \times 1\frac{1}{8} =$	$2\frac{1}{4}$
Total debit:	$-\frac{7}{8}$

Maximum profit: (difference between strikes) minus cost of spread:
$$(105 - 95) - \tfrac{7}{8} = 9\tfrac{1}{8}$$
Upper break-even level: higher strike minus cost of spread: $105 - \frac{7}{8} = 104\frac{1}{8}$
Lower break-even level: lower strike minus maximum profit: $95 - 9\frac{1}{8} = 85\frac{7}{8}$
Maximum loss: amount of stock decline below lower break-even level

The risk/return potential of this spread must consider that the potential loss is the full amount that the stock may decline below the lower break-even level.

In tabular form, the expiration profit/loss is as shown in Table 10.3.

Microsoft	(below)	80	85	$85\frac{7}{8}$	90	95	100	$104\frac{1}{8}$	105	110
Spread debit	$-\frac{7}{8}$									
Value of one by one spread at expiration		10	10	10	10	10	10	5	$\frac{7}{8}$	0	0
Value of extra short put at expiration	– full amt	–15	–10	$-9\frac{1}{8}$	–5	0	0	0	0	0
Profit/loss	– full amt	$-5\frac{7}{8}$	$-\frac{7}{8}$	0	$4\frac{1}{8}$	$9\frac{1}{8}$	$4\frac{1}{8}$	0	$-\frac{7}{8}$	$-\frac{7}{8}$

Table 10.3 ■ Microsoft long January 105–95 one by two put spread

In graphic form, the expiration profit/loss of this spread is shown in Figure 10.2.

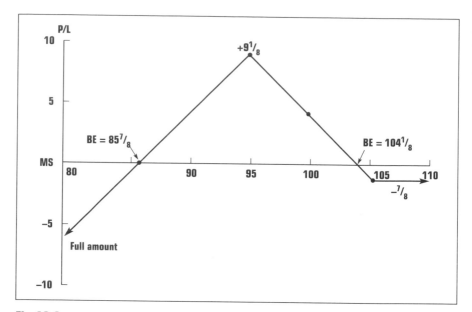

Fig 10.2 ■ **Microsoft long January 105–95 one by two put spread**

Long one by two put spread for a credit

Bearish strategy

Like the long one by two call spread, the long one by two put spread can often be done for a credit if the strikes are close or adjacent. The risk/return characterisitcs are similar, but with the opposite market direction. Bear in mind that declines in stock prices can be sudden and drastic, and accordingly this strategy is not recommended for beginners. It is advisable to consider that any long one by two spread done for a small debit, or for even, more closely matches the current volatility of the underlying.

How to manage the risk of the long one by two spreads

The return scenario for these spreads is a gradual underlying move from the long towards the short strike. If, however, the underlying makes a sudden move to the short strike, with no sign of a retracement, the spread becomes subject to the delta and vega risk of the extra short option. It is then advisable to cover the risk of this option. There are two practical solutions:

■ The first is simply to buy back the extra short. This cuts the loss on the position and leaves a net long call or put spread with limited risk.

■ The second solution is less costly, and it is to buy an out-of-the-money option that is the same distance from the two short options as they are from the long option. For example, if the spread is long one 105 call and short two 115 calls, and if XYZ rallies to 115, then the solution is to buy one 125 call. Likewise, if the spread is long one 95 put and short two 85 puts, and if XYZ breaks to 85, then the solution is to buy one 75 put.

In the first case, the resulting position is a long call butterfly, and in the second case, the resulting position is a long put butterfly. Both positions have limited risk, and they have the potential to recoup some of the loss through time decay. The butterfly spread is discussed in a separate chapter.

Before you trade any spread that is net short an option, you should *have a contingency plan* as part of your risk scenario. At the same time you place your spread order, you should also place a buy-stop, market order for a covering option that is activated at a predetermined level of the underlying.

Long call ladder (UK), or long call Christmas tree (US)

Bullish strategy

A variation of the long one by two is a spread that places the two short options at different strikes. The **long call ladder** is a long call spread with an extra short call at a third strike that is above the lower two strikes. If XYZ is at 100, then you can buy one 105 call, sell one 110 call, and sell one 115 call in the same transaction. This spread is also known as the long Christmas tree, or simply, the 'tree.'[10] In practice, it is placed out-of-the-money.

> Long call ladder is a long call spread with an extra short call at a third strike that is above the lower two strikes.

Using the preceding set of Microsoft options, you could pay 5 for one January 115 call, sell one January 120 call at $3\frac{1}{4}$, and sell one January 125 call at 2 for a net credit of $\frac{1}{4}$. Occasionally, this spread may be done for a small credit, but in practice, it would most likely trade at a small debit or at even, i.e., for no debit or credit. Like the one by two with adjacent strikes, a generous credit for this spread implies that the stock is sufficiently volatile to reach the upper break-even level. See the put ladder (page 119) for a more typical example.

---

[10] This term probably signifies that the options are placed at higher and higher levels, like ornaments on a Christmas tree. Remember that this spread is net short an option, so you will want to put out the fire before it reaches the top.

At expiration, the maximum profit for the ladder is earned when the stock or underlying closes between the upper two strikes, 120–125. In this case, because of the small spread credit, this profit is calculated as the difference between the lower two strikes plus the credit from the spread, or $(120 - 115) + \frac{1}{4} = 5\frac{1}{4}$. (If the spread is traded for a debit, this profit is calculated as the difference between the lower two strikes minus the debit. If the spread is traded for a debit, then there is a lower break-even level. This is calculated as the lowest strike plus the spread debit.)

The upper break-even level is the highest strike plus the maximum profit. In this case, the calculation is $125 + 5\frac{1}{4} = 130\frac{1}{4}$. Above the upper break-even level the spread loses point for point with the stock, and faces the possibility of unlimited loss. The expiration profit/loss is as follows:

Debit from long January 115 call:	–5
Credit from short January 120 call:	$3\frac{1}{4}$
Credit from short January 125 call:	2
Total credit:	$\frac{1}{4}$

Maximum profit: (middle strike minus lower strike) plus credit (or minus debit) from spread: here, $(120 - 115) + \frac{1}{4} = 5\frac{1}{4}$
Upper break-even level: highest strike plus maximum profit: $125 + 5\frac{1}{4} = 130\frac{1}{4}$
Maximum loss: potentially unlimited

You can compare the break-even level of this ladder to the one by twos with adjacent and non-adjacent strikes. As you might expect, this level is between the other two, at $130\frac{1}{4}$. This ladder is a fair compromise in terms of risk/return potential.

Note again the potential for unlimited loss compared to a maximum profit of $5\frac{1}{4}$. The expiration profit/loss of this spread is shown in Table 10.4.

Microsoft	110	115	120	125	130	$130\frac{1}{4}$	135	(above)
Spread credit	$\frac{1}{4}$							
Value of one by one spread at expiration	0	0	5	5	5	5	5	5
Value of extra short call at expiration	0	0	0	0	–5	$-5\frac{1}{4}$	–10	(– unlimited)
Profit/loss	$\frac{1}{4}$	$\frac{1}{4}$	$5\frac{1}{4}$	$5\frac{1}{4}$	$\frac{1}{4}$	0	$-4\frac{3}{4}$	(– unlimited)

Table 10.4 ■ Microsoft long January 115–120–125 call ladder

Figure 10.3 is a graph of this spread at expiration.

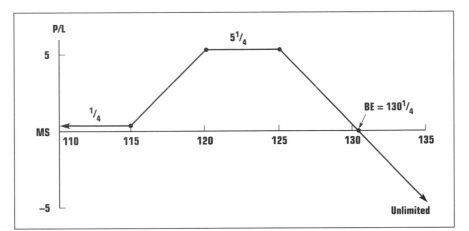

Fig 10.3 ■ **Microsoft long January 115–120–125 call ladder**

Long put ladder (UK), or long put Christmas tree (US)

Bearish strategy

The **long put ladder** is a long put spread with an extra short put at a third strike below the put spread. If XYZ is at 100, then you could buy one 95 put, sell one 90 put, and sell one 85 put in the same transaction. This spread is also known as the long put Christmas tree.

> The long put ladder is a long put spread with an extra short put at a third strike below the put spread.

In Microsoft you could pay $3\frac{1}{8}$ for one January 105 put, sell one January 100 put at $1\frac{7}{8}$, and sell one January 95 put at $1\frac{1}{8}$. Here, the spread trades for a net debit of $\frac{1}{8}$.

At expiration, the maximum profit is earned when the stock closes between the lower two strikes, 100 – 95. In this case, because of the small spread debit, this profit is calculated as the difference between the higher two strikes minus the cost of the spread, or $(105 - 100) - \frac{1}{8} = 4\frac{7}{8}$.

The upper break-even level is the highest strike minus the cost of the spread, or $105 - \frac{1}{8} = 104\frac{7}{8}$. The lower break-even level is the lowest strike minus the maximum profit, or $95 - 4\frac{7}{8} = 90\frac{1}{8}$.

The maximum loss can be significant; is the full amount that the stock declines below the lower break-even level. The expiration profit/loss for this spread is as follows.

Debit from long January 105 put: $\qquad$ $-3\frac{1}{8}$
Credit from short January 100 put: $\qquad$ $1\frac{7}{8}$
Credit from short January 95 put: $\qquad$ $1\frac{1}{8}$
Total debit: $\qquad$ $-\frac{1}{8}$

Maximum profit/loss: (highest strike minus middle strike) minus cost of spread: $(105 - 100) - \frac{1}{8} = 4\frac{7}{8}$
Upper break-even level: highest strike − cost of spread: $105 - \frac{1}{8} = 104\frac{7}{8}$
Lower break-even level: lowest strike minus maximum profit: $95 - 4\frac{7}{8} = 90\frac{1}{8}$
Maximum loss: amount of stock decline below lower break even level

The risk/return potential of this spread should account for a decline in the stock below the lower break-even level. The expiration profit/loss in tabular form is shown in Table 10.5.

Microsoft	(below)	85	90	$90\frac{1}{8}$	95	100	$104\frac{7}{8}$	105	110
Spread debit	$-\frac{1}{8}$								
Value of one by one spread at expiration	5	5	5	5	5	5	$\frac{1}{8}$	0	0
Value of extra short put at expiration	(full amt)	−10	−5	$-4\frac{7}{8}$	0	0	0	0	0
Profit/loss	(full amt)	$-5\frac{1}{8}$	$-\frac{1}{8}$	0	$4\frac{7}{8}$	$4\frac{7}{8}$	0	$-\frac{1}{8}$	$-\frac{1}{8}$

Table 10.5 ■ Microsoft long January 105–100–95 put ladder

Figure 10.4 is a graph of the expiration profit/loss:

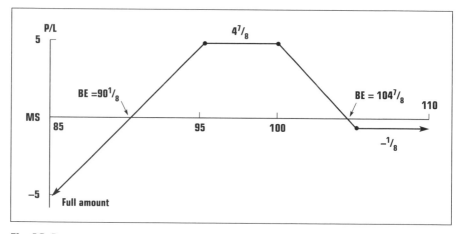

Fig 10.4 ■ Microsoft long January 105–100–95 put ladder

How to manage the risk of the long ladder

The risk of the long ladder is managed similarly to that of the long one by two. If the underlying suddenly moves to the short strike that was formerly farthest out-of-the-money, the first solution is to buy back that strike.

The second solution is to buy the out-of-the-money option that is as far from the ladder as the three options in the ladder are from each other. For example, if the ladder is long one 105 call, short one 110 call, and short one 115 call, and if XYZ quickly rallies to 115, then the solution is to buy one 120 call. Likewise, if the ladder is long one 95 put, short one 90 put, and short one 85 put, and if XYZ suddenly breaks to 85, then the solution is to buy one 80 put. In the first case, the resulting position is a **long call condor,** and in the second case, the resulting position is a **long put condor.** Both of these spreads have limited risk; they are discussed in Chapter 14.

Ladders at different strike prices

With the ladder the consecutive strike prices are usually equidistant from each other. The equidistance[11] may vary, however, from adjacent to any number of non-adjacent strikes. For example, if XYZ is at 100, a call ladder may have strike prices at 105, 110, and 115, or it may have strike prices at 105, 115, and 125. The second ladder costs more because the sum of the options sold is less. Its profit potential, however, is 10 points instead of five, less cost. Its upper break-even level, or point of potential unlimited risk, is farther from the underlying. With ladders, the major risk consideration is that the strike farthest out-of-the-money should be at a safe distance from the underlying.

Asymmetric ladder

Finally, there is no reason why the strikes of a ladder need to be equidistant from each other. Asymmetric ladders are occasionally traded, and they have different risk/return profiles. For example, you may wish to place the second short strike farther from the underlying. If XYZ is at 100, instead of placing your call ladder at 105, 110, and 115, you may place it at 105, 110, and 120. The second spread costs more and therefore has less profit potential, but it has less risk because its upper break-even level is farther from the underlying.

---

[11] i.e., the distance that is equal. This word, found in the Lenny Jordan Dictionary, will come in handy when we discuss spreads with four components.

Alternatively, you may place your ladder at 105, 115, and 120. This spread costs more than the two above because the two options sold are the least expensive, but it has the greatest profit potential. It also has the least potential risk because its upper break-even level is the farthest from the underlying. Just remember that the major risk of the ladder lies with the extra short option.

Comparing call spreads, 1x2's, and ladders

At this point, it will be constructive to compare the data from the spreads already discussed. We want to examine costs, profit potentials, risks and break-even levels. If we examine the call spreads, then we can apply the conclusions to the put spreads.

Microsoft at $111\frac{3}{4}$
January options, 60 days until expiration

	cost/ income	max profit	max. loss	low break-even	upper break-even (point of unlim. loss potential)
115–120 call spread	$1\frac{3}{4}$ debit	$3\frac{1}{4}$	$1\frac{3}{4}$	$116\frac{3}{4}$	none
115–125 call spread	3 debit	7	3	118	none
115–120, one by two	$1\frac{1}{4}$ credit	$6\frac{1}{2}$	unlim.	none	$126\frac{1}{2}$
115–125, one by two	1 debit	9	unlim.	116	134
115–120–125 ladder	$\frac{1}{4}$ credit	$5\frac{1}{4}$	unlim.	none	$130\frac{1}{4}$

Table 10.6 ■ Comparing call spreads, 1 x 2's and ladders

Try to develop your options awareness by taking a few minutes to analyze this data. Compare the costs or incomes to the potential profits, and compare the potential profits to the upper break-even levels, etc.

The most risk averse spreads are obviously the two one by one call spreads. Concerning the others, you may find that a short strike often seems to be a magnet for the underlying contract but in reality options strikes have little or no effect on the underlying, apart from rare occasions. But if the market moves in the direction of your short strike you may have to cover simply out of worry. **It is much easier to make trading decisions when your judgement is not impaired by proximate risk.**

An analysis procedure such as the above should always be used when deciding which spread to trade.

Questions for one by twos and ladders

1 It's now the third week in November, and the global stock markets have overcome their annual October nervousness and have begun to rally. You want to take a bullish position because you expect the rally to continue until Christmas. The S&P 500 index is currently at 1152.61, but its all-time high is 1186.75. you think that the index will eventually meet resistance and settle at approximately 1200 for December expiration. You want to give your assessment a try, but you don't want to risk too much.

At the CBOE the following SPX options on the S&P 500 are trading at the following prices. The contract multiplier is $100. This is a European-style option, so there is no early exercise.
S&P index at 1152.61
December options with 30 days until expiration

Strike	1175	1200	1225
Call prices	17	$7\frac{1}{2}$	$2\frac{1}{2}$

a) i)   What is the cost of the December 1175–1200, one by two call spread in ticks and in dollars?

  ii)   What is the lower break-even level?

  iii) At December expiration, what index level will give the maximum profit?

  iv)   What is the maximum profit?

  v)   What is the upper break-even level?

  vi)   What is the maximum loss?

  vii) What is your profit/loss if the index settles at 1212?

  viii) If, one week after you open this position, i.e., with approximately three weeks till expiration, the index reaches 1200, how can you manage the risk?

b) Suppose instead you want to pay more for your spread in exchange for less upside risk.

  i)   What is the cost of the Dec 1175–1200–1225 call ladder in ticks and in dollars?

  ii) What is the lower break-even level?

  iii) At December expiration, what index level will give the maximum profit?

  iv) What is the maximum profit?

  v)   What is the upper break-even level?

  vi) What is the maximum loss?

  vii) What is your profit/loss if the index settles at 1212?

c) Perhaps you think the upside risk of the above two spreads is still too great, and you think the index might reach 1225 before settling into a range. You are willing to pay more to reduce your exposure, and to profit more from the upside potential.

   i) What is the cost of the December 1175 – 1225, one by two call spread?

   ii) What is the lower break-even level?

   iii) At December expiration, what index level will give the maximum profit?

   iv) What is the maximum profit?

   v) What is the upper break-even level?

   vi) What is the maximum loss?

   vii) What is your profit/loss if the index settles at 1212?

2 Because of perennial lawsuits in the US, you are bearish on British American Tobacco. The current price of the shares is $479\frac{1}{2}$p (£4.79$\frac{1}{2}$). You think that the shares are well supported below 400p, and you note the prices of the following January puts. (Remember, the contract multiplier is £1,000.)

British American Tobacco at $479\frac{1}{2}$p
January puts with 70 days until expiry

Strike	390	420	460
January puts	$4\frac{1}{2}$	10	$22\frac{1}{2}$

a) i) What is the cost of the January 460–390, one by two put spread in ticks and in sterling?

   ii) What is the upper break-even level?

   iii) At January expiry, what price level of the shares will give the maximum profit?

   iv) What is the maximum profit?

   v) What is the lower break-even level?

   vi) What is the maximum loss?

   vii) At expiry, what is your profit/loss if the shares close at 370?

b) Suppose you decide to be more economical, and you don't mind raising your lower break-even level.

   i) What is the cost of the January 460–420–390 asymmetric put ladder in ticks and in sterling?

   ii) What is the upper break-even level?

     iii) At January expiry, what price level of the shares will give the maximum profit?

     iv) What is the maximum profit?

     v)   What is the lower break-even level?

     vi) What is the maximum loss?

     vii) At expiry, what is your profit/loss if the shares close at 370?

c) If instead you think that the maximum downside potential for the shares is approximately 420, you might buy the January 460–420, one by two put spread.

     i)   What is the cost of this spread in ticks and in sterling?

     ii)   What is the upper break-even level?

     iii) At January expiry, what price level of the shares will give the maximum profit?

     iv) What is the maximum profit?

     v)   What is the lower break-even level?

     vi) What is the maximum loss?

     vii) If, two weeks after you open this position, the shares are trading at 420, how can you manage the risk?

     viii) At expiry, what is your profit/loss if the shares close at 370?

d) For a favourable price you are willing to buy shares in British American Tobacco. This year's range for the shares is $584\frac{1}{2} - 329\frac{1}{2}$. You realize that by trading the above three spreads, you may be obligated to buy shares via your extra short put. What would be the effective purchase price of your shares with spreads a, b and c above?

Answers

1 **a)** i) $17 - [2 \times 7\frac{1}{2}] = 2$, or $200

      ii) $1175 + 2 = 1177$

      iii) 1200

      iv) $[1200 - 1175] - 2 = 23$

      v) $1200 + 23 = 1223$

      vi) potentially unlimited

      vii) $23 - 12 = 11$ profit

      viii) Buy either one 1200 call, or one 1225 call.

  b) i) $17 - 7\frac{1}{2} - 2\frac{1}{2} = 7$, or $700

      ii) $1175 + 7 = 1182$

      iii) 1200 to 1225

      iv) $[1200 - 1175] - 7 = 18$

      v) $1225 + 18 = 1243$

      vi) potentially unlimited

      vii) 18 profit

c) i) $17 - [2 \times 2\frac{1}{2}] = 12$, or \$1200

      ii) $1175 + 12 = 1187$

      iii) 1225

      iv) $[1225 - 1175] - 12 = 38$

      v) $1225 + 38 = 1263$

      vi) potentially unlimited

      vii) $[1212 - 1175] - 12 = 25$ profit

2 **a)** i) $22\frac{1}{2} - [2 \times 4\frac{1}{2}] = 13\frac{1}{2}$, or £135

      ii) $460 - 13\frac{1}{2} = 446\frac{1}{2}$

      iii) 390

      iv) $[460 - 390] - 13\frac{1}{2} = 56\frac{1}{2}$

      v) $390 - 56\frac{1}{2} = 333\frac{1}{2}$

      vi) $333\frac{1}{2}$, if the shares go to zero

      vii) $56\frac{1}{2} - [390 - 370] = 36\frac{1}{2}$p profit

b) i) $22\frac{1}{2} - 10 - 4\frac{1}{2} = 8$, or £80

      ii) $460 - 8 = 452$

      iii) 420 to 390

      iv) $[460 - 420] - 8 = 32$

      v) $390 - 32 = 358$

      vi) 358, if the shares go to zero

      vii) $32 - [390 - 370] = 12$p profit

c) i) $22\frac{1}{2} - [2 \times 10] = 2\frac{1}{2}$, or £25

      ii) $460 - 2\frac{1}{2} = 457\frac{1}{2}$

      iii) 420

      iv) $[460 - 420] - 2\frac{1}{2} = 37\frac{1}{2}$

      v) $420 - 37\frac{1}{2} = 382\frac{1}{2}$

      vi) $382\frac{1}{2}$, if the shares go to zero

      vii) Buy one 420 put, or buy one 390 put.

      viii) $37\frac{1}{2} - [420 - 370] = 12\frac{1}{2}$p loss

d) $390 - 56\frac{1}{2} = 333\frac{1}{2}$; $390 - 32 = 358$; $420 - 37\frac{1}{2} = 382\frac{1}{2}$

11

Combos and hybrid spreads for market direction

Bullish strategy

Still another way of financing a long call position is to sell a put. Usually both strikes are out-of-the-money, and this spread is called the **long call, short put combo**. It is also called the **cylinder**. If

> Another way of financing a long call position is to sell a put.

XYZ is at 100, you may buy the 110 call and sell the 85 put in the same transaction. In order to trade this spread, you must be reasonably certain that the underlying is due to increase in value, because the short put incurs the potential obligation to buy the underlying. The downside risk is great, but so is the upside potential. This spread is often traded by professionals who want to buy the underlying.

Again, we'll work with the previous set of Microsoft options.

Microsoft at $111\frac{3}{4}$
60 days until January expiration
Contract multiplier of $100

Strike	90	95	100	105	110	115	120	125	130
January calls				$10\frac{7}{8}$	$7\frac{5}{8}$	5	$3\frac{1}{4}$	2	$1\frac{1}{8}$
January puts		$\frac{15}{16}$	$1\frac{1}{8}$	$1\frac{7}{8}$	$3\frac{1}{8}$	$4\frac{7}{8}$	$7\frac{1}{4}$		

Table 11.1 ■ Microsoft January options

Here, you could pay $3\frac{1}{4}$ for one January 120 call, and sell one January 95 put at $1\frac{1}{8}$ for a net debit of $2\frac{1}{8}$. On the upside, the spread behaves like a long 120 call purchased for $2\frac{1}{8}$. The break-even level is the call strike price plus the cost of the spread, or $120 + 2\frac{1}{8} = 122\frac{1}{8}$. You are long a call, so you have unlimited upside potential.

On the downside, the spread behaves like a short 95 put for which you have *paid* $2\frac{1}{8}$. If at expiration, the stock closes below the put strike, or 95, you will be assigned on the short put, and you will be obligated to buy the stock at the strike price, or 95. The cost of your stock purchase will be effectively *increased* by the debit of the spread. For example, if the stock closes at 95 and you are assigned on the put, the purchase price of Microsoft would be $95 + 2\frac{1}{8} = 97\frac{1}{8}$. If the stock continues to decline, you are still obligated to make purchase for an effective price of $97\frac{1}{8}$. Because of the naked, short put position, the potential loss is large.

It is advisable to place the put at a greater distance from the underlying than the call, unless you are convinced that the stock has bottomed out.

If at expiration the stock closes between 95 and 120, the debit from the spread, or $2\frac{1}{8}$ in this case, is lost. The expiration profit/loss is summarized as follows:

Debit from January 120 call:	$-3\frac{1}{4}$
Credit from January 95 put:	$1\frac{1}{8}$
Total debit:	$-2\frac{1}{8}$

Upside break-even level: call strike plus cost of spread: $120 + 2\frac{1}{8} = 122\frac{1}{8}$
Maximum upside profit: potentially unlimited
Downside potential purchase price: cost of spread plus lower strike price: $2\frac{1}{8} + 95 = 97\frac{1}{8}$
Maximum downside loss: decline of stock below downside potential purchase price: $97\frac{1}{8}$
Profit/loss between strikes: loss of spread debit: $2\frac{1}{8}$ loss between 95 and 120

The risk/return potential is, practically speaking, equal and great. In tabular form, the expiration profit/loss is shown in Table 11.2:

Microsoft	(below)	90	95	100	120	$122\frac{1}{8}$	125	130	(above)
Spread debit	$-2\frac{1}{8}$								
Value of spread at expiration	(– full amt)	-5	0	0	0	$2\frac{1}{8}$	5	10	(unlimited)
Profit/loss	(– full amt)	$-7\frac{1}{8}$	$-2\frac{1}{8}$	$-2\frac{1}{8}$	$-2\frac{1}{8}$	0	$2\frac{7}{8}$	$7\frac{7}{8}$	(unlimited)

Table 11.2 ■ **Microsoft long January 120 call, short 95 put combo**

In graphic terms, the expiration profit/loss is shown in Figure 11.1.

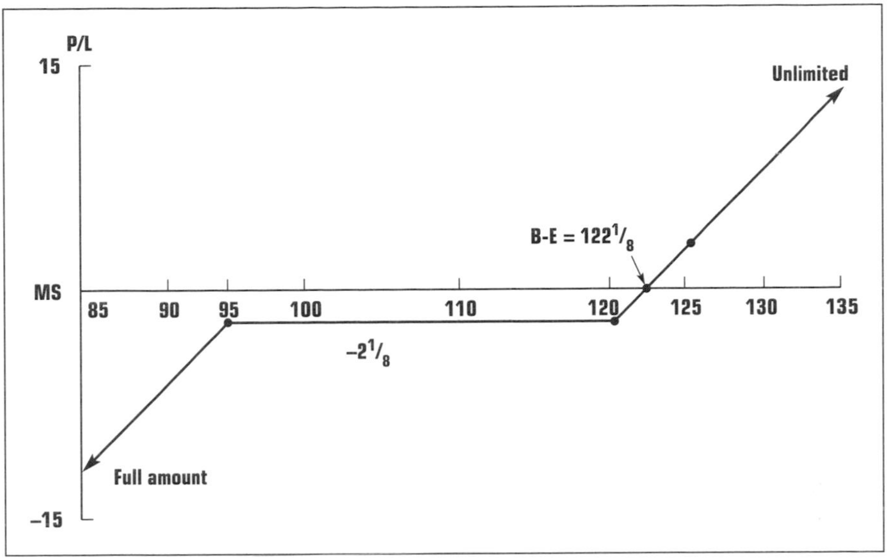

Fig 11.1 ■ **Microsoft January long 120 call, short 95 put combo**

The long call, short put combo is often traded in bull markets, and especially bull markets in commodities that are beginning from long-term support levels.

Long put, short call combo or cylinder

Bearish strategy

A long out-of-the-money put coupled with a short out-of-the-money call is known as the **long put, short call combo**. It is also called the **cylinder**. If XYZ is at 100, you could buy one 95 put and sell one 110 call in the same transaction. Both options positions are a potential sale of the underlying. This spread is often traded by stock holders in bear markets where there are significant levels of resistance to higher prices: the long put functions as a stop-loss sale, and the short call functions as a potential sale at a higher price.

> A long out-of-the-money put coupled with a short out-of-the-money call is known as the long put, short call combo.

This spread is often used as a hedge by holders of bonds: the short call effectively sells the bond at a favourable price while the long put insures against an unforeseen inflationary scenario. For both bond and stock holders, when used in this manner, this spread is called the **fence**.

In Microsoft you could pay $3\frac{1}{8}$ for one January 105 put and sell one January 125 call at 2 for a net debit of $1\frac{1}{8}$. On the downside, your spread behaves like a long 105 put purchased for $1\frac{1}{8}$. Your break-even level is the put strike minus the cost of the spread, or $105 - 1\frac{1}{8} = 103\frac{7}{8}$. Below this level you profit one to one with the decline of the stock.

On the upside, your spread behaves like a short 125 call for which you have *paid* $1\frac{1}{8}$. If the stock closes above 125 at expiration, you will be assigned on your short call, and you will be obligated to sell the stock at 125. The spread was traded for a net debit of $1\frac{1}{8}$, so your effective sale price would be the call strike minus the spread debit, or $125 - 1\frac{1}{8} = 123\frac{7}{8}$. No matter how far the stock rises above 125, you will still be obligated to sell it for an effective purchase price of $123\frac{7}{8}$. The loss, as with any short call position, is potentially unlimited.

At expiration, if the stock closes between the strike prices, the spread debit is taken as a loss. Here, if the stock closes between 105 and 125, the loss on the position is $1\frac{1}{8}$.

A summary of the expiration profit/loss is as follows:

Debit from long January 105 put: $-3\frac{1}{8}$
Credit from short January 125 call: 2
Total debit: $-1\frac{1}{8}$

Downside break-even level: put strike minus cost of spread: $105 - 1\frac{1}{8} = 103\frac{7}{8}$
Maximum downside profit: decline of stock below lower break-even level: $103\frac{7}{8}$
Upside potential sale price: higher strike minus debit from spread: $125 - 1\frac{1}{8} = 123\frac{7}{8}$
Maximum upside loss: potentially unlimited
Profit/loss if stock closes between strikes: loss of spread debit: $1\frac{1}{8}$

Again, the risk/return potential, practically speaking, is equal and great. The expiration profit/loss is shown in Table 11.3:

Microsoft	(below)	95	100	$103\frac{7}{8}$	105	125	130	(above)
Spread debit	$-1\frac{1}{8}$							
Value of spread								
at expiration	(full amt)	10	5	$1\frac{1}{8}$	0	0	-5	(-unlimited)
Profit/loss	(full amt)	$8\frac{7}{8}$	$3\frac{7}{8}$	0	$-1\frac{1}{8}$	$-1\frac{1}{8}$	$-6\frac{1}{8}$	(-unlimited)

Table 11.3 ■ **Microsoft January long 105 put, short 125 call combo**

Figure 11.2 shows a graph of this combo.

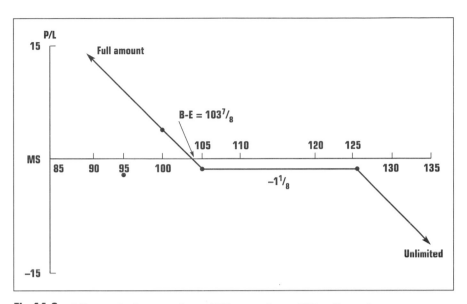

Fig 11.2 ■ Microsoft January long **105** put, short **125** call combo

If you were the owner of Microsoft stock, and if you applied this spread as a fence, then your effective selling levels at expiration would be either $103\frac{7}{8}$ or $123\frac{7}{8}$.

Directional hybrid spreads

The directional spreads that we have discussed are the most common, but they are not the only choices available. Many investors create spreads that combine components of the standard spreads in order to suit a particular outlook and strategy. There are no special terms for these hybrid spreads, but they can be traded in one transaction on most, if not all, open-outcry exchanges. You may not trade these spreads, but you might review them in order to improve your options awareness.

> Many investors create spreads that combine components of the standard spreads in order to suit a particular outlook and strategy.

As with all spreads, a hybrid can be created provided your outlook accounts for:

■ direction
■ level of support

■ level of resistance.

The risk/return potential should also be assessed, and any contingency plans prepared. The following is just one example of a hybrid spread.

Long call spread, short put (three-way hybrid)

Bullish strategy

If a call purchase can be financed by the sale of a put, then a call spread purchase can be financed by the sale of a put. If XYZ is at 100, you could buy the 105–115 call spread and sell the 85 put. On most open-outcry exchanges, this 3-way can be traded in one transaction, and the bid-ask spread for it will be marginally greater than with a single option.

The advantage of this spread is that the long call is financed with two options, but the disadvantage is that the short put contains the potential obligation to purchase the underlying in a declining market. Also, the upside is limited.

In Microsoft, you could pay 5 for one January 115 call, sell one January 130 call at $1\frac{1}{8}$, and sell one January 95 put at $1\frac{1}{8}$ in the same transaction for a net debit of $2\frac{3}{4}$. The profit range is 15 points at a cost of $2\frac{3}{4}$. Compare this to the January 115–125 call spread, in which the profit range is 10 points at a cost of 3. The three-way must account for the naked short put, however.

The upside of this spread behaves like a long 115-130 call spread purchased for a cost of $2\frac{3}{4}$. The break-even level at expiration is the lower strike plus the cost of the spread, or $115 + 2\frac{3}{4} = 117\frac{3}{4}$.

The maximum upside profit is the difference between strikes minus the cost of the spread, or $(130 - 115) - 2\frac{3}{4} = 12\frac{1}{4}$.

The downside of this spread behaves like a short 95 put traded for a *debit* of $2\frac{3}{4}$. If the stock closes below 95 at expiration, you will be assigned on the short put, and you will be obligated to pay 95 for the stock. Because your spread was traded for a debit of $2\frac{3}{4}$, your effective purchase price will be the strike price of the put *plus* the cost of the spread, or $95 + 2\frac{3}{4} = 97\frac{3}{4}$. No matter how far the stock declines below 95, you will still be obligated to purchase it for an effective cost of $97\frac{3}{4}$. Because of the naked short put, the potential loss is great.

If at expiration the stock closes between the middle strikes of the spread, or 95–115, a loss is taken equal to the cost of the spread, or $2\frac{3}{4}$. A summary of the profit/loss at expiration follows.

Debit from long January 115 call:	-5
Credit from short January 130 call:	$1\frac{1}{8}$
Credit from short January 95 put:	$1\frac{1}{8}$
Total debit:	$-2\frac{3}{4}$

Upside break-even level: lower call strike plus cost of spread: $115 + 2\frac{3}{4} = 117\frac{3}{4}$
Maximum upside profit: difference between strikes minus cost of spread: $(130–115) – 2\frac{3}{4} = 112\frac{1}{4}$.
Potential downside purchase price: Put strike plus cost of spread: $95 + 2\frac{3}{4} = 97\frac{3}{4}$
Maximum downside loss : $97\frac{3}{4}$
Profit/loss if stock closes between middle two strikes (95–115) is the cost of the spread, or $2\frac{3}{4}$ loss

Like the combo, this three-way is occasionally traded at the beginning of bull markets in commodities, when long-term support levels are well established. There are many other hybrids which are traded less often. The more sophisticated traders are continually inventing new ways to spread options.

Questions on combos and three-way hybrid spreads

1   It is July in the grain belt, and conditions are hot and dry. The December Corn futures contract at the CBOT has been trading in a range centered on 220 ($2.20 per bushel), with good support between 200 and 210. You know from experience that if a drought occurs, the December contract can reach 260 or more within several weeks.

On this day December Corn settles at $222\frac{3}{4}$, and you note the following set of December options. These options expire in the third week of November, and they are exercisable to the December futures contract. Their contract multiplier is $50, which means that the 260 call, priced at 2, costs 2 × $50, or $100.

December Corn at $222\frac{3}{4}$
December options, with 120 days until expiration.

Strike	200	210	220	230	240	250	260	270	280
Calls			$11\frac{1}{2}$	7	$4\frac{1}{2}$	3	2	$1\frac{1}{4}$	$\frac{7}{8}$
Puts		$1\frac{3}{4}$	$4\frac{1}{4}$	$8\frac{3}{4}$					

a) i) What is the cost of the long 230 call – short 200 put combo in ticks and in dollars?

ii) At expiration, what is the upside break-even level?

iii) What is the maximum upside profit?

iv) What is the downside price of a potential long position in the December futures contract?

v) What is the potential downside loss?

vi) What is the profit/loss if the December futures contract settles between 200 and 230 at the expiration of the December options?

b) Suppose, instead, your outlook for December corn calls for a maximum price appreciation of 260.

i) What is the cost of the long 230 – 260 call spread, short 200 put, three-way spread?

ii) At expiration, what is the upside break-even level?

iii) What is the maximum profit?

iv) What is the downside price of a potential long position in the December futures contract?

v) What is the potential downside loss?

vi) What is the profit/loss if the December futures contract settles between 200 and 230 at the expiration of the December options?

2 The CBOT December Treasury Bond futures contract is currently trading at 129.26 ($129 \frac{26}{32}$), which corresponds to a yield of 5.08 per cent. Lately Treasuries have attracted buying interest through a flight to quality based on problems in emerging markets. You think that the bullishness has run its course, however, and you note the following December options. These options expire in the third week of November and they are exercisable to the December futures contract. As specified earlier, they trade in 64ths, and the contract multiplier is $1,000, which means that the cost of the 132 call is $\frac{32}{64} \times \$1,000$, or $500.

December T-Bond futures at 129.26
December options with 22 days until expiration

Strike	128	129	130	131	132
Calls		1.46	1.12	.50	.32
Puts	.37	.58	1.24		

i) You decide to buy the 129 put and sell the 132 call as a combo. What is the cost of your spread in ticks and in dollars?

ii) At expiration, what is the downside break-even level?

iii) What is the maximum downside profit?

iv) If the December futures contract rallies, what is the price of your potential short position?

v) What is your potential upside loss?

vi) What is your profit/loss if the December futures contract is between 129 and 132 when the December options expire?

Answers

1 **a)** i) $7 - 1\frac{3}{4} = 5\frac{1}{4} \times \$50 = \$262.50$

ii) $230 + 5\frac{1}{4} = 235\frac{1}{4}$

iii) The full amount that the December futures contract rallies above $235\frac{1}{4}$

iv) $200 + 5\frac{1}{4} = 205\frac{1}{4}$

v) The full amount that the December futures contract declines below 200, plus $5\frac{1}{4}$. The maximum loss could theoretically be $205\frac{1}{4}$.

vi) $5\frac{1}{4}$ loss

b) i) $[7 - 2] - 1\frac{3}{4} = 3\frac{1}{4} \times \$50 = \$162.50$

ii) $230 + 3\frac{1}{4} = 233\frac{1}{4}$

iii) $[260 - 230] - 3\frac{1}{4} = 26\frac{3}{4}$

iv) $200 + 3\frac{1}{4} = 203\frac{1}{4}$

v) The full amount that the December futures contract declines below 200, plus $3\frac{1}{4}$. The maximum loss could theoretically be 203 $\frac{1}{4}$.

vi) $3\frac{1}{4}$ loss

2 **a)** i) $.58 - .32 = .26$; $\frac{26}{64} \times \$1,000 = \$406.25$

ii) 26 options ticks = 13 futures ticks. Futures trade in 32nds. $129.00 - .13 = 128.32 - .13 = 128.19$

iii) The full amount that the December futures contract declines below 128.19

iv) Futures price of $132.00 - .26$ options ticks $= 131.32 - .13 = 131.19$

v) The full amount that the December futures contract rallies above 132, plus the spread debit of 26 options ticks.

vi) Loss of spread debit, 26 options ticks

12 Volatility spreads

Options differ from most other kinds of investment products because they address market
volatility. Volatility is a function of absolute price
movement, i.e., price fluctuations in either direction. Options can be traded to profit from either
increasing or decreasing absolute movement. Often the price trend of an
underlying is more difficult to assess than its volatility trend. When this is
the case, volatility spreads are preferable.

Options can be traded to profit from either increasing or decreasing absolute movement.

If the volatility is increasing, we can often assume that the underlying
is expanding its range, and that it will be significantly higher or lower at
expiration than it is at present. The risk of our assumption is that the
underlying may increase its range but that at expiration it may settle at
the midpoint.

If the volatility is decreasing, we can often assume that the underlying
will be within its recent range at expiration. The risk of our assumption is
that the underlying may decrease its range but that by expiration the
range itself may shift to a higher or lower level.

If we wish to trade volatility, we can take positions that profit from
either increasing or decreasing absolute movement. In more conventional
terms, we say that we can take positions to profit from either volatile or
stationary markets. By convention, the word 'volatile' means high volatility, and by convention, the word 'stationary' means low volatility. These
conventional terms may not be precise, but now that we know their limitations, we can use them. Therefore, for our purpose we can set out the
following definitions:

- **Volatile** means increasing absolute price movement, high absolute price movement, increasing historical and implied volatility, and high historical and implied volatility.

- **Stationary** means decreasing absolute price movement, low absolute price movement, decreasing historical and implied volatility, and low historical and implied volatility.

Spreads for volatile markets, such as the long straddle, profit from increased volatility, both historical and implied. They incur a cost from time decay. They may or may not be net long options. They have net positive vega, positive gamma, and negative theta. These spreads are best opened when the market is quiet, or emerging from quiet conditions, and when absolute movement is expected to increase.

Spreads for stationary markets, such as the long at-the-money butterfly, profit from decreased volatility, both historical and implied. They profit from time decay. They may or may not be net short options. They have net negative vega, negative gamma, and positive theta. These spreads are best opened when the market has been active, and when absolute movement has started to decrease.

The same spread can often be traded in either volatile or stationary markets, depending on whether it is bought or sold. Practically speaking, some of these spreads are more suitable for the first or the second type of market, and some have more inherent risks. All beginners should trade the spreads with the least risk, and these are marked with an asterisk (*).

At some point, you may benefit from reviewing this introduction.

Long straddle

For volatile markets

The **long straddle** is a simultaneous purchase of the at-the-money call and put. This spread profits when the underlying, at expiration, has increased or decreased to a level that more than compensates for its cost. If XYZ is at 100, you could buy

> The long straddle is a simultaneous purchase of the at-the-money call and put.

the 100 call and the 100 put in the same transaction. The maximum risk of the spread is its cost, and the potential return is the full amount that the underlying increases or decreases above the upside, or below the downside, break-even levels.

Consider the following set of options on Microsoft, which has moved to a lower price, $108\frac{7}{8}$.

Microsoft at 108 $\frac{7}{8}$
60 days till January expiration

Strike	90	95	100	105	110	115	120	125	130
January calls				9	$6\frac{1}{8}$	4	$2\frac{1}{2}$	$1\frac{5}{8}$	1
January puts	1	$1\frac{5}{8}$	$2\frac{5}{8}$	$4\frac{1}{8}$	$6\frac{1}{4}$	$9\frac{1}{8}$			

Table 12.1 ■ Microsoft January options, 2

Here, you could purchase the January 110 straddle by paying $6\frac{1}{8}$ for the 110 call and $6\frac{1}{4}$ for the 110 put in a single transaction, for a total debit of $12\frac{3}{8}$. This debit is your maximum risk. With this spread you have the right to buy the stock at 110 also the right to sell the stock at 110.

At expiration, the upside break-even level is the strike price plus the cost of the spread, or $110 + 12\frac{3}{8} = 122\frac{3}{8}$. The downside break-even level is the strike price minus the cost of the spread, or $110 - 12\frac{3}{8} = 97\frac{5}{8}$.

Above $122\frac{3}{8}$ the spread profits point for point with an increase in the stock price, and the maximum return is potentially unlimited. Below $97\frac{5}{8}$ the spread profits point for point with a decline in the stock price, and the maximum return is potentially $97\frac{5}{8}$. (There are probably a few buyers for Microsoft before it gets to zero, however.)

Between the break-even levels, a partial loss is taken. On the upside, this equals the stock price, minus the strike price, minus the cost of the spread. In this case, if the stock at expiration closes at 120, the loss would be $(120 - 110) - 12\frac{3}{8} = -2\frac{3}{8}$. On the downside, the partial loss equals the strike price, minus the stock price, minus the cost of the spread. In this case, if the stock closes at 100, the loss would be $(110 - 100) - 12\frac{3}{8} = -2\frac{3}{8}$.

The expiration profit/loss is summarized as follows:

Debit from long January 110 call: $-6\frac{1}{8}$
Debit from long January put: $-6\frac{1}{4}$
Total debit: $-12\frac{3}{8}$

Upside break-even level: strike price plus cost of spread: $110 + 12\frac{3}{8} = 122\frac{3}{8}$
Downside break-even level: strike price minus cost of spread: $110 - 12\frac{3}{8} = 97\frac{5}{8}$
Maximum upside profit: potentially unlimited
Maximum downside profit: amount that stock declines below lower break-even level: $97\frac{5}{8}$
Maximum risk : cost of spread: $12\frac{3}{8}$

In order to determine the risk/return potential of this spread, you must consider the cost of the spread versus the potential for absolute price movement of the stock. In tabular form, the expiration profit/loss is as in Table 12.2.

Microsoft	(below)	85	97⅝	105	110	115	122⅜	135	(above)
Spread debit	−12⅜								
Value of spread at expiration	(full amt)	25	12⅜	5	0	5	12⅜	25	(unlimited)
Profit/loss	(full amt)	12⅝	0	−7⅜	−12⅜	−7⅜	0	12⅝	(unlimited)

Table 12.2 ■ Microsoft long January 110 straddle

A profit/loss graph of this spread at expiration is as shown in Figure 12.1.

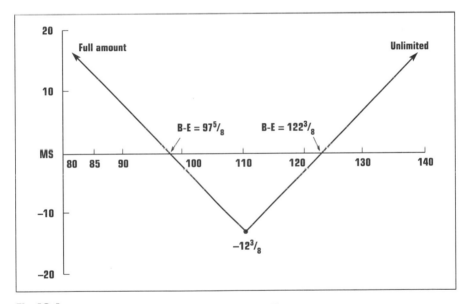

Fig 12.1 ■ Microsoft long January 110 straddle

The long straddle has the total positive vega of the call plus the put. It is extremely sensitive to a change in the implied volatility. If the underlying starts to move, and the implied volatility starts to increase, this spread profits on two accounts, direction and increased implied.

This spread has double the gamma of a single at-the-money call or put. If the market rallies, the increase of the call delta accelerates, the decrease of the put delta accelerates, and the spread gets longer quickly. If the market breaks, the spread gets shorter quickly for the opposite reasons.

The risk, or the trade-off, of the long straddle is that the market may stay in its present range, and that the implied volatility may decrease while time decay depreciates the investment. Remember that with at-the-money options time decay accelerates in the period of 60–30 days until expiration. The risk here is double that of a single at-the-money option, and even greater than with an out-of-the-money option. It is therefore advisable to take a long straddle position that is *half the size* of your usual position.

The long straddle is the most expensive options spread, and so it requires a great deal of market movement in order to profit. It can pay off handsomely, or it can result in a big let-down.

A spread that profits from volatile markets but that has less risk than the long straddle is the **long iron butterfly** (discussed in Chapter 13).

Short straddle

For stationary markets

> The short straddle is the opposite position of the long straddle, i.e., a simultaneous sale of the at-the-money call and put.

The **short straddle** is the opposite position of the long straddle, i.e., a simultaneous sale of the at-the-money call and put. If XYZ is at 100, you could sell both the 100 call and the 100 put. The risk/return characteristics are also opposite to the long straddle. The maximum return is the amount of the premium collected; the potential loss is unlimited. In order to sell the straddle, you must be convinced that the underlying will not exceed the range covered by the premium income, or the break-even levels, at expiration. You must also be prepared to meet large margin calls if the position goes against you. Because the potential risk is unlimited *it is not advisable to sell the straddle* until you are an experienced options trader.

Because the straddle is the most expensive options spread, it is often a tempting sale, and it is often profitable. It is justifiable only when probability is on the seller's side. Assessing probability is difficult, but the volatility trends are the most helpful guides.

The expiration profit/loss for the short straddle can be summarized by making the opposite calculations of the previous long straddle. This summary is as follows:

Credit from long January 110 call: $6\frac{1}{8}$
Credit from long January 110 put: $6\frac{1}{4}$
Total credit: $12\frac{3}{8}$

Upside break-even level: strike price plus cost of spread: $110 + 12\frac{3}{8} = 122\frac{3}{8}$
Downside break-even level: strike price minus cost of spread: $110 - 12\frac{3}{8} = 97\frac{5}{8}$
Maximum upside loss: potentially unlimited
Maximum downside loss: amount that stock declines below lower break-even level: $97\frac{5}{8}$
Maximum profit : income from spread: $12\frac{3}{8}$

The risk/return potential of this spread must be evaluated in terms of its income versus a loss that is potentially unlimited. In tabular form, the expiration profit/loss is as shown in Table 12.3.

Microsoft	(below)	85	$97\frac{5}{8}$	105	110	115	$122\frac{3}{8}$	135	(above)
Spread credit	$12\frac{3}{8}$								
Value of spread at expiration	(full amt)	-25	$-12\frac{3}{8}$	-5	0	-5	$-12\frac{3}{8}$	-25	(unlimited)
Profit/loss	(full amt)	$-12\frac{5}{8}$	0	$7\frac{3}{8}$	$12\frac{3}{8}$	$7\frac{3}{8}$	0	$-12\frac{5}{8}$	(unlimited)

Table 12.3 ■ Microsoft short January 110 straddle

In graphic form, the expiration profit/loss is as shown in Figure 12.2.

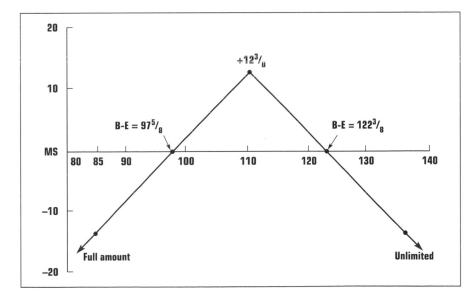

Fig 12.2 ■ Microsoft short January 110 straddle

Two similar spreads that profit from stationary markets but that have limited risk are the **long at-the-money butterfly** (discussed in Chapter 14) and the **short iron butterfly** (discussed in Chapter 13). They are among the spreads recommended for stationary markets.

Long strangle

For absolute market movement

> **The long strangle is the simultaneous purchase of an out-of-the-money call and put.**

The **long strangle** is the simultaneous purchase of an out-of-the-money call and put. Both the options are equidistant from the underlying. If XYZ is at 100, you could buy the 90 put and buy the 110 call in the same transaction. This spread is similar to the long straddle but costs less. The break-even levels are more distant from the underlying, and while there is less potential profit, there is also less risk.

Using the preceding set of Microsoft options, you could pay 4 for one January 115 call and pay $4\frac{1}{8}$ for one January 105 put in the same transaction for a total debit of $8\frac{1}{8}$. This debit is your maximum risk.

At expiration, the upside break-even level is the higher strike price plus the cost of the spread, or $115 + 8\frac{1}{8} = 123\frac{1}{8}$. The downside break-even level is the lower strike price minus the cost of the spread, or $105 - 8\frac{1}{8} = 96\frac{7}{8}$.

Like the long straddle, this spread profits the full amount that the stock closes outside the break-even levels at expiration. If the stock closes between the strike prices, the cost of the spread is taken as a loss. Between the strike prices and the break-even levels, a partial loss is taken.

The expiration profit/loss for this spread is summarized as follows:

Debit from long January 115 call: -4
Debit from long January 105 put: $-4\frac{1}{8}$
Total debit: $-8\frac{1}{8}$

Upside break-even level: upper strike price plus cost of spread: $115 + 8\frac{1}{8} = 123\frac{1}{8}$
Downside break-even level: lower strike price minus cost of spread: $105 - 8\frac{1}{8} = 96\frac{7}{8}$
Maximum upside profit: potentially unlimited
Maximum downside profit: amount of stock decline below lower break-even level: $96\frac{7}{8}$
Maximum risk: cost of spread: $8\frac{1}{8}$

In order to determine the risk/return potential of this spread, you must weigh its cost against the potential for the stock to move outside the break-even levels. The expiration profit/loss is as shown in Table 12.4.

Microsoft	(below)	85	96 $\frac{7}{8}$	105	110	115	123 $\frac{1}{8}$	135	(above)
Spread debit	$-8\frac{1}{8}$	----	----	----	----	----	----	----	----
Value of spread									
at expiration	(full amt)	20	8 $\frac{1}{8}$	0	0	0	8 $\frac{1}{8}$	20	(unlimited)
Profit/loss	(full amt)	11 $\frac{7}{8}$	0	$-8\frac{1}{8}$	$-8\frac{1}{8}$	$-8\frac{1}{8}$	0	11 $\frac{7}{8}$	(unlimited)

Table 12.4 ■ Microsoft long January 105–115 strangle

The expiration profit/loss is shown in Figure 12.3.

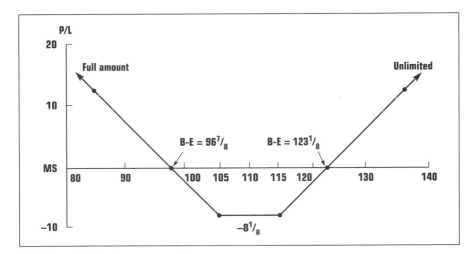

Fig 12.3 ■ Microsoft long January 105–115 strangle

As a spread for volatile markets, the long strangle can be placed at any distance from the underlying. The closer both strikes are to the underlying, the more this spread behaves like a long straddle, with increased exposure to time decay (via negative theta), and increased exposure to a decline in implied volatility (via positive vega). Because the maximum risk of this spread is known at the outset, it is not inadvisable to trade it, but because of the premium exposure, and because only one of the strikes is likely to profit, the risk may be unjustifiable for some investors. A similar spread with less premium risk is the **long iron condor**, discussed in Chapter 13.

The long strangle is preferable as a trade to profit from increasing implied volatility. If the current implied is low and/or increasing, this spread has an additional return scenario. It is therefore justifiable in itself, regardless of direction, and the wings, or each strike, can be placed far out of the money. As with all long vol positions, the days until expiration should be more than 60.

Short strangle

For stationary markets

The strangle is more often used as a short spread to profit from decreasing implied volatility. The short strangle is too often traded simply to gain income from time decay, which is a dangerous misapplication as we have already seen.

The short strangle has, like the short straddle, theoretically unlimited risk, but because the two strikes are at greater distances from the underlying, it is more manageable strategy. The positive theta, or the daily income form time decay, is not as great, but the negative vega, or exposure to increased implied volatility, is also not as great.

Because of the two short, naked options, it is advisable not to trade this spread until you have gained experience. A similar spread for stationary markets with less risk is the **short iron condor**, which is also discussed in Chapter 13.

Using the set of Microsoft options, a typical short strangle would be a sale of the 100 put at $2\frac{5}{8}$ and a sale of the 120 call at $2\frac{1}{2}$ in the same transaction, for a net credit of $5\frac{1}{8}$.

At expiration, the upside break-even level is the upper strike price plus the income from the spread, or $120 + 5\frac{1}{8} = 125\frac{1}{8}$. Above this level the potential loss is unlimited. The downside break-even level is the lower strike price minus the income from the spread, or $100 - 5\frac{1}{8} = 94\frac{7}{8}$. Below this level the potential loss is the full value of the stock. The expiration profit/loss is summarized as follows:

Credit from January 120 call:	$2\frac{1}{2}$
Credit from January 100 put:	$2\frac{5}{8}$
Total credit	$5\frac{1}{8}$

Upside break-even level: higher strike plus income from spread: $120 + 5\frac{1}{8}$ = $125\frac{1}{8}$

Downside break-even level: lower strike minus income from spread: $100 - 5\frac{1}{8} = 94\frac{7}{8}$

Maximum loss: potentially unlimited

Maximum profit: income from spread: $5\frac{1}{8}$

The expiration profit/loss is shown in Table 12.5.

Microsoft	(below)	85	94⅞	100	110	120	125⅛	135	(above)
Spread credit	5⅛								
Value of spread at expiration	(full amt)	–15	–5⅛	0	0	0	–5⅛	–15	(unlimited)
Profit/loss	(full amt)	–9⅞	0	5⅛	5⅛	5⅛	0	–9⅞	(unlimited)

Table 12.5 ■ Microsoft short January 100–120 strangle

Figure 12.4 is a graph of the profit/loss at expiration.

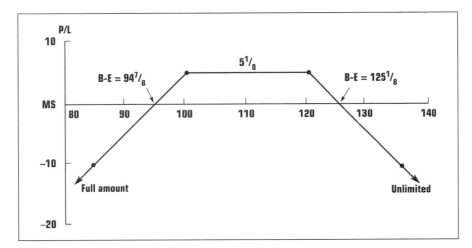

Fig 12.4 ■ Microsoft short January 100–120 strangle

Questions on straddles and strangles

1 Intel's earnings prospects are good, but the stock market as a whole has been bearish and volatile lately. The market could rally, or it could retrace to recent lows, dragging Intel with it. The stock price is 90, and the following January options are listed:

Intel at 90
January options with 80 days until expiration

Strike	75	80	85	90[12]	95	100	105
Calls				6¼	3⅞	2¼	1⅜
Puts	1⅜	2⅛	3¾	5½			

---

[12] You may question why the call and the put are not priced the same. This is because the price of Intel, as implied by the options, is actually 90¾. The reason is that the options prices include the cost of carry on the stock for 80 days. This is explained in Part Four.

a) i)   What is the cost of the January 90 straddle?

    ii)   At expiration, what is the upside break-even level?

    iii) What is the downside break-even level?

    iv) What is the maximum profit?

    v)   What is the maximum loss?

    vi) What is the profit/loss if the stock closes at 95 at expiration?

b) i)   What is the cost of the January 85–95 strangle?

    ii)   At expiration, what is the upside break-even level?

    iii) What is the downside break-even level?

    iv) What is the maximum profit?

    v)   What is the maximum loss?

    vi) What is the profit/loss if the stock closes at 95 at expiration?

2   In the UK, the outlook for Sainsbury during the next several months is for continued good, but not spectacular, trading, and you expect the shares to be stable. The implied volatility for the options is 38 per cent, down from over 50 per cent. It is November, and the January options are entering their accelerated time decay period. Sainsbury is trading at $537\frac{1}{2}$, and the following options prices are listed:

Sainsbury at $537\frac{1}{2}$

January options with 70 days until expiry

Strike	420	460	500	550	600	650	700
Calls				34	$17\frac{1}{2}$	8	3
Puts	3	8	$17\frac{1}{2}$	$39\frac{1}{2}$			

i)   What is the income from selling the January 500–600 strangle?

ii) At expiry, what is the upside break-even level?

iii) What is the downside break-even level?

iv) What is the maximum profit?

v) What is the maximum loss?

Answers

1   **a)** i) $6\frac{1}{4} + 5\frac{1}{2} = 11\frac{3}{4}$

      ii) $90 + 11\frac{3}{4} = 101\frac{3}{4}$

      iii) $90 - 11\frac{3}{4} = 78\frac{1}{4}$

      iv) upside unlimited; downside $78\frac{1}{4}$

      v) $11\frac{3}{4}$

      vi) $[95 - 90] - 11\frac{3}{4} = 6\frac{3}{4}$ loss

b) i) $3\frac{3}{4} + 3\frac{7}{8} = 7\frac{5}{8}$

ii) $95 + 7\frac{5}{8} = 102\frac{5}{8}$

iii) $85 - 7\frac{5}{8} = 77\frac{3}{8}$

iv) upside unlimited; downside $77\frac{3}{8}$

v) $7\frac{5}{8}$

vi) $7\,5\frac{5}{8}$ loss

2 i) $17\frac{1}{2} + 17\frac{1}{2} = 35$

ii) $600 + 35 = 635$

iii) $500 - 35 = 465$

iv) 35

v) unlimited upside, 465 on the downside.

Iron butterflies and iron condors: combining straddles and strangles for reduced risk

Introduction

Often, the risk of unlimited loss from being short two naked options cannot be justified. This is especially true for new traders. Occasionally, the

> **Occasionally, the risk of premium loss from being long two options cannot be justified.**

risk of premium loss from being long two options cannot be justified. By combining straddles and strangles, you can take the same approaches to volatile or stationary markets, but you can limit and quantify your risks. Your potential returns may not be as great, but you can sleep more soundly, and you'll be easier to live with. The following spreads all have more manageable risk.

Again, all these spreads can be traded in one transaction on most exchanges. Their bid – ask market should be marginally greater than that of a single option.

* Long iron butterfly

For absolute market movement

A long straddle can be financed by the sale of a strangle. If XYZ is at 100, you could buy the 100 straddle and simultaneously sell the 90 – 110 strangle in order to create the **long iron butterfly**. You can also think of this spread as a long at-the-money call spread at the 100 and 110 strikes, plus a long at-the-money put spread at the 100 and 90 strikes.

Compared to the long straddle, this spread has reduced premimum exposure, but it also has reduced potential return.

Using the previous set of Microsoft options:

Microsoft at $108\frac{7}{8}$

60 days until January expiration

Strike	90	95	100	105	110	115	120	125	130
January calls		$16\frac{1}{2}$		9	$6\frac{1}{8}$	4	$2\frac{1}{2}$	$1\frac{5}{8}$	1
January puts	1	$1\frac{5}{8}$	$2\frac{5}{8}$	$4\frac{1}{8}$	$6\frac{1}{4}$	$9\frac{1}{8}$		$16\frac{3}{4}$	

Table 13.1 ■ **Microsoft January options**

Here, you could pay $12\frac{3}{8}$ for the 110 straddle, and sell the 95–125 strangle at $3\frac{1}{4}$, for a net debit of $9\frac{1}{8}$. This is similar to paying $4\frac{1}{2}$ for the 110–125 call spread plus paying $4\frac{5}{8}$ for the 110–95 put spread.

Like the long call spread and the long put spread, the distance between strikes of the long iron butterfly can be varied in order to adjust the risk/return potential. Practically speaking, underlyings do not move to zero or infinity within the life of an options contract; there are always levels of support and resistance. It is realistic to place the short wings of this spread at these levels. The above choice of strikes views support/resistance at approximately 13 per cent below or above the current price. This is a large but not unreasonable move for Microsoft. If you choose this strategy in the first place, then you are expecting something out of the ordinary to happen.

Note that the above strikes are widely separated, and as a result the straddle component has a large exposure to the Greeks. This spread has a better return potential when the implied is increasing. A profit/loss summary at expiration is as follows:

Debit from January 110 straddle:	$-12\frac{1}{2}$
Credit from January 95–125 strangle:	$\underline{3\frac{1}{4}}$
Total debit:	$-9\frac{1}{8}$
Upside break-even level:	
straddle strike plus spread debit:	$110 + 9\frac{1}{8} = 119\frac{1}{8}$
Downside break-even level:	
straddle strike minus spread debit:	$110 - 9\frac{1}{8} = 100\frac{1}{8}$
Maximum upside profit:	
(highest strike minus middle strike)	
minus spread debit:	$(125 - 110) - 9\frac{1}{8} = 5\frac{7}{8}$
Maximum downside profit:	
(middle strike minus lowest strike)	
minus spread debit:	$(110 - 95) - 9\frac{1}{8} = 5\frac{7}{8}$
Maximum loss: cost of spread:	$9\frac{1}{8}$

The risk/return ratio of this spread is $9\frac{1}{8} \div 5\frac{7}{8} = 1.55$, or $1.55 potential risk for each potential return of $1. Admittedly, this is not an optimum risk/return ratio, but it is better than that of the long 110 straddle if you expect the stock to range at a maximum of 13 per cent.

The expiration profit/loss for this spread is shown in Table 13.1.

Microsoft	90	95	100	100 $\frac{7}{8}$	105	110	115	119 $\frac{1}{8}$	120	125	130
Spread debit	$-9\frac{1}{8}$										
Value of spread at expiration	15	15	10	$9\frac{1}{8}$	5	0	5	$9\frac{1}{8}$	10	15	15
Profit/loss	$5\frac{7}{8}$	$5\frac{7}{8}$	$\frac{7}{8}$	0	$-4\frac{1}{8}$	$-9\frac{1}{8}$	$-4\frac{1}{8}$	0	$\frac{7}{8}$	$5\frac{7}{8}$	$5\frac{7}{8}$

Table 13.2 ■ Microsoft long January 95–110–125 Iron butterfly

In graphic form, the profit/loss at expiration is as shown in Figure 13.1.

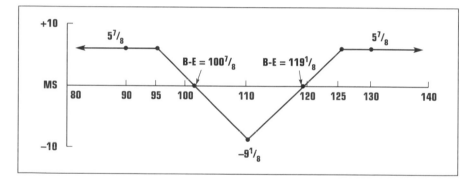

Fig 13.1 ■ Microsoft long January 95–110–125 iron butterfly

Suppose you think that the upside potential for the stock is greater than its downside potential. You might create a long *asymmetric* iron butterfly by substituting a short January 130 call at 1 for the short January 125 call at $1\frac{3}{8}$. Your spread debit increases to $9\frac{3}{4}$, but your profit potential is now $4\frac{3}{8}$ greater.

Alternatively, you might create a *hybrid* spread by buying the January 110 straddle at $12\frac{3}{8}$, and selling only the January 95 put at $1\frac{5}{8}$ for a total debit of $10\frac{3}{4}$. Here, your upside profit potential is unlimited.

✳ Short iron butterfly

For stationary markets

Suppose premium levels are high and trending downward. You would like to sell a straddle but you don't want the risk of unlimited loss. Instead, you could sell the above iron butterfly. You are then short the January 110 straddle and long the January 95–125 strangle, which acts as two stop-loss orders at guaranteed levels. You are effectively short the 110–125 call spread and short the 110–95 put spread. The profit/loss summary and table at expiration for this spread are exactly opposite to those of the above, while the expiration graph is the inverse.

Credit from January 110 straddle:	$12\frac{3}{8}$
Debit from January 95–125 strangle:	$-3\frac{1}{4}$
Total credit:	$9\frac{1}{8}$
Upside break-even level:	
straddle strike plus spread credit:	$110 + 9\frac{1}{8} = 119\frac{1}{8}$
Downside break-even level:	
straddle strike minus spread credit:	$110 - 9\frac{1}{8} = 100\frac{7}{8}$
Maximum profit: credit from spread:	$9\frac{1}{8}$
Maximum upside loss:	
(highest strike minus middle strike)	
minus spread credit:	$(125 - 110) - 9\frac{1}{8} = 5\frac{7}{8}$
Maximum downside loss:	
(middle strike minus lowest strike)	
minus spread credit:	$(110 - 95) - 9\frac{1}{8} = 5\frac{7}{8}$

Note that the risk/return ratio is also opposite to the former spread, at $5\frac{7}{8} \div 9\frac{1}{8} = .64$. This is a preferred ratio for most investors, provided volatility is declining. Note also that the break-even levels are an average of 8.3 per cent above or below the current stock price. The profit/loss table at expiration is shown in Table 13.2.

Microsoft	90	95	100	$100\frac{7}{8}$	105	110	115	$119\frac{1}{8}$	120	125	130
Spread credit	$9\frac{1}{8}$										
Value of spread at expiration	−15	−15	−10	$-9\frac{1}{8}$	−5	0	−5	$-9\frac{1}{8}$	−10	−15	−15
Profit/loss	$-5\frac{7}{8}$	$-5\frac{7}{8}$	$-\frac{7}{8}$	0	$4\frac{1}{8}$	$9\frac{1}{8}$	$4\frac{1}{8}$	0	$-\frac{7}{8}$	$-5\frac{7}{8}$	$-5\frac{7}{8}$

Table 13.3 ■ Microsoft short January 95–110–125 iron butterfly

The profit/loss at expiration is shown in Figure 13.2.

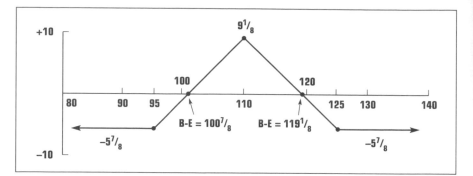

Fig 13.2 ■ **Microsoft short January 95–110–125 iron butterfly**

Looking ahead, we will learn that the profit/loss characteristics of this spread are identical to the long January 95–110–125 call or put butterfly. Personally, I would rather trade the above spread because the out-of-the-money call and put are usually more liquid than either the corresponding in-the-money put and call of the straight butterfly. i.e., the January 125 call is probably more liquid than the January 125 put. This usually results in a tighter bid – ask market for the spread as a whole.

Lastly, there is every reason to vary the wings of the short or long iron butterfly depending on your outlook. For example, you may sell the January 110 straddle at $12\frac{3}{8}$ and instead pay $5\frac{1}{8}$ for the January 100–120 strangle, resulting in a net credit of $7\frac{1}{4}$. Your break-even levels are then $102\frac{3}{4}$ and $117\frac{1}{4}$. Your maximum loss is only $2\frac{3}{4}$, bringing your risk/return ratio down to .38. The trade-off is that your profit range is reduced from $18\frac{1}{4}$ points to $14\frac{1}{2}$ points.

*Short iron condor

For stationary markets

> The risks of the short strangle can be limited by buying a long strangle at strikes that are farther out-of-the-money.

The risks of the short strangle can be limited by buying a long strangle at strikes that are farther out-of-the-money. If XYZ is at 100, you could sell the 90–110 strangle, and buy the 85–115 strangle in the same transaction. You might think of this four-way spread as a short out-of-the-money call spread at 110–115, plus a short out-of-the-money put spread at 90–85. This spread is known as the **short iron condor**.

The maximum profit here is the combined credit from the short call and put spreads. Like the short call and put spread, the maximum loss is here limited and quantifiable at the outset. Like all premium selling strategies, this spread is most profitable when used with accelerated time decay. Declining implied and historical volatilities are also profitable scenarios for this spread. If your outlook calls for lower market volatility, this spread is one of the best choices.

Using the previous set of Microsoft options, you could sell the January 100–120 strangle at $5\frac{1}{8}$, and pay $3\frac{1}{4}$ for the January 95–125 strangle, for a net credit of $1\frac{7}{8}$.

On the upside, this spread behaves like a short 120–125 call spread for which you have collected $1\frac{7}{8}$. At expiration, the upside break-even level is the strike price of the lower call plus the total income from the spread, or $120 + 1\frac{7}{8} = 121\frac{7}{8}$. The maximum upside loss is the difference between call strikes minus the income from the spread, or $(125 - 120) - 1\frac{7}{8} = 3\frac{1}{8}$.

On the downside, this spread behaves like a short 100–95 put spread for which you have collected $1\frac{7}{8}$. At expiration, the downside break-even level is the strike price of the higher put minus the total income from the spread, or $100 - 1\frac{7}{8} = 98\frac{1}{8}$. The maximum downside loss is the difference between put strikes minus the income from the spread, or $(100 - 95) - 1\frac{7}{8} = 3\frac{1}{8}$. The profit/loss at expiration is summarized as follows:

Credit from short January 100 put:	$2\frac{5}{8}$
Credit from short January 120 call:	$2\frac{1}{2}$
Debit from long January 95 put:	$-1\frac{5}{8}$
Debit from long January 125 call:	$-1\frac{5}{8}$
Total credit:	$1\frac{7}{8}$

Maximum profit: income from spread: $1\frac{7}{8}$

Upside break-even level: lower call strike plus spread credit: $120 + 1\frac{7}{8} = 121\frac{7}{8}$

Downside break-even level: higher put strike minus spread credit: $100 - 1\frac{7}{8} = 98\frac{1}{8}$

Maximum upside loss: difference between call strikes minus spread credit: $(125 - 120) - 1\frac{7}{8} = 3\frac{1}{8}$

Maximum downside loss: Difference between put strikes minus spread credit: $(100 - 95) - 1\frac{7}{8} = 3\frac{1}{8}$

The risk/return ratio for this spread is maximum loss ÷ maximum profit, or

$\dfrac{3\frac{1}{8}}{1\frac{7}{8}} = 1.67$ at risk for each potential return of 1. Although the profit potential of this spread is not spectacular, neither is the maximum loss. Also consider that the profit range is $121\frac{7}{8} - 98\frac{1}{8} = 23\frac{3}{4}$ points. The stock would need to settle more than +/− 11 per cent at expiration before a loss would result. Remember, you are trading this spread because you expect the stock to range, and for volatility to come down.

Again, there are asymmetric and hybrid possibilities. If you are range-bullish, you might sell the 105–120 strangle and buy the 95–125 strangle for a net credit of $3\frac{3}{8}$. Here, your maximum loss increases to $6\frac{5}{8}$, however, because of the downside risk.

The expiration profit/loss is shown in Table 13.3.

Microsoft	90	95	98$\frac{1}{8}$	100	120	121$\frac{7}{8}$	125	130
Spread credit	1$\frac{7}{8}$							
Value of spread at expiration	−5	−5	−1$\frac{7}{8}$	0	10	−1$\frac{7}{8}$	−5	−5
Profit/loss	−3$\frac{1}{8}$	−3$\frac{1}{8}$	0	1$\frac{7}{8}$	1$\frac{7}{8}$	0	−3$\frac{1}{8}$	−3$\frac{1}{8}$

Table 13.4 ■ Microsoft short January 95–100–120–125 iron condor

The expiration profit/loss is graphed as in Figure 13.3.

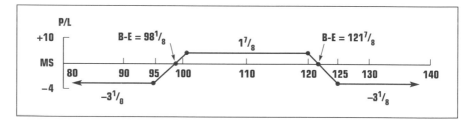

Fig 13.3 ■ Microsoft short January 95–100–120–125 iron condor

※ Long iron condor

For volatile markets

The opposite form of the above four-way spread is occasionally used as a way of financing the long strangle. If XYZ is at 100, you could buy the 95–105 strangle and sell the 90–110 strangle in one transaction. You might think of this as a long out-of-the-money call spread at 105–110, plus a long out-of-the-money put spread at 100–95. This spread is known as the **long iron condor**. As with long call and put spreads, the long options here can be placed closer to the underlying because they are financed by short options that are farther out-of-the-money. There is less potential return than with the long strangle, but there is also less cost and less premium risk.

With the previous set of Microsoft options, you could trade this spread with non-adjacent strikes on both the call and put sides in order to extend the profit range. You could pay $8\frac{1}{8}$ for the January 105–115 strangle, and sell the January 95–125 strangle at $3\frac{1}{4}$, for a net debit of $4\frac{7}{8}$.

On the upside, this spread behaves like a long January 115–125 call spread for which you have paid $4\frac{7}{8}$. At expiration, the upside break-even level is the lower call strike plus the cost of the spread, or $115 + 4\frac{7}{8} = 119\frac{7}{8}$. The maximum upside profit is the difference between call strikes minus the cost of the spread, or $(125 - 115) - 4\frac{7}{8} = 5\frac{1}{8}$. The maximum risk is the cost of the spread, or $4\frac{7}{8}$.

On the downside, this spread behaves like a long January 105–95 put spread for which you have paid $4\frac{7}{8}$. At expiration, the downside break-even level is the higher put strike minus the cost of the spread, or $105 - 4\frac{7}{8} = 100\frac{1}{8}$. The maximum downside profit is the difference between put strikes minus the cost of the spread, or $(105 - 95) - 4\frac{7}{8} = 5\frac{1}{8}$. The maximum risk is again the cost of the spread, or $4\frac{7}{8}$. The expiration profit/loss is summarized as follows:

Debit from long January 115 call:	-4
Debit from long January 105 put:	$-4\frac{1}{8}$
Credit from short January 125 call:	$1\frac{5}{8}$
Credit from short January 95 put:	$1\frac{5}{8}$
Total debit:	$-4\frac{7}{8}$

Upside break-even level:	
lower call strike plus spread debit:	$115 + 4\frac{7}{8} - 119\frac{7}{8}$
Downside break-even level:	
higher put strike minus spread debit:	$105 - 4\frac{7}{8} = 100\frac{1}{8}$
Maximum upside profit:	
difference between call strikes	
minus spread debit:	$(125 - 115) - 4\frac{7}{8} = 5\frac{1}{8}$
Maximum downside profit:	
difference between put strikes	
minus spread debit:	$(105 - 95) - 4\frac{7}{8} = 5\frac{1}{8}$
Maximum loss: cost of spread: $4\frac{7}{8}$	

The risk/return potential is maximum loss/maximum profit: $\dfrac{4\frac{7}{8}}{5\frac{1}{8}} = .95$ at risk for each potential profit of 1. Table 13.5 shows the expiration profit/loss.

Microsoft	90	95	100 $\frac{1}{8}$	105	115	119 $\frac{7}{8}$	125	130
Spread debit	-4 $\frac{7}{8}$							
Value of spread at expiration	10	10	4 $\frac{7}{8}$	0	0	4 $\frac{7}{8}$	10	10
Profit/loss	5 $\frac{1}{8}$	5 $\frac{1}{8}$	0	-4 $\frac{7}{8}$	-4 $\frac{7}{8}$	0	5 $\frac{1}{8}$	5 $\frac{1}{8}$

Table 13.5 ■ Microsoft long January 95–105–115–125 iron condor

A graph of the expiration profit/loss is shown in Figure 13.4.

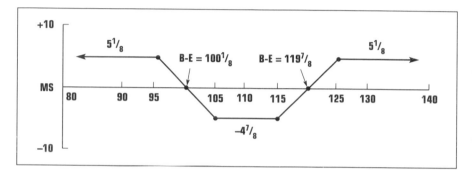

Fig 13.4 ■ Microsoft long January 95–105–115–125 iron condor

Questions on combined straddles and strangles

1   Refer to the previous set of Sainsbury January options:

Sainsbury at 537 $\frac{1}{2}$
January options with 70 days until expiry

Strike	420	460	500	550	600	650	700
Calls				34	17 $\frac{1}{2}$	8	3
Puts	3	8	17 $\frac{1}{2}$	39 $\frac{1}{2}$			

a) i)   What is the income from the short January 460 – 500 – 600 – 650 iron condor? This is an asymmetric spread.
   ii)   At expiry, what is the upside break-even level?
   iii) What is the downside break-even level?
   iv) What is the maximum upside loss?
   v)   What is the maximum downside loss?
   vi) What is the maximum profit from this spread?
   vii) What is the profit range?

b) i) What is the income from the short January 460 – 550 – 650 iron butterfly? This is also an asymmetric spread.

   ii) At expiry, what is the upside break-even level?

  iii) What is the downside break-even level?

  iv) What is the maximum upside loss?

   v) What is the maximum downside loss?

  vi) What is the maximum profit?

 vii) What is the profit range?

2 Given the previous set of Intel options.

Intel at 90

January options with 80 days until expiration

Strike	75	80	85	90	95	100	105
Calls				$6\frac{1}{4}$	$3\frac{7}{8}$	$2\frac{1}{4}$	$1\frac{3}{8}$
Puts	$1\frac{3}{8}$	$2\frac{1}{8}$	$3\frac{3}{4}$	$5\frac{1}{2}$			

a) i) What is the cost of the long January 75 – 85 – 95 – 105 iron condor?

  ii) At expiration, what is the upside break-even level?

 iii) What is the downside break-even level?

  iv) What is the maximum upside profit?

   v) What is the maximum downside profit?

  vi) What is the maximum loss?

b) i) What is the cost of the long January 75 – 90 – 105 iron butterfly?

  ii) At expiration, what is the upside break-even level?

 iii) At expiration, what is the downside break-even level?

  iv) What is the maximum upside profit?

   v) What is the maximum downside profit?

  vi) What is the maximum loss?

Answers

1 a) i) $17\frac{1}{2} + 17\frac{1}{2} - 8 - 8 = 19$ credit

  ii) $600 + 19 = 619$

 iii) $500 - 19 = 481$

  iv) $[650 - 600] - 19 = 31$

   v) $[500 - 460] - 19 = 21$

  vi) 19

 vii) $619 - 481 = 138$

b) i) $34 + 39\frac{1}{2} - 8 - 8 = 57\frac{1}{2}$ credit

ii) $550 + 57\frac{1}{2} = 607\frac{1}{2}$

iii) $550 - 57\frac{1}{2} = 492\frac{1}{2}$

iv) $[650 - 550] - 57\frac{1}{2} = 42\frac{1}{2}$

v) $[550 - 460] - 57\frac{1}{2} = 32\frac{1}{2}$

vi) $57\frac{1}{2}$

vii) $607\frac{1}{2} - 492\frac{1}{2} = 115$

2 a) i) $3\frac{3}{4} + 3\frac{7}{8} - 1\frac{3}{8} - 1\frac{3}{8} = 4\frac{7}{8}$ debit

ii) $95 + 4\frac{7}{8} = 99\frac{7}{8}$

iii) $85 - 4\frac{7}{8} = 80\frac{1}{8}$

iv) $[105 - 95] - 4\frac{7}{8} = 5\frac{1}{8}$

v) $[85 - 75] - 4\frac{7}{8} = 5\frac{1}{8}$

vi) $4\frac{7}{8}$

b) i) $6\frac{1}{4} + 5\frac{1}{2} - 1\frac{3}{8} - 1\frac{3}{8} = 9$ debit

ii) $90 + 9 = 99$

iii) $90 - 9 = 81$

iv) $[105 - 90] - 9 = 6$

v) $[90 - 75] - 9 = 6$

vi) 9

14 Butterflies and condors: combining call spreads and put spreads

Introduction

The spreads in this chapter are used most often to profit from stationary or range-bound markets. All consist of either calls or puts, and they all combine a long one by one spread with a short one by one spread that is farther out-of-the-money. For one example, if XYZ is at 100, you could buy the 95–100 call spread and sell the 100–105 call spread to create a **long call butterfly**.

All these spreads have four components. They are most commonly bought, and are used to profit from declining volatility and/or premium erosion. There are other uses, however, which we will discuss.

All these spreads can be traded in one transaction on most, if not all, exchanges. Their bid – ask markets are only marginally greater than those of single options. When purchased, they have minimal risk, and are therefore recommended for new traders.

*Long at-the-money call butterfly

For stationary markets

The **long at-the-money call butterfly** is most easy to understand as the combination of a long call spread whose higher strike is at the money, plus a short call spread whose lower strike is also at the money. For example, if XYZ is at 100, the long at-the-money call butterfly would be a long 95–100 call spread plus a short 100–105 call spread. The combined spread is long one 95 call, short two 100 calls, and long one 105 call.

The spread is done for a debit, usually small, and the debit is the maximum potential loss. The profit/loss graph at expiration resembles a butterfly. If the following discussion seems complicated, keep in mind that this spread is basically two call spreads combined.

The return scenario is for the underlying to close at the middle strike at expiration. There, the long, lower call spread is worth its maximum, or the difference between the lower two strikes, and the short, upper call spread expires worthless. Taking the example above, if XYZ closes at 100, then the 95–100 call spread is worth 5, and the 100–105 call spread is worth zero. The cost of the butterfly is then subtracted from 5 to calculate the net profit.

There are two common risk scenarios.

■ The first is that at expiration the underlying closes at or below the lowest strike, leaving all options out-of-the-money and worthless. If XYZ closes at 93, then all the above options will settle at zero. The cost of the butterfly is then taken as a loss.

■ The second risk scenario is that at expiration the underlying closes at or above the highest strike. There, both call spreads expire at full and equal value, making their sum zero. For example, with the long 95 - 100–105 call butterfly above, if XYZ closes at 108, both call spreads are worth 5. The profit on the long 95–100 call spread pairs off against the loss on the short 100–105 call spread. The butterfly is then worthless, and the cost of the butterfly is taken as a loss.

There are other, less common risks, and they are discussed at the end of the section on butterflies.

A long at-the-money butterfly increases in value as it approaches expiration and when the underlying remains between the outermost strikes. Because it is a premium selling strategy, it is best opened when the options contract has 60 days or less till expiration. Because there is minimum risk to the butterfly, it can be opened close to expiration, for example, under 30 days, and it can be held until several days before an options contract expires. The risk remains mimimal provided the spread remains at the money, i.e., with no short strike deeply in the money and therefore subject to early assignment.

> A long at-the-money butterfly increases in value as it approaches expiration and when the underlying remains between the outermost strikes.

Taking again the set of Microsoft options:

Microsoft at $108 \frac{7}{8}$

60 days till January expiration

Strike	90	95	100	105	110	115	120	125	130
January calls				9	$6\frac{1}{8}$	4	$2\frac{1}{2}$	$1\frac{5}{8}$	1
January puts	1	$1\frac{5}{8}$	$2\frac{5}{8}$	$4\frac{1}{8}$	$6\frac{1}{4}$	$9\frac{1}{8}$			

Here, you could pay 9 for one January 105 call, sell two January 110 calls at $6\frac{1}{8}$, and pay 4 for the January 115 call for a net debit of $\frac{3}{4}$. You are then long the January 105–110–115 call butterfly. The premium outlay is small, but so is the possibility of the stock closing at 110, 60 days from now. On the other hand, the potential profit is $4\frac{1}{4}$, and the profit range, which we will discuss, is $8\frac{1}{2}$ points. The value of the spread grows as expiration approaches and the stock remains centered at approximately 110.

At expiration, the maximum profit occurs if the stock closes at 110. There, the lower call spread is worth its maximum, 5, and the upper call spread is worth its minimum, 0. The profit is calculated as the difference between the lower two strikes minus the cost of the butterfly, or $(110 - 105) - \frac{3}{4} = 4\frac{1}{4}$. The maximum loss is the cost of the butterfly, or $\frac{3}{4}$.

At expiration, there are two break-even levels with the call butterfly. The lower level is where the value of the long call spread pays for the cost of the butterfly. This is calculated as the lowest strike price plus the spread debit, or $105 + \frac{3}{4} = 105\frac{3}{4}$.

The higher break-even level is where the profit on the long call spread equals the loss on the short call spread. This could be calculated as the difference between the lower two strikes, minus the butterfly debit, plus the middle strike, or $(110 - 105) - \frac{3}{4} + 110 = 114\frac{1}{4}$. However, it is more easily calculated as the highest strike minus the butterfly debit, or $115 - \frac{3}{4} = 114\frac{1}{4}$. At this level, the value of the 105–110 call spread at 5, less the butterfly debit of $\frac{3}{4}$, equals the value of the 110–115 call spread at $4\frac{1}{4}$.

The profit range of this butterfly is then $114\frac{1}{4} - 105\frac{3}{4} = 8\frac{1}{2}$. It is important to think about profit ranges when trading volatility because in essence we are trading a range of probable outcomes for the underlying at expiration.

The expiration profit/loss is summarized as follows:

Debit from one long January 105 call:	-9
Debit from one long January 115 call:	-4
Credit from two short January 110 calls: $2 \times 6\frac{1}{8} =$	$12\frac{1}{4}$
Total debit:	$-\frac{3}{4}$

Downside break-even level: lowest strike plus cost of butterfly: $105 + \frac{3}{4} = 105\frac{3}{4}$

Upside break-even level: highest strike minus cost of butterfly: $115 - \frac{3}{4} = 114\frac{1}{4}$

Maximum profit: difference between lower two strikes minus cost of butterfly: $(110 - 105) - \frac{3}{4} = 4\frac{1}{4}$

Level of maximum profit: middle strike: 110

Maximum loss: cost of butterfly: $\frac{3}{4}$

The risk/return ratio for this spread is $\frac{3}{4} \div 4\frac{1}{4}$, or .18 at risk for each potential profit of 1. This low ratio is the particular advantage of the long butterfly. The expiration profit/loss is shown in Table 14.1

Microsoft	100	105	105$\frac{3}{4}$	110	114$\frac{1}{4}$	115	120
Spread debit	$-\frac{3}{4}$						
Value of long 105–110 call spread at expiration	0	0	$\frac{3}{4}$	5	5	5	5
Value of short 110–115 call spread at expiration	0	0	0	0	$-4\frac{1}{4}$	-5	-5
Profit/loss	$-\frac{3}{4}$	$-\frac{3}{4}$	0	$4\frac{1}{4}$	0	$-\frac{3}{4}$	$-\frac{3}{4}$

Table 14.1 ▪ Microsoft long January 105–110–115 call butterfly

The graph of the expiration profit/loss is as follows:

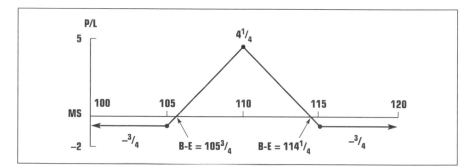

Fig 14.1 ▪ Microsoft long January 105–110–115 call butterfly

*Long at-the-money put butterfly

For stationary markets

The **long at-the-money put butterfly** has the identical profit/loss characterisitics of a long at-the-money call butterfly. (This fortunate occurrence has brought relief to many options trainers.) If both spreads are exactly at the money, their cost is usually the same. The same strikes are used, but with puts instead of calls. For example, if XYZ is at 100, you could buy one 105 put, sell two 100 puts, and buy one 95 put to create the butterfly. You can think of this spread as a long in-the-money put spread at the 105 and 100 strikes, plus a short at-the-money put spread at the 100 and 95 strikes.

At expiration the maximum profit occurs if the underlying closes at the middle strike. The maximum loss is the cost of the spread.

With the above Microsoft options, you could pay $9\frac{1}{8}$ for the January 115 put, sell two January 110 puts at $6\frac{1}{4}$, and pay $4\frac{1}{8}$ for the January 105 put order to go long the January 115 – 110 – 105 put butterfly. Your net debit is $\frac{3}{4}$, and this is your maximum potential loss.

At expiration, the upside break-even level is the highest strike minus the cost of the butterfly, or $115 - \frac{3}{4} = 114\frac{1}{4}$. The downside break-even level is the lowest strike plus the cost of the butterfly, or $105 + \frac{3}{4} = 105\frac{3}{4}$. Note that the profit range is $114\frac{1}{4} - 105\frac{3}{4} = 8\frac{1}{2}$, the same as with the long at-the-money call butterfly.

The maximum profit is the difference between the two highest strikes minus the cost of the spread, or $(115 - 110) - \frac{3}{4} = 4\frac{1}{4}$. The expiration profit/loss is summarized as follows:

Debit from one long January 115 put:	$-9\frac{1}{8}$
Debit from one long January 105 put:	$-4\frac{1}{8}$
Credit from two short January 110 puts: $2 \times 6\frac{1}{4} =$	$12\frac{1}{2}$
Total debit:	$-\frac{3}{4}$

Maximum profit: difference between two higher strikes minus spread debit: $(115 - 110) - \frac{3}{4} = 4\frac{1}{4}$
Level of maximum profit: middle strike: 110
Upside break-even level: highest strike minus cost of spread: $115 - \frac{3}{4} = 114\frac{1}{4}$
Downside break-even level: lowest strike plus cost of spread: $105 + \frac{3}{4} = 105\frac{3}{4}$
Maximum loss: cost of spread: $\frac{3}{4}$

The risk/return ratio of this spread is maximum loss ÷ maximum profit, or $\dfrac{\frac{3}{4}}{4\frac{1}{4}} = .18$ at risk for each potential profit of 1. In tabular form the expiration profit/loss is summarized in Table 14.2.

Microsoft	100	105	$105\frac{3}{4}$	110	$114\frac{1}{4}$	115	120
Spread debit	$-\frac{3}{4}$						
Value of long 115 - 110 put spread at expiration	5	5	5	5	$\frac{3}{4}$	0	0
Value of short 110 - 105 put spread at expiration	-5	-5	$-4\frac{1}{4}$	0	0	0	0
Profit/loss	$-\frac{3}{4}$	$-\frac{3}{4}$	0	$4\frac{1}{4}$	0	$-\frac{3}{4}$	$-\frac{3}{4}$

Table 14.2 ■ Microsoft 115–110–105 put butterfly

The graph of the expiration profit/loss is identical to the one shown in Figure 14.1 for the call butterfly.

Short at-the-money call and put butterflies

For volatile markets

For each spread traded there are two opposing outlooks. Intsead of buying an at-the-money butterfly in order to profit from a stationary market, a trader may sell the same butterfly because his outlook calls for the underlying to be outside the spread's range at expiration.

For example, instead of buying, you could sell the above call or put butterfly at $\frac{3}{4}$. This is your maximum profit at expiration if the stock closes at or below 105, or at or above 115. Practically spreaking, this $\frac{3}{4}$ income is small, but in a volatile market so is the risk of the stock expiring within the butterfly's range. Your position would be short one January 105 call, long two January 110 calls, and short one January 115 call. In order to leave no stone unturned, the expiration profit/loss for this short call butterfly is summarized below:

Credit from one long January 105 call:	9
Credit from one long January 115 call:	4
Debit from two short January 110 calls: $2 \times 6\frac{1}{8} =$	$-12\frac{1}{4}$
Total credit:	$\frac{3}{4}$

Downside break-even level: lowest strike plus credit from butterfly: $105 + \frac{3}{4} = 105\frac{3}{4}$

Upside break-even level: highest strike minus credit from butterfly: $115 - \frac{3}{4} = 114\frac{1}{4}$

Maximum profit: credit from butterfly: $\frac{3}{4}$

Two levels of maximum profit: below lowest strike, 105; above highest strike, 115

Maximum loss: difference between lower two strikes minus credit from butterfly: $(110 - 105) - \frac{3}{4} = 4\frac{1}{4}$

Price range of potential loss: $114\frac{1}{4} - 105\frac{3}{4} = 8\frac{1}{2}$ points

The risk/return ratio for this spread is $\dfrac{4\frac{1}{4}}{\frac{3}{4}} = 5.67$ at risk for each potential profit of 1. This extremely high ratio is only justifiable in volatile markets and trending markets. This is not a spread for range-bound markets. On the other hand, this high risk/return ratio together with a low potential profit indicates that the underlying has a greater probability than not to be at this level at expiration.

The expiration profit/loss is shown in Table 14.3.

Microsoft	100	105	105¾	110	114¼	115	120
Spread credit	¾	-	-	-	-	-	-
Value of short 105–110 call spread at expiration	0	0	-¾	-5	-5	-5	-5
Value of long 110–105 call spread at expiration	0	-	-	-	4¼	5	5
Profit/loss	¾	¾	0	-4¼	0	¾	¾

Table 14.3 ■ Microsoft short January 105–110–115 call butterfly

The profit/loss at expiration is graphed as follows:

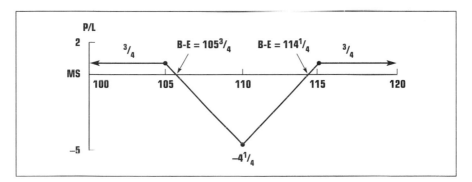

Fig 14.2 ■ Microsoft short January 105–110–115 call butterfly

If you wanted to assume more risk you might instead sell the 105–110–115 call butterfly in the December contract which has 30 days until expiration. The at-the-money December call butterfly would be worth approximately 1¾, and the break-even levels would be 106¾ and 113¼. Just be prepared to close the position several days before expiration.

*Long out-of-the-money call butterfly

For upside direction followed by stationary market

A butterfly can be used with a directional outlook. Suppose you think that a stock has recently become oversold because of an unfavorable analyst's report, or because of less than expected earnings. You know, however, the stock is fundamentally sound, and it will most likely rally

back to its former level. In order to profit from
your outlook, you could buy an out-of-the-
money call butterfly. This spread costs less than
an at-the-money butterfly, and its price will increase as the stock enters
its range. All the better if the rally is slow and time consuming, because
the butterfly, when it finally becomes at-the-money, will be worth more
through time decay.

For example, if you expect Microsoft to increase from its current price of
$108\frac{7}{8}$ to the 120 range, you could pay $\frac{5}{8}$ for the January 115–120–125 call butterfly. You do this by paying 4 for one 115 call, selling two 120 calls at $2\frac{1}{2}$,
and paying $1\frac{5}{8}$ for one 125 call. If the stock increases to 120 in 30 days' time
your butterfly will be worth approximately $1\frac{3}{4}$. You know this because the
current December at-the-money butterfly, with 30 days until expiration, is
worth $1\frac{3}{4}$. If the stock then settles into a range centered on 120, you have a
profitable and low-risk options position. You may decide to take your
profit at this point.

The expiration profit/loss for this butterfly is as follows.

Debit from one long January 115 call:	−4
Debit from one January 125 call:	$-1\frac{5}{8}$
Credit from two short January 120 calls: $2 \times 2\frac{1}{2} =$	5
Total debit:	$-\frac{5}{8}$

Maximum profit: difference between two lower strikes minus spread
debit: $(120 - 115) - \frac{5}{8} = 4\frac{3}{8}$.
Level of maximum profit: middle strike of spread: 120
Lower break-even level: lowest strike price plus spread debit: $115 + \frac{5}{8} = 115\frac{5}{8}$
Upper break-even level: highest strike price minus spread debit: $125 - \frac{5}{8}$
$= 124\frac{3}{8}$
Profit range: $124\frac{3}{8} - 115\frac{5}{8} = 8\frac{3}{4}$
Maximum loss: cost of spread: $\frac{5}{8}$

The risk/return ratio is $\dfrac{\frac{5}{8}}{4\frac{3}{8}} = .14$ at risk for each potential profit of 1.

Through knowing the basics of butterflies, the table and graph of the
profit/loss at expiration can be constructed.

*Long out-of-the-money put butterfly

For downside direction followed by stationary market

Just as the long out-of-the-money call butterfly can profit from oversold conditions, the long out-of-the-money put butterfly can profit from over-bought conditions. This situation often occurs in commodities, but it is common to all markets, especially bear markets, for those of us who remember them.

For example, if you expect Microsoft to retrace to 100, you could pay $\frac{1}{2}$ for the January 105–100–95 put butterfly. You do this by paying $4\frac{1}{8}$ for the 105 put, selling two 100 puts at $2\frac{5}{8}$, and paying $1\frac{5}{8}$ for one 95 put. If the stock eventually settles into a range centered at 100, then you have a low-risk profit opportunity. The expiration profit/loss is summarized as follows.

Debit from one January 105 put:	$-4\frac{1}{8}$
Debit from one January 95 put:	$-1\frac{5}{8}$
Credit from two January 100 puts: $2 \times 2\frac{5}{8} =$	$5\frac{1}{4}$
Total debit:	$-\frac{1}{2}$

Maximum profit: difference between two higher strikes minus spread debit: $(105 - 100) - \frac{1}{2} = 4\frac{1}{2}$

Level of maximum profit: middle strike: 100

Upper break-even level: highest strike minus spread debit: $105 - \frac{1}{2} = 104\frac{1}{2}$

Lower break-even level: lowest strike plus spread debit: $95 + \frac{1}{2} = 95\frac{1}{2}$

Profit range: $104\frac{1}{2} - 95\frac{1}{2} = 9$

Maximum loss: Cost of spread: $\frac{1}{2}$

The risk/return ratio of this butterfly is $= \dfrac{\frac{1}{2}}{4\frac{1}{2}}$ .11 at risk for each potential

profit of 1. Again, note the excellent risk/return ratios for this group of spreads.

Additional risks with the butterfly

There are other risks with the butterfly. The first is pin risk, which is unlikely, but theoretically possible. The two short strikes may conceivably expire at-the-money. It is best to close the butterfly several days before expiration. You may refer to the section on pin risk in Part One.

Another risk is that of early exercise with American-style-options such as the OEX, the FTSE-100 American-style contract, and most options on individual stocks in the US and UK. If your short strike becomes deep in-the-money close to expiration, you may be assigned to cash in the indexes, therefore leaving your long options unhedged. With a long call butterfly in stocks, you may be assigned an unwanted short stock position, and with a long put butterfly in stocks, you may be assigned an unwanted long stock position. In all these cases, if your butterfly becomes deep in-the-money close to expiration, it will have lost its value, and you should close the position.

If you hold the long butterfly until expiration there are two additional risks. For a call butterfly, if the underlying settles between the two higher strikes, then you will be assigned one more short underlying contract than the one which you will exercise to. Most likely you will not want this position.

Second, if the underlying settles between the two lower strikes, then you or your clearing firm will exercise to one long underlying contract, which you may not want.

For the long put butterfly, if the underlying settles between the two lower strikes, then you will be assigned one more long underlying contract than the one which you will exercise to. If the underlying settles between the two higher strikes, then you or your clearing firm will exercise to one short underlying contract.

There is an additional risk in that the deep in-the-money puts on stocks and American-style stock indexes generally have more early exercise premium, and are more frequently subject to early exercise and assignment. Perhaps for this reason, the at-the-money call butterfly is more often traded than the put butterfly, especially in stocks.

The most prudent way to avoid these risks is to close your butterfly position if it becomes deeply in the money, or close it several days before expiration.

*Long out-of-the-money call condor

For upside direction followed by stationary market

If the expected upside range of an underlying is too difficult to assess for the use of an out-of-the-money call butterfly, then you can increase the range of the spread by shifting the short call spread to the next two higher strikes that are out of the money. This creates a **long out-of-the-money call condor**. For example, if XYZ is at 100 you could buy one 105 call, sell one 110 call, sell one 115 call, and buy one 120 call. While the maximum profit is the same as with the butterfly, the profit range is extended by 5 points. This spread costs more, but it has an increased probability to profit. It is similar to the long call ladder or Christmas tree, but it has the protection of the extra long call at the highest strike.

For example, in Microsoft January options you could pay 4 for one 115 call, sell one 120 call at $2\frac{1}{2}$, sell one 125 call at $1\frac{5}{8}$, and pay 1 for one 130 call. Your net debit is $\frac{7}{8}$. Here, the maximum profit is taken if the stock is between 120–125 at expiration. The break-even levels are $115\frac{7}{8}$ and $129\frac{1}{8}$. The profit/loss calculations are practically the same as with the call butterfly. The expiration profit/loss for this condor is summarized as follows:

Debit from one long January 115 call:	-4
Debit from one long January 130 call:	-1
Credit from one short January 120 call:	$2\frac{1}{2}$
Credit from one short January 125 call:	$1\frac{5}{8}$
Total debit	$-\frac{7}{8}$

Maximum profit: difference between lowest two strikes minus spread debit: $(120 - 115) - \frac{7}{8} = 4\frac{1}{8}$
Range of maximum profit: 120 – 125
Lower break-even level: lowest strike plus spread debit: $115 + \frac{7}{8} = 115\frac{7}{8}$
Upper break-even level: highest strike minus spread debit: $130 - \frac{7}{8} = 129\frac{1}{8}$
Profit range: $129\frac{1}{8} - 115\frac{7}{8} = 13\frac{1}{4}$
Maximum loss: cost of spread: $\frac{7}{8}$

The risk/return ratio of this long call iron butterfly is $\dfrac{\frac{7}{8}}{4\frac{1}{8}} = .21$ at risk for

each potential profit of 1. A table of the profit/loss at expiration is shown in Table 14.4.

Microsoft	110	115	$115\frac{7}{8}$	120	125	$129\frac{1}{8}$	130	135
Spread debit	$-\frac{7}{8}$							
Value of long 115 - 120 call spread at expiration	0	0	$\frac{7}{8}$	5	5	5	5	5
Value of short 125 - 130 call spread at expiration	0	0	0	0	0	$-4\frac{1}{8}$	-5	-5
Profit/loss		$-\frac{7}{8}$	$-\frac{7}{8}$	0	$4\frac{1}{8}$	$4\frac{1}{8}$	0	$-\frac{7}{8}$	$-\frac{7}{8}$

Table 14.4 ■ Microsoft long January 115–120–125–130 call condor

A profit/loss graph of this condor at expiration appears in Figure 14.3.

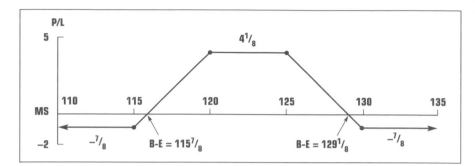

Fig 14.3 ■ **Microsoft long January 115 – 120 – 130 call condor**

*Long at-the-money call condor

For stationary markets

Like the butterfly, the call condor can be placed at many different strikes, depending on your outlook for the price range of the underlying.

Like the butterfly, the call condor can be placed at many different strikes, depending on your outlook for the price range of the underlying. If you think that the underlying has made its move for the near future, then you might trade the at-the-money call condor. For example, if XYZ is at 100, you could buy one 95 call, sell one 100 call, sell one 105 call, and buy one 110 call. This spread costs more than the at-the-money butterfly, and consequently its maximum profit is the less than the at-the-money butterfly, but its profit range is greater.

Using our now familiar set of Microsoft January options, you could pay 9 for one 105 call, sell one 110 call at $6\frac{1}{8}$, sell one 115 call at 4, and pay $2\frac{1}{2}$ for one 120 call. Your net debit is $1\frac{3}{8}$. The expiration profit/loss is summarized as follows:

Debit from one January 105 call:	–9
Debit from one January 120 call:	$-2\frac{1}{2}$
Credit from one January 110 call:	$6\frac{1}{8}$
Credit from one January 115 call:	4
Total debit:	$-1\frac{3}{8}$

Maximum profit: difference between two lowest strikes minus spread debit: $(110 - 105) - 1\frac{3}{8} = 3\frac{5}{8}$
Range of maximum profit: 110 – 115
Lower break-even level: lowest strike plus spread debit: $105 + 1\frac{3}{8} = 106\frac{3}{8}$

Upper break-even level: highest strike minus spread debit: $120 - 1\frac{3}{8} = 118\frac{5}{8}$
Profit range: $118\frac{5}{8} - 106\frac{3}{8} = 12\frac{1}{4}$
Maximum loss: cost of spread: $1\frac{3}{8}$

The risk/return ratio for this spread is $\dfrac{1\frac{3}{8}}{3\frac{5}{8}} = .38$ for 1. By knowing how the condor works, you can make a table and a graph of the profit/loss at expiration.

*Long out-of-the-money put condor

For downside direction followed by stationary market

If the profit range of an out-of-the-money put butterfly is too limited, it can be extended by shifting the short put spread to the next two lower strikes. If XYZ is at 100, you could buy one 100 put, sell one 95 put, sell one 90 put, and buy one 85 put. The resulting spread is the **long out-of-the-money put condor.** This spread costs more than the butterfly and its maximum profit is consequently less, but its profit range is greater. It is similar to the long put ladder or long put Christmas tree, but it has the protection of the long put at the lowest strike.

For example, in Microsoft January options you could pay $4\frac{1}{8}$ for one 105 put, sell one 100 put at $2\frac{5}{8}$, sell one 95 put at $1\frac{5}{8}$, and pay 1 for one 90 put. Your total debit is $\frac{7}{8}$.

Note that this put ladder has several features in common with the long January $115 - 120 - 125 - 130$ call ladder: Both maximum profits are $4\frac{1}{8}$, the profit ranges are $13\frac{1}{4}$, the ranges of maximum profit are 5 points, the risk/return ratios are .21, and of course, the spread debits are $\frac{7}{8}$.

The expiration profit/loss for this put condor is summarized as follows.

Debit from long January 105 put:	$-4\frac{1}{8}$
Debit from long January 90 put:	-1
Credit from short January 100 put:	$2\frac{5}{8}$
Credit from short January 95 put:	$1\frac{5}{8}$
Total debit:	$-\frac{7}{8}$

Maximum profit: difference between highest two strikes minus spread debit: $(105 - 100) - \frac{7}{8} = 4\frac{1}{8}$

Range of maximum profit: 100 − 95
Upper break-even level: highest strike minus spread debit: $105 - \frac{7}{8} = 104\frac{1}{8}$
Lower break-even level: lowest strike plus spread debit: $90 + \frac{7}{8} = 90\frac{7}{8}$
Profit range: $104\frac{1}{8} - 90\frac{7}{8} = 13\frac{1}{4}$
Maximum loss: Cost of spread: $\frac{7}{8}$

The risk/return ratio is again favourable at $\dfrac{\frac{7}{8}}{4\frac{1}{8}} = .21$ for 1. The profit/loss at expiration is shown in Table 14.5.

Microsoft	85	90	90⅞	95	100	104¼	105	110
Spread debit		$-\frac{7}{8}$						
Value of long 105–100 put spread at expiration	5	5	5	5	5	$\frac{7}{8}$	0	0
Value of short 95–90 put spread at expiration	−5	−5	$-4\frac{1}{8}$	0	0	0	0	0
Profit/loss		$-\frac{7}{8}$	$-\frac{7}{8}$	0	$4\frac{1}{8}$	$4\frac{1}{8}$	0	$-\frac{7}{8}$	$-\frac{7}{8}$

Table 14.5 ■ Microsoft long January 105–100–95–90 put condor

The graph of the profit/loss at expiration is shown in Figure 14.4.

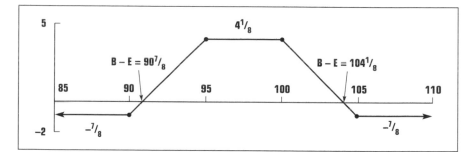

Fig 14.4 ■ Microsoft long January 105–100–95–90 put condor

*Long at-the-money put condor

For stationary markets

Put condors, like call condors, can be placed at many different strikes, depending on your near-term outlook for the underlying. If your outlook calls for a stationary market, but you wish to leave room for error on the downside, you can substitute the long at-the-money put condor for the at-the-money put butterfly. You might, for example, buy the above January 115 – 110 – 105 – 100 put condor for a debit of $1\frac{3}{8}$. The downside profit potential of this spread

Put condors, like call condors, can be placed at many different strikes, depending on your near-term outlook for the underlying.

is the same as the upside profit potential of the long January 105 – 110 – 115 – 120 call condor. The profit/loss at expiration is summarized as follows:

Debit from long January 115 put:	$-9\frac{1}{8}$
Debit from long January 100 put:	$-2\frac{5}{8}$
Credit from short January 110 put:	$6\frac{1}{4}$
Credit from short January 105 put:	$4\frac{1}{8}$
Total debit:	$-1\frac{3}{8}$

Maximum profit: difference between highest two strikes minus spread debit: $(115 - 110) - 1\frac{3}{8} = 3\frac{5}{8}$
Range of maximum profit: 110 – 105
Upper break-even level: highest strike minus spread debit: $115 - 1\frac{3}{8} = 113\frac{5}{8}$
Lower break-even level: lowest strike plus spread debit: $100 + 1\frac{3}{8} = 101\frac{3}{8}$
Profit range: $113\frac{5}{8} - 101\frac{3}{8} = 12\frac{1}{4}$
Maximum loss: Cost of spread: $1\frac{3}{8}$

The risk/return ratio is again favourable at $\dfrac{1\frac{3}{8}}{3\frac{3}{8}}$ = .38 for 1.

By now you should be an expert at tabulating and graphing the expiration profit/loss levels of condors and butterflies.

Short at-the-money put condor

For volatile markets

Like the butterfly, the condor can be sold in order to profit from a volatile or trending market.

Like the butterfly, the condor can be sold in order to profit from a volatile or trending market. For example, you could sell the above January 115 – 110 – 105 – 100 put condor at $1\frac{3}{8}$. If Microsoft closes above 115 or below 100 at expiration, you earn the credit from the spread. In this case you are taking a slightly bullish position.

The profit/loss figures are exactly the opposite of the above long put condor, but in order to minimize confusion, the expiration summary is:

Credit from long January 115 put:	$9\frac{1}{8}$
Credit from long January 100 put:	$2\frac{5}{8}$
Debit from short January 110 put:	$-6\frac{1}{4}$
Debit from short January 105 put:	$-4\frac{1}{8}$
Total credit:	$1\frac{3}{8}$

Maximum profit: spread credit: $1\frac{3}{8}$

Range of maximum profit: above 115 and below 100

Upper break-even level: highest strike minus spread credit: $115 - 1\frac{3}{8} = 113\frac{5}{8}$

Lower break-even level: lowest strike plus spread credit: $100 + 1\frac{3}{8} = 101\frac{3}{8}$

Maximum loss: difference between highest two strikes minus spread credit: $(115 - 110) - 1\frac{3}{8} = 3\frac{5}{8}$

Price range of stock for potential loss: $113\frac{5}{8} - 101\frac{3}{8} = 12\frac{1}{4}$ points

The risk/return ratio is again high at $\dfrac{3\frac{5}{8}}{1\frac{3}{8}}$ = 2.64 to 1. This spread is only suitable for volatile markets. The expiration profit/loss is shown in Table 14.6

Microsoft	95	100	$101\frac{3}{8}$	105	110	$113\frac{5}{8}$	115	120
Spread credit	$1\frac{3}{8}$	- - -	- - -	- - -	- - -	- - -	- - -	- - -
Value of short 115–110								
put spread at expiration	-5	-5	-5	-5	-5	$-1\frac{3}{8}$	0	0
Value of long 105–100								
put spread at expiration	5	5	$3\frac{5}{8}$	0	0	0	0	0
Profit/loss	$1\frac{3}{8}$	$1\frac{3}{8}$	0	$-3\frac{5}{8}$	$-3\frac{5}{8}$	0	$1\frac{3}{8}$	$1\frac{3}{8}$

Table 14.6 ■ Microsoft short January 115–110–105–100 put condor

In graphic form, the profit/loss at expiration is shown in Figure 14.5.

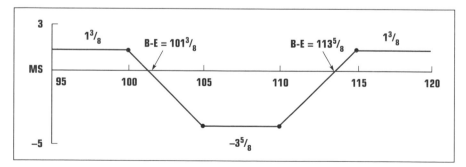

Fig 14.5 ■ Microsoft short January 115–110–105–100 put condor

We might compare this condor to the short $105 - 110 - 115$ call or put butterfly. The risk with the condor is that the stock's price range for a potential loss at expiration is extended from $8\frac{1}{2}$ to $12\frac{1}{4}$ points. The maximum loss is less, at $3\frac{5}{8}$ versus $4\frac{1}{4}$. The potential income, of course, is greater.

Short at-the-money call condor for volatile markets

If instead your outlook is for volatile conditions and you are slightly bearish, you might sell the January $105 - 110 - 115 - 120$ call condor at $1\frac{3}{8}$. (Don't be surprised if you earn your profit on the upside.) If at expiration Microsoft closes below 105 or above 120, then you earn the credit from the spread. Your profit/loss summary is as follows.

Credit from short January 105 call:	9
Credit from short January 120 call:	$2\frac{1}{2}$
Debit from long January 110 call:	$-6\frac{1}{8}$
Debit from long January 115 call:	-4
Total credit:	$1\frac{3}{8}$

Maximum profit: spread credit: $1\frac{3}{8}$
Range of maximum profit: below 105 and above 120
Lower break-even level: lowest strike plus spread credit: $105 + 1\frac{3}{8} = 106\frac{3}{8}$
Upper break-even level: highest strike minus spread credit: $120 - 1\frac{3}{8} = 118\frac{5}{8}$
Maximum loss: difference between lowest two strikes minus spread credit: $(110 - 105) - 1\frac{3}{8} = 3\frac{5}{8}$
Price range of stock for potential loss: $118\frac{5}{8} - 106\frac{3}{8} = 12\frac{1}{4}$ points

The risk/return ratio is $\dfrac{3\frac{5}{8}}{1\frac{3}{8}} = 2.64$ to 1.

*Butterflies and condors with non-adjacent strikes

Butterflies are flexible spreads which can profit from a variety of trading ranges. You can extend the profit range of a butterfly by extending the equidistance of the strikes. If XYZ is at 100, and you expect it to rally into a range of between 105

> **Butterflies are flexible spreads which can profit from a variety of trading ranges.**

and 115, then you can buy the $100 - 110 - 120$ call butterfly. This spread costs more than the adjacent strike, $105 - 110 - 115$ call butterfly, but it has a greater profit range.

Using the set of Microsoft January options, you could pay $6\frac{1}{8}$ for the 110 call, sell two 120 calls at $2\frac{1}{2}$, and pay 1 for the 130 call, for a net debit of $2\frac{1}{8}$. Your profit range is then $112\frac{1}{8}$ to $127\frac{7}{8}$, or $15\frac{3}{4}$ points. The expiration profit/loss is summarized as follows:

Debit from long January 110 call:	$-6\frac{1}{8}$
Debit from long January 130 call:	-1
Credit from two short January 120 calls: $2 \times 2\frac{1}{2} =$	$\underline{5}$
Total debit:	$-2\frac{1}{8}$

Maximum profit: difference between lowest two strikes minus spread debit: $(120 - 110) - 2\frac{1}{8} = 7\frac{7}{8}$
Lower break-even level: lowest strike plus spread debit: $110 + 2\frac{1}{8} = 112\frac{1}{8}$
Upper break-even level: highest strike minus spread debit: $130 - 2\frac{1}{8} = 127\frac{7}{8}$
Profit range: $127\frac{7}{8} - 112\frac{1}{8} = 15\frac{3}{4}$ points
Maximum loss: cost of spread: $2\frac{1}{8}$

The risk/return ratio is $\dfrac{2\frac{1}{8}}{15\frac{3}{4}}$, or .13 to 1.

Condors can also increase their profit ranges by increasing the equidistance of the strikes. This is especially feasible now that stock indexes and as a result, options premiums, are at high levels. In fact, this feasibility seems to increase with each blink of the eyes. Consider the set of FTSE options below.

June FTSE–100 options
June Future at 6250
106 days until expiry
ATM implied at 26 per cent

Strike	6225	6325	6425	6525	6625	6725	6825	6925
Calls	$359\frac{1}{2}$	303	$253\frac{1}{2}$	205	165	131	$102\frac{1}{2}$	80

If you discern that the path of least resistance is up, or if you're simply bullish, you may wish to take a long call position in the UK market. But if the thought of spending £2000 to £3000 for one options contract gives you pause, then you may instead consider financing your call purchase with a spread.

For £470, the 6325 – 6525 – 6725 – 6925 call condor can be purchased without selling your cottage in the Cotswolds. The maximum profit is 200 – 47 =

153 ticks. The break-even levels, at 6372 and 6878, provide a profit range of 506 points. The risk/return for this spread is favourable, at $\frac{47}{153} = .31$.

The trade-off with this spread is that if the FTSE rallies quickly, then the spread will show only a modest profit. Like all butterflies and condors, this spread needs time decay to work for it.

Non-adjacent strike butterflies and condors are preferred alternatives in the OEX or SPX as well. They are sensible ways of reducing premium exposure while minimizing risk. Perhaps the exchanges may consider reducing the tick size of these three contracts in order to accommodate the individual investor, and to improve liquidity and price discovery.

Volatility, days until expiration, and butterflies and condors

Likewise when volatilities are high, you can often find inexpensive adjacent strike butterflies and condors, such as in the above FTSE example. This is because the underlying is trading in a wide range, and the probability of it settling near a particular strike at expiration is small. The same factors apply to these spreads when there are many days until expiration. At times like these, it is preferable to trade butterflies and condors with non-adjacent strikes. They cost more, but their profit range is greater.

Conclusion

In this chapter we have covered butterflies and condors in depth. The reasons for this are twofold: when purchased, these spreads have low risk/return ratios; also, they can easily be opened and closed in one transaction. They are therefore justifiable trading strategies under many market conditions. It is worth learning how to use them.

Questions on butterflies and condors

1   In the UK, the FTSE-100 index has been bullish since the end of October, and you expect this trend to continue through the end of the year. The December futures contract is currently at 5470. Using technical analysis, you determine that there is resistance at a former support area between 5700 and 5800. Because you want to avoid the risk of early exercise in the American-style options, you note the following European-style December call options.

December FTSE contract at 5470
December options with 40 days until expiry

Strike	5625	5675	5725	5775	5825	5875	5925	5975	6025
Calls	$159\frac{1}{2}$	$137\frac{1}{2}$	117	$97\frac{1}{2}$	81	68	57	$46\frac{1}{2}$	$35\frac{1}{2}$

a) What is the cost of the long 5675 – 5775 – 5875 call butterfly?
  i)   At expiry, what is the maximum profit of the spread?
  ii) What is the lower break-even level?
  iii) What is the uper break-even level?
  iv) What is the profit range?
  v)   What is the maximum loss?

b) What is the cost of the long 5625 – 5725 – 5825 – 5925 call condor?
  i)   At expiry, what is the maximum profit of the spread?
  ii) What is the lower break-even level?
  iii) What is the upper break-even level?
  iv) What is the profit range?
  v)   What is the maximum loss?

c) How do you account for the greater profit range of the condor?

2 Because of problems with the UN weapons inspectors in Iraq, the price of crude oil has been volatile lately. The issue has been temporarily resolved, however, and the inspectors have returned to their duties. The price of January crude oil as traded at the New York Mercantile Exchange has retraced from approximately $15 per barrel to the present $11.86.

You expect crude oil to enter a range centered at $12 per barrel for the next month, by which time the January options will have expired on December 16. The current January implied volatility is still high, at 58 per cent, so you think this is a good premium selling opportunity. You observe the following settlement prices for the January options. The contract multiplier is $10 per tick, meaning that the 13.00 call is worth $27 \times \$10 = \$270$.

January crude oil at $11.86
January options with 22 days until expiration

Strike	11.00	11.50	12.00	12.50	13.00
Calls	1.17	.84	.61	.41	.27
Puts	.31	.50	.75	1.05	1.41

a) i) What is the cost, in ticks and dollars, of the long January 11.50 – 12.00 – 12.50 call butterfly?

ii) At expiration, what is the maximum profit?

iii) What is the lower break-even level for this butterfly?

iv) What is the upper break-even level?

v) What is the profit range?

vi) What is the maximum loss?

b) i) Because January crude is making new lows this week, you decide to leave a margin of error on the downside. What is the cost of the long January 12.50 – 12.00 – 11.50 – 11.00 put condor?

ii) At expiration, what is the maximum profit?

iii) What is the upper break-even level?

iv) What is the lower break-even level?

v) What is the profit range?

vi) What is the maximum loss?

3 i) Returning to Microsoft, what is the cost of the long January 110 – 105 – 100 – 95 put condor?

ii) At expiration, what is the maximum profit?

iii) What is the upper break-even level?

iv) What is the lower break-even level?

v) What is the profit range?

vi) What is the maximum loss?

Answers

1 **a)** i) $137\frac{1}{2} + 68 - [2 \times 97\frac{1}{2}] = 10\frac{1}{2}$

ii) $[5775 - 5675] - 10\frac{1}{2} = 89\frac{1}{2}$

iii) $5675 + 10\frac{1}{2} = 5685\frac{1}{2}$

iv) $5875 - 10\frac{1}{2} = 5864\frac{1}{2}$

v) $5864\frac{1}{2} - 5685\frac{1}{2} = 179$ points

vi) $10\frac{1}{2} = £105$

b) i) $159\frac{1}{2} + 57 - 117 - 81 = 18\frac{1}{2}$

ii) $[5725 - 5625] - 18\frac{1}{2} = 81\frac{1}{2}$

iii) $5625 + 18\frac{1}{2} = 5643\frac{1}{2}$

iv) $5925 - 18\frac{1}{2} = 5906\frac{1}{2}$

v) $5906\frac{1}{2} - 5643\frac{1}{2} = 263$ points

vi) $18\frac{1}{2} = £185$

c) The condor has a gross profit range that is 100 points greater. The 8p extra cost reduces eight points of profit from both the lower and

upper break-even levels. The net profit range of the condor is therefore 84p greater.

2 a) i) $.84 + .41 - [2 \times .61] = .03 \times \$10 = \$30$

  ii) $[12.00 - 11.50] - .03 = .47$

  iii) $11.50 + .03 = 11.53$

  iv) $12.50 - .03 = 12.47$

  v) $12.47 - 11.53 = .94$

  vi) $.03$, or $\$30$

  b) i) $1.05 + .31 - .75 - .50 = .11 \times \$10 = \$110$

  ii) $[12.50 - 12.00] - .11 = .39$

  iii) $12.50 - .11 = 12.39$

  iv) $11.00 + .11 = 11.11$

  v) $12.39 - 11.11 = 1.28$

  vi) $.11$, or $\$110$

3 i) $6\frac{1}{4} + 1\frac{5}{8} - 4\frac{1}{8} - 2\frac{5}{8} = 1\frac{1}{8}$, or $\$112.50$

  ii) $[110 - 105] - 1\frac{1}{8} = 3\frac{7}{8}$

  iii) $110 - 1\frac{1}{8} = 108\frac{7}{8}$

  iv) $95 + 1\frac{1}{8} = 96\frac{1}{8}$

  v) $108\frac{7}{8} - 96\frac{1}{8} = 12\frac{3}{4}$

  vi) $1\frac{1}{8}$

The covered write, the calendar spread and the diagonal spread

The diagonal spread for trending markets

Introduction

There are two additional spreads that profit from stationary markets. The **covered write** involves selling a call against a long underlying position, and the **calendar** or **time spread** involves selling a near-term at-the-money option, usually a call, and buying a farther-term at-the-money option, again usually a call. Both spreads profit from time decay.

The covered write or the buy-write

If an investor owns or is long an underlying contract, he may sell or write a call on it to earn additional income. This strategy is known as the **covered write** and it is often used by long-term holders of stocks that are temporarily underperforming. It is often traded in bear markets.

When the underlying is bought and the call is sold in the same transaction, this spread is also known as the **buy-write.**

> When the underlying is bought and the call is sold in the same transaction, this spread is also known as the buy-write.

For example, if you own XYZ at a price of 100 you may sell one 105 call at perhaps 3. The maximum profit is the premium earned from the sale of the call plus the amount that the underlying appreciates to the strike price of the call. Here, this would be 5 + 3 = 8. The downside break-even level is the price of the underlying at the time of the call sale less the call income. Here, this would be 100 − 3 = 97.

There are two risks:

■ The first is that the underlying may decline below the downside break-even level, and the you will take a loss on the total position.

■ The second is that the underlying may advance above the call strike price, the underlying will be called away, and you will relinquish the upside profit from the underlying.

■ This spread is best used by investors who have purchased the underlying at significantly lower levels, who think that there is little or no upside potential, and who can tolerate short-term declines in the underlying.

For example, GE is currently trading at $92\frac{1}{16}$, and the December 95 calls, with 30 days until expiration, are priced at $1\frac{7}{8}$. You may sell one call on each 100 GE shares that you own. Alternatively, you may pay $92\frac{1}{16}$ for one hundred shares, while selling the call, as a spread.

At expiration, the maximum profit for your spread occurs at the strike price of the call. There, you gain the price appreciation of the stock plus the full income from the call. The maximum profit is calculated as the strike price minus the purchase price of the stock plus the income from the call, or $(95 - 92\frac{1}{16}) + 1\frac{7}{8} = 4\frac{13}{16}$.

Above the call strike price, the profit from the stock is offset by the loss on the call, on a point for point basis. The maxium profit is earned, no more, no less. The stock will be called away from you at expiration.

The lower break-even level for your position is the price at which the call income equals the decline in the stock price. This is calculated as the price of the stock minus the income from the call, or $92\frac{1}{16} - 1\frac{7}{8} = 90\frac{3}{16}$. Below this level the spread loses point for point with the stock.

The expiration profit/loss for this covered write is summarized as follows.

Maximum profit: strike price minus stock price, plus income from call: $(95 - 92\frac{1}{16}) + 1\frac{7}{8} = 4\frac{13}{16}$.
The maximum profit occurs at or above the strike price of the call.
Break-even level: stock price minus income from call: $92\frac{1}{16} - 1\frac{7}{8} = 90\frac{3}{16}$.
Maximum loss: full amount of stock price decline below break-even level: $90\frac{3}{16}$.

The expiration profit/loss is summarized in Table 15.1.

GE	(below)	85	90	90 $\frac{3}{16}$	92 $\frac{1}{16}$	95	100
Credit from 95 call	1 $\frac{7}{8}$	---	---	---	---	---	---
Value of call at expiration	0	0	0	0	0	0	-5
Stock profit/loss at expiration	(–full amt)	-7 $\frac{1}{16}$	-2 $\frac{1}{16}$	-1 $\frac{7}{8}$	0	2 $\frac{15}{16}$	7 $\frac{15}{16}$
Total profit/loss	(–full amt)	-5 $\frac{3}{16}$	-$\frac{3}{16}$	0	1 $\frac{7}{8}$	4 $\frac{13}{16}$	4 $\frac{13}{16}$

Table 15.1 ■ GE covered write: pay 92 $\frac{1}{16}$ for GE, sell December 95 call at 1 $\frac{7}{8}$

The expiration profit/loss is shown in Figure 15.1.

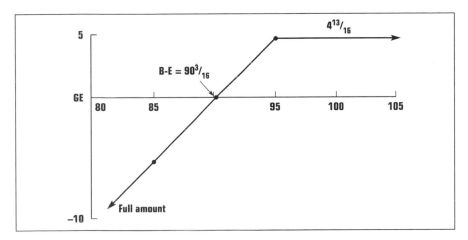

Fig 15.1 ■ GE covered write: pay 92 $\frac{1}{16}$ for GE, sell December 95 call at 1 $\frac{7}{8}$[13]

How to manage the risk of the covered write

The covered write is best suited to long-term stock holders who can tolerate a decline in the stock price below the break-even level.

There are two solutions to the upside risk. Using the above spread, first note that with GE at 92 $\frac{1}{16}$, the Dec 90 calls are priced at 4 $\frac{5}{8}$. Let's assume that GE immediately rallies 5 dollars, to 97 $\frac{1}{16}$. At this point, your short 95 calls will be worth approximately 4 $\frac{5}{8}$, and you may simply buy them back. Your profit/loss is as follows.

---

[13] The above graph is almost identical to that of a short, in-the-money December 95 put. This put could be sold for approximately 4 $\frac{7}{16}$. The $\frac{3}{8}$ seemingly greater profit potential for the covered write includes the cost of carry on the stock purchase for 30 days at 5 per cent interest. This covered write is actually a synthetic short 95 put. Synthetics are discussed in Part Four.

Sale of 95 call:	$1\frac{7}{8}$ credit
Purchase of 95 call:	$4\frac{5}{8}$ debit
Profit on stock:	5 credit
profit/loss:	$2\frac{1}{4}$ credit

With this solution you have revised your outlook. You have concluded that there is significant upside potential for GE.

The second solution is to maintain your outlook. You conclude that you have erred in your estimate for GE's upside potential, but that the stock's new level is the top for the time being. Your stategy is to write calls for the next few expirations, and you expect to profit in the end.

With GE at $97\frac{1}{16}$, the value of the 95 call will be, as we said, approximately $4\frac{5}{8}$. The 100, or 'par' call will then be approximately $1\frac{7}{8}$. The 95 – 100 call spread will be approximately $4\frac{5}{8} - 1\frac{7}{8} = 2\frac{3}{4}$. You can then buy this spread, and by doing so, roll your short call to the 100 strike.

The options summary is as follows.

Sale of 95 call:	$1\frac{7}{8}$
Purchase of 95 call:	$-4\frac{5}{8}$
Sale of 100 call:	$1\frac{7}{8}$
Total options debit:	$-\frac{7}{8}$

Here, the profit equals the five points appreciation on the stock minus the total options debit, or $5 - \frac{7}{8} = 4\frac{1}{8}$.

The total profit/loss summary at expiration is as follows:

Maximum profit: new strike price minus stock purchase price, minus debit from call position: $(100 - 92\frac{1}{16}) - \frac{7}{8} = 7\frac{1}{16}$

The maximum profit occurs at or above the strike price, 100, of the open December call.

Break-even level: stock purchase price plus total options debit: $92\frac{1}{16} + \frac{7}{8} = 92\frac{15}{16}$. Note that this level is $2\frac{3}{4}$ points above the former B-E level.

Maximum loss: full amount of stock price decline below break-even level: $92\frac{15}{16}$.

The risk here is that at the new price level, $97\frac{1}{16}$, GE contains five points of downside loss potential for which you have received a credit of only $4\frac{1}{8}$. The potential return, of course, is improved.

The expiration profit/loss is summarized in Table 15.2:

GE	(below)	85	90	$92\frac{1}{16}$	$92\frac{15}{16}$	95	$97\frac{1}{16}$	100	105
Total options debit	$-\frac{7}{8}$	—	—	—	—	—	—	—	—
Value of 100 call at expiration	0	0	0	0	0	0	0	0	-5
Stock profit/loss at expiration	(–full amt)	$-7\frac{1}{16}$	$-2\frac{1}{16}$	0	$\frac{7}{8}$	$2\frac{15}{16}$	5	$7\frac{15}{16}$	$12\frac{15}{16}$
Total profit/loss	(–full amt)	$-7\frac{15}{16}$	$-2\frac{15}{16}$	$-\frac{7}{8}$	0	$2\frac{1}{16}$	$4\frac{1}{8}$	$7\frac{1}{16}$	$7\frac{1}{16}$

Table 15.2 ■

With the covered write, it is important *not* to think in terms of the short call as 'downside protection'. Remember 'portfolio insurance'? A form of this now discredited strategy was a variation of the covered write. During the 1980s portfolio insurance was sold to investors as a means of 'downside protection', in other words, calls were written against a stock portfolio in order to compensate for a price decline, and in the mean time, to earn income.

Have you ever heard of an insurance policy that *paid* you to be insured? On October 19, 1987, no amount of calls sold protected stockholders from the enormous loss of their assets' values. With options, the only form of full downside protection is the purchase of a put.

The long calendar spread or long time spread

Calendar spreads in particular can be complicated, and their return potentials can in many cases be duplicated by other stationary market spreads. However, learning about them is an excellent way to improve your understanding of options, and to improve your risk awareness.

Because an option's decay accelerates with time it is possible to sell a near-term option and buy a farther-term option at the same strike in order to profit from the different rates of decay. The resulting position is termed either the **long calendar spread** or the **long time spread**. Usually this spread is traded with both options at the money. For example, if XYZ is at 100, you could sell one June 100 call and buy one September 100 call in the same transaction. Apart from extraordinary circumstances, this spread is done for a debit. Your outlook should call for a stationary market with both options remaining at-the-money.

This spread is best opened when the near-term option has between 60 to 30 days till expiration. The time distance between the two options can vary. A greater distance increases the cost of the spread, and reduces the hedge value of the farther-term option, while a shorter distance reduces the difference in rates of decay, which in turn lowers the profit potential. Optimally, there should be 30 to 90 days between options. This spread should be closed before the near-term option expires.

A preferable opportunity is when the relationship between the near-term implied volatility and the farther-term volatility is at a discrepancy, i.e., the near-term volatility is at a higher level than usual in comparison to the farther-term volatility. This often occurs when the underyling has reacted suddenly to an event that is of short-term significance, or perhaps when the longer-term significance of an event is not fully accounted for. The underlying has moved to a level at which it is expected to remain for the near term.

Consider the following set of options on Rolls-Royce.

Rolls-Royce at $223\frac{1}{2}$

November options with 9 days until expiry, November implied at 52 per cent

February options with 98 days until expiry, February implied at 46 per cent (Feb − Nov = 89 days)

May options with 188 days until expiry, May implied at 44 per cent (May − Feb = 90 days)

Strike	180	(CS)	220	(CS)	260	(CS)
November calls	44		$8\frac{1}{2}$		cab	
		(7)		(17)		$(10\frac{1}{2})$
February calls	51		$25\frac{1}{2}$		$10\frac{1}{2}$	
		(5)		(7)		$(6\frac{1}{2})$
May calls	56		$32\frac{1}{2}$		17	

The values of the calendar spreads are given in parentheses (CS). Note that the calendar spread with the most value is the February − November 220 call calendar spread. There the characteristic of at-the-money, accelerated time decay is most in evidence. By comparing the February − November 220 call calendar spread to the February − November 180 and 260 call calendar spreads it can be seen that as the underlying moves away from the strikes, the calendar spreads have less value.

Because of this latter fact, many traders buy calendar spreads that are out of the money. Their outlook calls for the underlying to approach the strike of the spread as the front month option reaches 30 or fewer days until expiration. For example, you could pay $6\frac{1}{2}$ for the May − February 260 call calendar, and if the stock rises to 260 at the point when February has 9 days until expiration, then the spread will be worth approximately 17, or the present value of the February − November 220 call calendar.

To get an accurate profit/loss assessment at expiration requires simulation by computer, which can determine the value of the calendar at various points in time and at various price levels of the underlying. The above set of options, however, indicate the basic profit/loss behaviour of this spread.

Except under unusual circumstances, the maximum loss is the debit of the spread.

Risks of calendar spreads

Because the calendar spread includes options on two contract months there are several risk scenarios, and these are different for options on stocks, interest rate contracts, and commodities. Calendar spreads must often be evaluated as two separate positions, and therefore a proper risk/return profile can only be obtained with the aid of a risk analysis program. However, the major risks can be noted.

> Calendar spreads must often be evaluated as two separate positions, and therefore a proper risk/return profile can only be obtained with the aid of a risk analysis program.

One risk common to all is that the implied volatility may increase more for the short, near-term option than for the long, farther-term option, causing the spread to lose its value. This is usually due to an unforseen event. The underlying may then move away from the strikes before profit is made from time decay.

Another possible risk is that the historical volatility of the underlying may decrease, bringing the implied volatilities of all the options contracts down with it. Because the long, farther-term contract has the greater vega, the spread will lose its value.

If a stock makes a large upside move, both calls may go to parity, and the spread will become worthless. If a stock makes a large downside move, both calls, and the spread, will become worthless.

With stocks and stock indexes, takeovers, changes in dividends, or a change in the current level of interest rates can affect the delta spread between the two options contracts.

Short-term interest rate and other interest rate contracts have their own risks. A central bank may unexpectedly announce a change in interest rates, or the change may be greater or less than expected. Economic indicators may change the market's assessment of the interest rate outlook. This will cause the spreads between the underlying futures contracts, and consequently the options spreads, to change. Caution must be exercised when spreading options between contracts with different delivery months.

There is significant risk in spreading agricultural commodities from old crop to new crop. For example, with CBOT corn early in the growing season you should avoid selling September calls against December calls. This is because a shortage may develop in September which will cause its underlying futures contract to rally while the December underlying remains practically unchanged. Many commodities have seasonal volatility trends which should be studied.

Most calendars traded are call calendars, but there is no reason not to trade put calendars. The profit/loss characteristics are practically identical, except in the OEX and FTSE, where American-style calls and puts have different behaviour due to early exercise. Puts on stocks are more likely to be exercised early if trading at parity, because a put is the right to sell the stock and raise cash.

Because there are more variables with a calendar spread, it is simpler to buy a butterfly or condor if your outlook calls for decreased volatility and for the underlying to close near a particular strike. A better reason to trade the long calendar as opposed to the long butterfly is to profit from a discrepancy in the implied volatilities from month to month.

Long diagonal call spread for a bullish market followed by a stationary market

It is possible to alter the strikes of the calendar spread. The most common variation is to sell a near-term, out-of-the-money call and buy a far-term at-the-money call. For example, you might pay $32\frac{1}{2}$ for the May 220 call above, while selling the February 260 call at $10\frac{1}{2}$, for a net debit of 22.

The return scenario for this spread is for the shares to rally gradually to 260 towards February expiration. At 9 days until February expiration, the value of the spread would be similar to the current February 180 – November 220 call calendar, at $42\frac{1}{2}$. The diagonal calendar is a combination of the long, far term, at-the-money call spread plus the long, out-of-the-money call calendar spread:

(Long May 220 call + short May 260 call) + (long May 260 call + short February 260 call) = Long May 220 call + short February 260 call

Diagonal spreads may also be traded with puts. Here, you can buy a far-term put and sell a near-term put that is at a strike farther out-of-the-money.

Questions on covered writes and calendar spreads

1 Your shares in Boeing have performed well in the past, but now, with the possibility of a global recession, aircraft orders are down, and the stock is in a trading range. You are looking to supplement your dividend by writing one call on 100 shares of your stock. You realize that if the stock rallies above the call strike price, it will be called away from you. Boeing is currently trading at $42\frac{13}{16}$, and the December 45 calls, with 30 days until expiration, are trading at $\frac{13}{16}$.

i)   What is the maximum profit from writing one Dec 45 call?
ii)   What happens if at expiration the stock closes above 45?
iii) What is the break-even level?
iv)   What is your percentage return over the next 30 days with your stock valued at $42\frac{13}{16}$.

2 Sainsbury's range this past year is no less than 370 to $588\frac{1}{2}$. You have held onto your shares, riding the market turbulence. Because supermarkets are currently cutting prices, you forsee reduced profit margins for the near term.

Sainsbury is currently trading at $537\frac{1}{2}$. With 70 days until expiration, the January 550 calls are trading at 34, and the January 600 calls are trading at $17\frac{1}{2}$. You would like to sell one of these as a covered write on 1,000 shares that you own.

a) i)   What is the maximum profit from writing one January 550 call?
ii)   What happens if at expiry the shares closes above 550?
iii) What is the break-even level?
iv)   What is your percentage return over the next 70 days with your shares valued at $537\frac{1}{2}$?

b) i)   What is the maximum profit from writing one January 600 call?
ii)   What happens if at expiry the shares closes above 600?
iii) What is the break-even level?
iv)   What is your percentage return over the next 70 days with your shares valued at $537\frac{1}{2}$?

3 It is late November, and IBM is currently trading at $159\frac{3}{4}$. You expect IBM to remain at approximately 160 for the next month while investors frantically chase internet stocks. You note the following prices for 160 calls.

November 160 calls, with one day until expiration: $\frac{11}{16}$
December 160 calls, with 29 days until expiration: $5\frac{1}{8}$
Jan 160 calls, with 64 days until expiration: $7\frac{1}{2}$

a) What is the cost of the December – January 160 call calendar?

b) Barring a special dividend or takeover within the next 29 days, what is the maximum loss of your calendar spread?

c) i) Although there are 28 days between November and December expirations, and 35 days between December and January expirations, you would like to estimate the profit potential of the December – January spread. What is your estimate for the value of this spread with IBM at 160 and one day until December expiration?

ii) Would you expect the December – January spread to be worth more or less than the November – December spread?

Answers

1 i) $[45 - 42\frac{13}{16}] + \frac{13}{16} = 3$

ii) Your stock will be called away, or sold, but you will still have your maximum profit.

iii) $42\frac{13}{16} - \frac{13}{16} = 42$

iv) $\frac{13}{16} \div 42\frac{13}{16} = 1.9\%$

2 a) i) $[550 - 537\frac{1}{2}] + 34 = 46\frac{1}{2}$

ii) Your shares will be called away, or sold, but you will still have your maximum profit.

iii) $537\frac{1}{2} - 34 = 503\frac{1}{2}$

iv) $34 \div 537\frac{1}{2} = 6.33\%$

2 b) i) $[600 - 537\frac{1}{2}] + 17\frac{1}{2} = 80$

ii) Your shares will be called away, or sold, but you will still have your maximum profit.

iii) $537\frac{1}{2} - 17\frac{1}{2} = 520$

iv) $17\frac{1}{2} \div 537\frac{1}{2} = 3.26\%$

3 a) $7\frac{1}{2} - 5\frac{1}{8} = 2\frac{3}{8}$

b) $2\frac{3}{8}$

c) i) Estimate would equal the November – December spread's value, $5\frac{1}{8} - \frac{11}{16} = 4\frac{7}{16}$

ii) More, because the long January call will have more days until expiration than the long December call. This doesn't imply greater profit potential, however, because the November – December spread would have cost less to begin with. This analysis assumes that the three implied volatilities are equal and will remain constant.

Part

3

Thinking about options

16 The interaction of the Greeks

17 Options performance based on cost

18 Options talk 1

19 Options talk 2: trouble shooting and common problems

20 Volatility skews

16 The interaction of the Greeks

The Greeks, the time until expiration, and the implied volatility interact with each other in ways that work together and in ways that trade off. They work differently for each options position. By knowing how they interact you can test your position for market scenarios. You can anticipate what may happen under the best, or return, scenario, or under the worst, or risk, scenario. You can know what to expect.

This chapter summarizes what you have previously learned about the Greeks. It places them all into perspective and describes their interaction.

Comparing options 1: The Greeks and time

Let's look again at the December Corn options that we have previously discussed. Tables 16.1 and 16.2 show two sets of options with different days until expiration, and with the corresponding deltas, gammas, thetas, and vegas. The price of the underlying is held constant.

You may compare the effect of time on options with the same strike, and on options with different strikes. Note, for example, the 230 call, a one-strike out-of-the-money option. As it approaches expiration, its delta becomes smaller, its gamma becomes greater, its theta becomes greater, and its vega becomes smaller. Note the 240 call, whose delta, theta, and vega become less, but whose gamma remains practically the same. Note that with time passing the gamma of the at-the-money option increases significantly more than the out-of and the in-the-money options. These are all consequences of the characteristics discussed in previous chapters.

90 DTE Implied Volatility at 20 per cent
Dec Corn at 220, options multiplier at $50

Strike	Call value	Call delta	Call Theta ($)	Put value	Put delta	Put Theta ($)	Gamma	Vega ($)	Vega (ticks)
190	$30\frac{1}{8}$	.92	.50	$\frac{5}{8}$	.06	.74	.006	6.70	$\frac{1}{8}$
200	$21\frac{1}{2}$	.83	1.26	$1\frac{7}{8}$	.15	1.42	.011	12.90	$\frac{1}{4}$
210	$14\frac{1}{4}$	.69	1.97	$4\frac{3}{8}$	.30	2.05	.016	18.77	$\frac{3}{8}$
220	$8\frac{5}{8}$	.51	2.31	$8\frac{5}{8}$	.47	2.31	.018	21.44	$\frac{3}{8}$
230	$4\frac{3}{4}$	.34	2.17	$14\frac{5}{8}$	.65	2.09	.017	19.84	$\frac{3}{8}$
240	$2\frac{3}{8}$	.20	1.68	$22\frac{1}{8}$	.78	1.52	.013	15.26	$\frac{1}{4}$
250	$1\frac{1}{8}$	.11	1.10	$30\frac{5}{8}$	.88	.86	.008	9.98	$\frac{1}{4}$

Table 16.1 ■ **December corn options, 90 days until expiration**

30 DTE, Implied Volatility at 20 per cent
Dec Corn at 220

Strike	Call value	Call delta	Call Theta ($)	Put value	Put delta ($)	Put Theta	Gamma	Vega ($)	Vega (ticks)
190	$29\frac{7}{8}$	.99	0	0	0	0	0	0	0
200	$20\frac{1}{8}$	.95	.83	$\frac{1}{4}$	.05	1.00	.008	3.00	0
210	$11\frac{3}{8}$	.80	2.84	$1\frac{1}{2}$	.20	2.92	.022	8.80	$\frac{1}{8}$
220	5	.51	4.13	5	.49	4.13	.031	12.51	$\frac{1}{4}$
230	$1\frac{5}{8}$	.23	3.14	$11\frac{1}{2}$	.77	3.06	.024	9.47	$\frac{1}{4}$
240	$\frac{3}{8}$	.07	1.37	$20\frac{1}{4}$	.93	1.21	.010	4.13	$\frac{1}{8}$
250	0	0	0	$29\frac{7}{8}$	.98	.13	0	0	0

Table 16.2 ■ **December corn options, 30 days until expiration**
(Tables 16.1 and 16.2 coutesy of FutureSource – Bridge.)

Table 16.3 is a generalized summary of the effect of time on the Greeks. Again, the underlying is held constant. The terms 'in-the-money' (ITM), 'at-the-money' (ATM), and 'out-of-the-money' (OTM) are used in abbreviated form.

		Delta	Gamma	Theta	Vega
Time forward:	OTM call	down	up	up	down
	put	down	up	up	down
	ATM call	unch'd	up	up	down
	put	unch'd	up	up	down
	ITM call	up	up	up	down
	put	up	up	up	down

Table 16.3 ■ The effect of time passing on the Greeks

The exceptions to the above generalizations are the deep in-the-money and far out-of-the-money options, such as the December 190 calls and puts, and the December 250 calls and puts. When these options have 40–50 DTE, most of their time premium has been expended, and changes in the Greeks are of little consequence (except when you're short them).

> A long options position has positive gamma, negative theta, and positive vega.

Remember that a long options position has positive gamma, negative theta, and positive vega. As time passes, it benefits more from price movement, it costs more in time decay, and it benefits less from an increase in implied volatility. A short options position has the opposite profile with respect to the Greeks.

By knowing how the Greeks interact, we can evaluate a position from just two variables. Traders often do this with delta and the number of days until expiration. 'I'm long a hundred, twenty-delta calls with thirty days out', has a very different meaning than 'I'm long a hundred, twenty-delta calls with ninety days out'. The former call position has a strike price that is closer to the money, higher (positive) gamma, greater (negative) theta, and smaller (positive) vega. It indicates that the trader is looking for a large move in the underlying, soon. The latter position indicates that the trader is looking for a large eventual move and/or an increase in implied volatility.

December Corn at 220

90 DTE		30 DTE	
December 240 calls		December 230 calls	
Delta	.20	Delta	.23
Gamma	.013	Gamma	.024
Theta	$1.42	Theta	$3.14
Vega	$15.26	Vega	$9.47

Table 16.4 ■ December Corn options with approx. .20 deltas

Understandably, traders seldom discuss their positions except with their risk managers. Consider the characteristics of the Greeks and the outlook of the traders who have positions opposite to those above.

Understandably, traders seldom discuss their positions except with their risk managers.

Comparing options 2: Delta versus gamma, theta and vega

The above tables also summarize what we already know about the relationship between delta and the other Greeks. Gamma, theta, and vega are all greatest with .50 delta options. Therefore, as the underlying moves, the Greeks of all options increase or decrease together, although not at the same rate. This simplifies the risk/return analysis of gamma, theta and vega with respect to delta, or underlying price movement.

Traders often speak of gamma, theta and vega when discussing how their positions have fared with a change in the underlying. 'Everything was fine until my gammas started kicking in, and now vol's getting pumped', means the opposite of 'I was getting hammered on time decay but now my gammas and vegas are helping me out'. (Traders are fond of complaining, even while they are making money.)

The first trader has positive theta and he has been collecting time decay. He has been short out-of-the-money options that have now become at-the-money options. His deltas are changing rapidly because of his negative gamma, making his position difficult to manage. In addition, he has negative vega and the implied volatility is increasing.

The second trader has been long out-of-the-money options and his negative theta has cost him in time decay. Now his options are at-the-money. His positive gamma has caused his deltas, and therefore the value of his options, to increase rapidly. Because the implied is increasing, his positive vega is paying off.

In both cases, the market has behaved the same. It was formerly quiet, it recently moved to a new price range, and now it is more volatile. This change of underlying level and corresponding change of options characteristics is illustrated in Table 16.5. It happens every day with all options contracts to a greater or lesser degree.

Position: December 230 calls

Position then		Position now	
December corn at 220		December corn at 230	
December 230 calls:		December 230 calls:	
Delta	.23	Delta	.51
Gamma	.024	Gamma	.031
Theta	$3.06	Theta	$4.13
Vega	$9.47	Vega	$12.51

Table 16.5 ■ December Corn with 30 DTE, position: December 230 calls

Comparing options 3: Implied volatility versus the Greeks

Because the implied volatility often trends, and occasionally makes a sudden change, it is essential to know how an options position can change accordingly. The interaction between implied volatility and the Greeks has some unusual characteristics which take time to fully understand. To know how the deltas change is the priority, because a change in the implied often changes the options position with respect to the underlying.

Table 16.6 is our now familiar set of December Corn options. The underlying is again at 220 and there are 90 days until expiration. The implied volatility, however, is increased to 30 per cent. This table should be compared to Table 16.1 on page 194, where the implied is 20 per cent.

December Corn at 220, implied volatility at 30 per cent

Strike	Call value	Call delta	Call Theta ($)	Put value	Put delta	Put Theta ($)	Gamma	Vega ($)	Vega (ticks)
190	32 1/8	.84	1.78	2 5/8	.14	2.02	.007	12.26	1/4
200	24 5/8	.75	2.57	4 7/8	.23	2.73	.009	16.64	3/8
210	18 1/8	.64	3.17	8 1/4	.34	3.25	.011	19.92	3/8
220	12 7/8	.52	3.46	12 7/8	.46	3.46	.012	21.41	3/8
230	8 7/8	.41	3.42	18 5/8	.58	3.34	.012	20.94	3/8
240	5 7/8	.30	3.10	25 1/2	.69	2.94	.011	18.86	3/8
250	3 3/4	.21	2.60	33 1/4	.77	2.36	.009	15.79	3/8

Table 16.6 ■ December Corn options with 90 DTE

(All data courtesy of FutureSource – Bridge.)

With an increase in implied volatility, we can make the following observations.

The deltas of out-of the-money options increase while the deltas of in-the-money options decrease. The reason is that with an increase in implied volatility, out-of-the-money options have a greater probability of becoming in-the-money, while in-the-money options have less of a probability of staying in-the-money. Similar changes occur when options have more days until expiration.

Gammas decrease. Note that with increased volatility, the difference between the deltas from strike to strike is decreased. This indicates that the underlying passes through strikes more readily, and as a consequence, the deltas of these strikes change less radically. Their corresponding gammas are therefore lowered. This occurrence is also similar in options with more days until expiration.

There are exceptions to the above. Far out-of- and in-the-money options, like the 190s and 250s above, increase their gamma before decreasing. They have low gammas to begin with because their deltas change very little when the underlying is at a low volatility. If vol suddenly increases, they wake up. This characteristic becomes more pronounced with approximately 30 days until expiration.

Thetas increase. Because options premiums increase while the time until expiration continues to decrease, there is increased time decay per day. Theta is therefore greater.

The vegas of the out-of-the-money and the in-the-money options increase. As the underlying increases its range, these options are more likely to become at-the-money. Their vegas approach that of the at-the-money options, and they become more sensitive to a change in the implied volatility.

The principle here is that an increased implied signifies that the underlying is increasing its range. This makes the distinctions between strikes less, and therefore the Greeks become more alike.

Table 16.7 is a generalized summary of the effect of increased implied volatility on the Greeks.

	Delta	Gamma	Theta	Vega
Implied volatility up: OTM call	up	down	up	up
OTM put	up	down	up	up
ATM call	unch'd	down	up	unch'd
ATM put	unch'd	down	up	unch'd
ITM call	down	down	up	up
ITM put	down	down	up	up

Table 16.7 ■ Effect of increased implied volatility on the Greeks

Like all generalizations, the above are subject to modifications. Note the set of options shown in Table 16.8 with 30 DTE at 30 per cent implied. You may compare this data to that shown in Table 16.2 which has the December Corn implied at 20 per cent.

30 DTE, Implied at 30 per cent
December Corn at 220

Strike	Call value	Call delta	Call Theta ($)	Put value	Put delta	Put Theta ($)	Gamma	Vega ($)	Vega (ticks)
190	$30\frac{1}{8}$	.96	1.11	$\frac{3}{8}$	.04	1.36	.005	2.72	0
200	$21\frac{1}{8}$	.87	3.05	$1\frac{1}{4}$	.12	3.22	.011	6.45	$\frac{1}{8}$
210	$13\frac{3}{8}$	.72	5.17	$3\frac{3}{8}$	.28	5.25	.018	10.56	$\frac{1}{4}$
220	$7\frac{1}{2}$	.52	6.19	$7\frac{1}{2}$	.48	6.19	.021	12.51	$\frac{1}{4}$
230	$3\frac{3}{4}$	.32	5.56	$13\frac{5}{8}$	.68	5.48	.019	11.19	$\frac{1}{4}$
240	$1\frac{5}{8}$	.17	3.90	$21\frac{1}{2}$	.83	3.74	.013	7.83	$\frac{1}{8}$
250	$\frac{5}{8}$	.07	2.20	$30\frac{1}{2}$	.92	1.96	.007	4.42	$\frac{1}{8}$

Table 16.8 ■ December Corn options

(Data courtesy of FutureSource – Bridge.)

The exceptions to the generalized summary are that now the gammas at the 190, 200, 240, and 250 strikes are increased. This is a function of the wake-up effect discussed above. With vol at 20 per cent and 30 DTE these strikes were theoretically out of play, but now with vol at 30 per cent they are showing signs of life. Suppose it's mid-October and the new crop is plentiful and on its way, what could possibly go wrong?

A few practical observations on how implied volatility changes

Most of the time an increase in the implied volatility is the result of an increase in the historical volatility

Most of the time an increase in the implied volatility is the result of an increase in the historical volatility, but often it is not. Shortly before the publication of government economic reports, crop forecasts, earnings announcements, and the results of central bank meetings, the prices of options often rise in anticipation of market movement. The resulting changes to the Greeks change the exposure of a position, and therefore change the risk/return profile.

Occasionally, the implied increases because the options market suspects that there is trouble brewing, and this situation of expectancy can last for months, even though there is no significant change in the underlying's daily price action.

Occasionally, an underlying may increase its volatility over the course of one or two days after a published earnings report or other event, but the implied will exhibit little change. This is because the options market views the event as falling within the range of expectations, and having no significance beyond a few trading sessions.

More troublesome, and at the same time potentially rewarding, is a change of implied volatilty due to an unexpected event. For example, a trader may be comfortably short out-of-the-money calls in stocks or a stock index when a central bank suddenly lowers its overnight lending rate. His position is similar to that in Table 16.5.

If the stock market rallies, as it usually does with an unexpected rate cut, this position becomes shorter in deltas not only because it is trending toward the money but because the deltas are being given an added push by the increase in the implied. In addition, this trader's formerly manageable, negative vega position suddenly grows with the implied. The price of, and loss on, his short calls is therefore increasing by three factors:

■ the increasing deltas,

■ the increasing implied volatility,

■ the increasing vegas. The options are growing teeth.

Meanwhile, the trader who has patiently held the opposite position, paying time decay for his long calls, is rewarded manifoldly.

An out-of-the-money put position behaves in a similar manner if the market takes a sudden hit on the downside. Suppose the central bank suddenly raises its rate. If the market breaks downward, and if, as usual, the implied increases, what is the effect on the out-of-the-money puts?

The other Greeks

There are additional Greeks which some trading firms use to monitor their positions. They are all based on the four that we have discussed, and are more useful in assessing the risk of large hedge funds or institutional portfolios. One of these is **Rho** which is the change of an option's value with respect to a change in the interest rate. With the low levels of interest rates in 1999 this is not a significant factor. It will become significant if in the future interest rates reach 10 per cent or more.

The Greeks, implied volatility, and the options calculator

You can calculate the Greeks of most options by using an options calculator. With this device you input the strike price, price of the underlying, time until expiration, volatility, interest rate, and dividends if applicable, and it uses the pricing model to calculate the theoretical value of the option with the Greeks.

The options calculator is an invaluable device, especially for beginners. It is advisable to spend at least a few hours with it.

> The options calculator is an invaluable device, especially for beginners.

With the options calculator you can also determine the implied volatility of an option from the option's price. Suppose you're reading the daily options price reports in your newspaper. The closing prices of the options and the underlyings are often listed. The near-term eurodollar or short sterling interest rate can be used. In the US, the amount and date of the dividends are consistant and widely reported, but in the UK this requires more of an estimate. The days until expiration are also often listed, and when not, you can check them on the exchange website. For stocks you can generally use the third Friday of the expiration month. The strike price you know.

If you plug these variables into the options calculator, it produces the implied volatility of the option.

Many options websites and some exchange websites have options calculators. Data vendors include the Greeks with their price reports, and most brokerage firms subscribe to one or more data services. Many brokerage and trading firms also have options calculators on their websites. It's a lot easier than it used to be.

Questions on the Greeks and implied volatility

1   Procter and Gamble is trading at 89. For the January 95 calls with 90
    days until expiration, note whether time passing causes the following
    Greeks to increase, decrease, or remain unchanged.

    a) delta

    b) gamma

    c) vega

    d) theta

2   Answer the above questions for the January 90 calls.

    a) delta

    b) gamma

    c) vega

    d) theta

3   **a)**   If the manager of your pension fund wants to hedge a portfolio of
             stocks and Treasury Bills against a possible interest rate increase
             during the next two weeks, which options position or positions
             might he employ?

    b) In terms of the Greeks, compare the advantages and disadvantages
           that he might consider by employing out-of-, or at-the-money options.

    i)   delta
    ii)   gamma
    iii)   vega
    iv)   theta

    c) Suppose he considers an at-the-money option. In terms of the
           Greeks, compare the advantages of employing a 30-day option to a
           60-day option.

    i)   delta
    ii)   gamma
    iii)   vega
    iv)   theta

    d) Now suppose he considers an out-of-the-money option. In terms of
           the Greeks, compare the advantages of employing a 30-day option
           to a 60-day option, each at the same strike.

    i)   delta
    ii)   gamma

    iii) vega

    iv) theta

e) Using a daily financial journal, and employing either OEX, SPX (CBOE) or FTSE options, make a choice from among the four possibilities above. Note also the options that you have not chosen. Follow all four for the next two weeks. (Options on all the above contracts expire on the third Friday of the month.)

4 Gillette is currently trading at $51\frac{9}{16}$. This year's trading range for Gillette is $62\frac{5}{8}$ to $38\frac{15}{16}$. With no new products coming to market in the near future and a recession possible in the near term, you expect the price of Gillette to be stable to slightly lower for the next few months. You own stock in Gillette as a sound long-term investment. For the time being, however, you would like to earn additional income by writing a call on your shares.

You are looking through your newspaper on Sunday morning and you note two calls for possible writing. Because you know options theory you can estimate the Greeks for these options before getting out of your easy chair to use your options calculator.

The September $52\frac{1}{2}$ calls, with approximately 45 days until expiration, are trading at $2\frac{3}{16}$, and the December $57\frac{1}{2}$ calls, with approximately 135 days till expiration, are trading at $2\frac{1}{16}$. First compare the break-even levels of the two calls. Then in terms of the Greeks, compare the advantages and disadvantages of writing one of either of the calls per each 100 shares you own.

a) Break-even September
    Break-even December

b) delta

c) gamma

d) vega

e) theta

5 The December FTSE futures contract is currently at 5530 and you are long one the December 5575 call which is currently trading at 190. A rumour circulates that a certain tabloid baron has dropped his opposition to European monetary union because he has formed a partnership with an Italian media mogul, and the December futures contract rallies to 5620. You know that your call position has made a profit, and while awaiting a price quote (and a possible change in the tabloid's editorial policy), you decide to evaluate the effect of the market move on your call's Greeks. How will they be affected by the change in the December futures contract?

a) delta

b) gamma

c) vega

d) theta

6 Intel is currently trading at 94 ½. The January options have 60 days until expiration and the December options have 30 days until expiration. Is each of the following statements true or false.

a) If the implied volatility increases, then the delta and theta of the January 85 put will also increase.

b) If the implied increases, then the gamma of the January 100 call will increase, and the vega will decrease.

c) If the implied decreases, then the vega of the December 95 call will decrease.

d) If the implied decreases, then the gamma and delta of the January 85 call will increase.

7 Under what circumstances can an increase in the implied cause an increase in an out-of-the-money option's gamma?

8 Suppose the S&P 500 index is at 1030, and you are long a number of 975 puts. The chairman of the US Federal Reserve bank, who is liked by the financial markets, announces that he is to retire when his term expires. What may happen to the implied volatility of your put options?

Answers

1 a) decrease

b) increase

c) decrease

d) increase

2 a) practically unchanged

b) increase

c) decrease

d) increase

3 **a)** Purchase puts on a stock index and/or eurodollars.

   b) i)   ATM puts provide more coverage per option.

   ii)   ATM puts respond more to market movement.

   iii)   ATM puts are more sensitive to an increase or decrease in the implied.

   iv)   OTM puts cost less in time decay.

   c) i)   no difference.

   ii)   near-term has greater gamma, it responds more to market movement.

   iii)   not-so-near is more sensitive to change in the implied.

   iv)   near-term costs more in daily time decay.

   d) i)   60-day has larger delta, therefore more coverage per option.

   ii)   30-day has greater gamma.

   iii)   60-day is more sensitive to change in the implied.

   iv)   30-day costs more in daily time decay.

4 **a)** $52\frac{1}{2} + 2\frac{3}{16} = 54\frac{11}{16}$
   $57\frac{1}{2} + 2\frac{1}{16} = 59\frac{9}{16}$

   b) September call has larger delta, which makes assignment more probable.

   c) December call has lower gamma, therefore the delta will change less from day to day, and position will be easier to monitor and manage.

   d) December call has higher vega, and if volatility declines because the stock remains in a stable range, then December will profit more than September.

   e) September call has significantly greater time decay.

   It is advisable not to think of this strategy in terms of annualized rate of return, or you may be tempted to employ it habitually, and then eventually you will have your investment called away. You could, however, consider employing this strategy when the implied volatility of the options contracts are decreasing.

5 **a)** increased.

   b) practically unchanged because the call is now as equally far in-the-money as it was formerly out-of-the money.

   c) unchanged, for the above reason.

   d) unchanged, for the above reason.

6   **a)** True

    b) False, the gamma will decrease but the vega will increase.

    c) False, it will remain practically unchanged.

    d) True

7   If the implied is increasing from a very low level then the gammas of the far out-of-the-money options will increase.

8   If his retirement is unexpected, then the implied may increase; if his retirement is expected, then the implied will most likely remain unchanged.

Options performance based on cost

So far, we have discussed a number of different ways of analyzing straight options and options spreads. We can take this a step further by examining which options are preferable choices given a specific amount to invest. In this chapter we look at a group of straight options and compare their risk-return potentials to their price. We can do this with the help of the Greeks.

Delta price ratio

The cost of trading price movement

Another way to think of delta is that it indicates the potential for price change in the option. If you compare the delta to the price of the option itself, you can determine the option's potential price change given the amount that you wish to invest. Table 17.1 shows our familiar set of Corn options at 90 DTE with their deltas. Let's assume that we have an upside directional outlook; only the calls are listed.

In the last column the delta of each option is divided by its price. The ratio is then expressed as a percentage. My term for this figure is the delta price ratio.[14] If December Corn moves plus or minus one point, then the 190 call increases or decreases by plus or minus .92 of a point. .92 is 3.05 per cent of $30\frac{1}{8}$, the amount invested.

By comparing the delta/price ratios we find that the out-of-the-money options have the greatest potential for price movement per amount invested. Note that this potential is for increased as well as decreased price movement. Here, both risk and return increase. But because the

---

[14] The term 'delta price ratio' is not in standard use. It is applied here because it is logical and convenient.

December Corn at 220, 90 DTE, implied volatility at 20 per cent			
Strike	Call value	Call delta	D/P (%)
190	$30\frac{1}{8}$	.92	3.05
200	$21\frac{1}{2}$	.83	3.86
210	$14\frac{1}{4}$	.69	4.84
220	$8\frac{5}{8}$	.51	5.91
230	$4\frac{3}{4}$	.34	7.16
240	$2\frac{3}{8}$	.20	8.42
250	$1\frac{1}{8}$	.11	9.78

Table 17.1 ■ December Corn options, with delta price ratio

amount invested is less than with in- or at-the-money options, investors often find this risk worth taking.

The trade-off is with time decay. The delta/price ratio increases as options move closer to expiration, but eventually an out-of-the-money option has very little probability of profiting from underlying price movement. The option's delta and the number of days until expiration are the best guides to this trade-off. A short-term, .30 delta option of less than 30 days, for example, has a greater delta/price ratio than a .30 delta option of more than 100 days, but the former is in a rapid decay time period.

Theta price ratio

The cost of trading time

We have previously discussed the time decay variable, or theta. We said that an option's time decay accelerates as expiration approaches. Before you decide which option to buy or sell, it is important to know the time decay of the option as a percentage of the option's value. You can then better choose the strike to trade. Table 17.2 shows our set of Corn options, each followed by its theta price ratio expressed in percentage terms.[15] Remember that here the call must be multiplied by $50 in order to give its price in dollars, while the theta is already expressed in dollars.

Here, the price of the 250 call is $1\frac{1}{8}$ × $50 = $56.25. The present daily decay of this option is $1.10, making the theta price ratio 1.10/56.25 = 1.96%. In percentage terms the 250 call is the most expensive to hold, while in absolute terms it is the least expensive.

---

[15] Again, the term 'theta price ratio' is applied because it is logical and convenient.

December Corn at 220, 90 DTE, implied volatility at 20 per cent				
Strike	**Call value (ticks)**	**Call delta**	**D/P (%)**	**Call Theta ($)**	**T/P (%)**
190	30 $\frac{1}{8}$	.92	3.05	.50	.03
200	21 $\frac{1}{2}$	.83	3.86	1.26	.12
210	14 $\frac{1}{4}$	.69	4.84	1.97	.28
220	8 $\frac{5}{8}$	.51	5.91	2.31	.54
230	4 $\frac{3}{4}$	.34	7.16	2.17	.91
240	2 $\frac{3}{8}$	.20	8.42	1.68	1.41
250	1 $\frac{1}{8}$	.11	9.78	1.10	1.96

Table 17.2 ■ December Corn options with theta/price ratios

Vega price ratio

The cost of trading volatility

In Chapter 8 we discussed implied volatility and its relation to vega, and we noted that an option's vega increases with more days until expiration. Table 17.3, using the contract multipler, compares the vega of an option to its price in order to determine how an investment may perform in per-centage terms due to a one per cent change in the implied. The vega/price ratio, as a percentage, is listed in the last column.[16]

December Corn at 220, 90 DTE, implied volatility at 20 per cent							
Strike	**Call value (ticks)**	**Call delta**	**D/P (%)**	**Call theta ($)**	**T/P (%)**	**Call vega ($)**	**V/P (%)**
190	30 $\frac{1}{8}$	.92	3.05	.50	.03	6.70	.44
200	21 $\frac{1}{2}$	.83	3.86	1.26	.12	12.90	1.20
210	14 $\frac{1}{4}$	.69	4.84	1.97	.28	18.77	2.63
220	8 $\frac{5}{8}$	.51	5.91	2.31	.54	21.44	4.97
230	4 $\frac{3}{4}$	.34	7.16	2.17	.91	19.84	8.35
240	2 $\frac{3}{8}$	.20	8.42	1.68	1.41	15.26	12.85
250	1 $\frac{1}{8}$	.11	9.78	1.10	1.96	9.98	17.74

Table 17.3 ■ December Corn options with vega/price ratios

---

[16] The term 'vega price ratio' is again a convenient and logical application.

Again, the largest percent trade-off is with the 250 calls. They may increase or decrease 17.74 per cent of their value with a one per cent change in the implied.

For the purpose of comparison, the same table of figures is given in Table 17.4, but with 30 DTE.

	30 DTE, implied at 20 per cent December Corn at 220						
Strike	Call value (ticks)	Call delta	D/P (%)	Call theta	T/P (%) ($)	Call vega ($)	V/P (%)
190	29 7/8	.99	3.31	0	–	0	–
200	20 1/8	.95	4.72	.83	.08	3.00	.30
210	11 3/8	.80	7.03	2.84	.50	8.80	1.55
220	5	.51	10.2	4.13	1.65	12.51	5.00
230	1 5/8	.23	14.15	3.14	3.86	9.47	11.66
240	3/8	.07	18.67	1.37	7.31	4.13	22.00
250	0	0	–	0	–	0	–

Table 17.4 ■ December Corn options

As we might expect with time passing, most of the delta price ratios, theta price ratios, and vega price ratios have increased for all the options that contain time premium. Note that the vega/price ratio for the ATM call remains at approximately five per cent. The risk-return trade-off with all the other options is clear.

Conclusions

In this chapter we have examined risk and return in terms of delta/price theta/price, and vega/price ratios. We have found that both the risk and return per amount invested increase as the option becomes farther out-of-the-money and as the option approaches expiration. These ratios vary with options on each underlying contract, and you will need to examine them for the contracts that you wish to trade.

There are two approaches to consider:

■ The first is obviously to limit your risk by limiting the number of contracts you wish to trade. There is a greater amount at risk by buying one December 220 call with 90 DTE at $431.25 than there is by buying one

250 call at $56.25, but the latter has greater per cent risk. Perhaps you are a natural risk taker, often taking long odds. Then the 250 call has the advantage of greater potential return, and $56.25 is the smaller loss to take if your investment fails to succeed.

■ The second approach is to limit the amount you wish to invest. For example, if you have $500 to invest, you may pay $431.25 for one of the above 220 calls, or you may pay $450 for eight of the above 250 calls. In this case both the amount and the percentage risk are greater with the 250 call position.

> In all cases, be clear about your market assessment and your goals.

Given a fixed amount to invest, we can draw the following conclusions:

■ If the market is accelerating to the upside, then your best choice is the D/P ratio of the 250s.

■ If the market is trending up, but volatility is stable or perhaps declining, then you'll prefer the lower V/P ratio of the 220s.

■ If volatility is increasing but it's getting close to expiration, you may prefer the T/P ratio of the 230's or 240's.

■ You might also use the above tables to evaluate risk-return for selling options.

■ In all cases, **be clear about your market assessment and your goals**.

Options talk 1

Introduction

Chapters 18 and 19 are more informal than those previous; their purpose is to provide general insight. As stated in the introduction to this book, it may be impossible to coach you via long distance given the varied conditions that occur in the markets, but the more knowledge you have, the more resources you'll have in order to take advantage of opportunities as they arise. What follows is not gospel, but it is based on a good deal of experience.

Trading delta and time decay

By knowing that delta indicates the probability of an option expiring in-the-money, you can assess the effect of time decay on probability. This can help you decide whether to open or close a position, and which strike prices to consider trading in the first place.

Buying an option

For example, if your outlook is for a large, directional move, you might consider buying a .30 delta option, call or put, with 90 to 120 days until expiration. You know that if time passes and the underlying remains stable, the delta decreases. This implies that the large move you are looking for becomes less probable as well. Remember that an option's time decay accelerates as it approaches expiration. You may consider, at some point between 60 and 30 days until expiration, rolling your position into a contract month with more time until expiration, even though it may cost more. A longer-term option gives you more time to be right.

A .30 delta option with 30 days until expiration will cost less than a .30 delta option with 90 days until expiration, but if your outlook is not soon realized, it will soon become a .10 delta option, and it will have cost you in time decay.

A near-term, .10 delta option is affordable, and if the market suddenly moves in its direction, it will profit handsomely, but it should be bought or held by those who feel comfortable making a short-term trade against ten to one odds. A more prudent use of this option is to hedge another position.

Don't make the mistake of buying an option just because it is cheap. A low-priced, far out-of-the-money option also has a low probability of expiring in the money. It also has higher delta, theta and vega price ratios. If you want to reduce the cost of your call or put, you can do this by spreading.

Suppose you have bought a .30 delta option, and as a result of market movement, it now has a .60 delta, and you have a profit. This often happens sooner than you expect. Did your original outlook call for this option have a .80 delta? Don't kid yourself; if the market move has met your expectations, then the option has done its work. Rather than risk exposure to theta, you should close the position.

Selling an option

Options sellers should have declining volatility on their side, which means that the probability of smaller inter- and intraday price movement is increasing.

It is also advisable for options sellers to take advantage of time decay whenever possible by taking a short position close to expiration. How close depends on the delta of the option and the risk that is justifiable. As illustrated in Part One, the farther the strike is from the underlying, the more days until expiration its daily time decay accelerates.

If the underlying makes a sudden, unforeseen move that results in a loss, you must have sufficient capital to maintain your short strategy in order to take advantage of a return to stable market conditions. In any case, it is prudent to roll your short position to a farther contract when your current contract has 30 DTE or less. A probability assessment least accounts for short-term price fluctuations, and an unexpected move when the underlying is close to expiration can severely damage your profit.

Should you wish to take advantage of decreasing probability, you may wish to sell a .20 delta option that is near-term, approximately 60 DTE.

This option has less theta than a .30 or .50 delta option, but its delta indicates that it has a greater probability (80 per cent) of remaining out-of-the money, and therefore has less potential risk.

If this option's delta eventually becomes .05, either through underlying price movement or through time decay, then you have a profit. You may now be tempted to hold this position in order to continue to collect a small amount of theta, but instead you should ask yourself if your previous outlook for the underlying has been realized. If so, it is better to close your position than to risk exposure to an increased delta, i.e., an underlying move in the direction of your short call or put.

But suppose our short .20 delta option becomes a .50 delta option through an adverse market move. Clearly our outlook did not lead to success, and we have incurred a loss. We may hope for a market retracement, and we may fear a continued adverse market move, but instead we should use all available means to formulate a new outlook. We may even use our old outlook as a starting point; it may have been flawed in some respects, but it may have been accurate in others.

If our new outlook calls for a stable market in the near term, then our .50 delta option presents an opportunity to recoup some and possibly all of our loss through greater theta, and we should retain our position. Again, let's not kid ourselves; if we are uncertain, or too unsettled to formulate a new outlook, then we should close our position.

The major risk of a naked short call position is a sudden, unforeseen increase in the price of the underlying. Likewise the major risk of a naked short put position is a sudden, unforeseen decrease in the price of the underlying. Both of these risks can and should be limited by spreading.

Trading volatility trends

When trading vega, and therefore volatility, it is important to take advantage of, and not to fight, the volatility trend. Volatility can increase and decrease for long periods of time, just as stock, bond and commodity markets have their bull and bear trends.

It may seem obvious, but it is always preferable to buy options when volatility is increasing and to sell options when it is decreasing. Many options traders ignore the trend, perhaps because they are accustomed to, or simply better at, buying or selling premium. This makes for frustrating and difficult trading.

To be fair, it is often difficult to trade volatility because, like any other market trend, it can be erratic. When this is the case, you are fully justified to *stay out of the market*.

Remember that the vega itself of an out-of-the-money option increases or decreases as the implied volatility changes, whereas the vega of an at-the-money option remains unchanged. There needs to be a gamma of the vega calculation in the options business. Perhaps it might be interesting to research this topic.

Durational outlook

A proper outlook tells you not only when to open a position, but also when to close a position, either by taking a profit or by cutting a loss with a stop order. There are many excellent books that describe how to trade the various types of markets; this guide teaches you how to be more flexible in your approach.

When trading options you should always have a duration for your outlook because options work for a limited time. In all cases keep your duration in mind, and when it has ended, either close your position or formulate a revised outlook. A revised outlook can be formulated by asking yourself the

> A proper outlook tells you not only when to open a position, but also when to close a position, either by taking a profit or by cutting a loss with a stop order.

following question: *If I wanted to enter the market now, is this the position I would take?* If the answer is no, then close your position. Otherwise, you are paying to hope.

19 Options talk 2: trouble shooting and common problems

Investing with leverage

Options are leveraged investments

Options are leveraged investments: the risk/return potential is far greater per amount invested than with standard investment strategies. It is therefore advisable to apportion less capital than with standard investments, unless you are very confident of your outlook.

One of the most prudent options strategies for trading a straight call or put position is to determine the amount of stock or shares that you are comfortably able to afford, then buy the number call options that leverage the same number of shares and no more. The rest of your capital is then placed in a cash deposit.

For example, suppose you are bullish on Intel, and you are considering paying $95 for 500 shares. You could instead pay 10 for 5, April 95 calls with 180 DTE, and place the remainder in a 6-month cash deposit. Your expenditure and cash deposit break down accordingly.

Amount to invest: $95 × 500 = $47,500
Cost of options: $10 × 100 × 5 = $5,000
Amount deposited in CD: $85 × 500 = $42,500

Of course, investors frequently leverage to a greater degree. The point to keep in mind is that a call can potentially expire worthless, and if it does, then you have still risked no more capital than you can afford.

The above guide to leverage is essential for those who sell calls naked. If you are the seller of the above 5, Intel 95 calls, you incur the potential obligation to buy 500 shares in order to transfer them to the long call holder. You should have at least the amount of the break-even

level times the number of shares leveraged on deposit in order to meet
the obligation of your short calls.

Short call break-even level: $10 + $95 = $105
Multiplied by number of shares: $105 × 500 = $52,500 on deposit

A short call spread faces the same potential capital requirement, although
the risk is limited.

Covered call writing assumes that the short call holder has already purchased shares to deliver, and so the capital requirement is already on deposit.

The seller of a naked put incurs the potential obligation to buy stock at
the break-even level. Therefore, this level of capital should be on deposit.
For example, if you are bullish in Intel you might, if compelled by the
devil to sell premium, sell 5, Intel April 95 puts at 10. You may also wish
to buy Intel on a price decline, but in either case, your prudent capital
requirement would be as follows.

Short put break-even level: $95 − $10 = $85
Multiplied by number of shares: $85 × 500 = $42,500

The put buyer is in an advantageous position in terms of capital requirement. He has the potential right to sell the stock at a higher level than the
market price at expiration.
Note that clearing firms often require less capital on deposit than we have
mentioned. The above are merely prudent suggestions. They will also
lead to more disciplined trading.

Contract liquidity and market making

Generally speaking, the more liquid an options contract, the tighter is
the bid/ask spread for an option's price. The greater the bid/ask spread,
the greater is the cost of opening and closing a position. This spread is
often simply called 'the market' for the option. Eurodollar options, for
example, have markets that are half to one tick wide, or $12.50 to $25.00.
The markets for options on thinly traded stocks can be three or more
ticks wide, or $300+.

The width of a bid/ask spread is a product of the opportunities for
spreading risk, either with the underlying or with other options. If the
underlying or the other options contracts are not liquid, then the options
market makers cannot hedge the positions that retail customers want
them to assume. They may be forced to carry the positions in their inven-

tory for periods of weeks or months, and during this time they are exposed to risk. In order to cover their risk, the market makers need to widen their bid/ask spreads. Under these circumstances, to ask the market makers to tighten their spreads is to ask them to put their jobs in jeopardy. No sensible trader, including yourself, will do this.

Bid/ask spreads also widen during highly volatile markets. If the underlying is leaping wildly, then the options market makers cannot hedge. In order to cover their risk, they need to widen their markets to correspond to the wide range of the underlying's prices. You would do the same.

Common problems with straight call or put positions

This section offers observations on what may happen to a straight call or put position. The circumstances here presented are not those that necessarily will happen. These observations are given in case similar circumstances occur to you. The purpose is simply for you to have a basis for understanding the behaviour of your options position if one of these situations arises.

Stocks up, calls practically unchanged or underperforming

Occasionally when a stock or stock index rallies, purchased out-of-the-money calls underperform. This can occur when the implied volatility has been extremely high, after a sell-off, and long call positions have been seen either as defensive alternatives to buying the stock or as synthetic puts. This is discussed in Part Four. As the market rallies, the downside protection that the calls afford is needed less, and the market probably thinks that the potential upside is limited. As a result the implied volatility of the calls declines, and premium levels fall. The options still gain in value because they are trending towards the money, but profits are not optimum.

Under these circumstances, an alternative strategy would be the long call spread. With this strategy the long call position's exposure to declining volatility is offset by that of the short, farther out-of-the-money call. Refer to Chapter 9 on this spread.

Stocks down, calls practically unchanged or down slightly (the opposite of the above)

Sometimes when an underlying breaks, short out-of-the-money calls in stocks or stock indexes stubbornly cling to their value. This can be due to a general rise in the implied volatility as traders seek downside protection from both calls and puts. The calls are losing value because the stock is moving away from them, but they are gaining value as the increasing implied volatility increases their premium. There is increased demand for them because they are alternatives to a stock purchase and because they can be converted into synthetic puts. This also discussed in Part Four.

When this occurs, it is advisable simply to hold the position until the market stabilizes. This requires strong nerves, but keep in mind that the stock's price direction and time decay are on your side. If the stock rebounds, the implied volatility often decreases, and if so, the calls' premiums will also decrease. The potential problem is that the stock may suddenly rebound to a higher level than where you sold the calls. Be ready with a buy-stop order. The more prudent strategy is the short call spread.

Stocks down, puts practically unchanged or underperforming

Occasionally a stock or stock index sells off and long, out-of-the-money puts underperform. This is often due to the fact that the stock has retraced to the lower end of its trading range, and the market thinks that it will remain supported at its present level. The implied remains stable, or decreases somewhat, because the stock decline has met expectations. This problem may also be due to a decrease in the implied volatility of the put because of a shift in the volatility skew, and for this, you should consult Chapter 10 on volatility skews.

An alternative strategy is the call sale, above, if properly managed. The long put spread is a better alternative because any decline in the implied, via the skew or otherwise, affects both the long and short put strikes. You are then taking advantage of downside price movement with little exposure to a change in the implied. Refer to Chapter 9 on the long put spread.

Personally, I have a different approach to buying a straight put. I use technical analysis to note the support level of the stock or index. If I think that the stock is more likely to break support than the market is indicating, I buy puts below the level of support. Not only are these puts cheaper, but more importantly, if the stock does break support, the implied often increases because the market is then uncertain of the extent of the downside potential. If I am uncertain that the stock will break support, which I am most often, I use the long put spread.

Stocks up, puts down slightly or unchanged

Often when the stock market rallies, puts lose very little of their premium. This occurs when the market fears a retracement. A rally in the stocks may be seen as a put buying opportunity, and demand remains strong. This can be nerve-racking for put sellers, and they feel like sitting ducks. Often the market retraces and stabilizes, and time decay begins to eat away at the puts, but by then the put sellers are only too glad to close their positions at a break-even level.

Another reason for this occurrence is that with a rally, the put skew often shifts horizontally with the underlying, causing the implieds of the puts to increase. Refer to Chapter 20 on volatility skews.

A sensible alternative to being short puts is the short put spread. This spread limits downside risk while still preserving the opportunity for income through time decay. The exposure to changes in the implied, via the skew or otherwise, is also limited. As we said before, you shouldn't sell naked puts unless you want to buy the stock or other underlying.

Straight calls and puts with commodities

Although it is difficult to generalize, with commodities you can often substitute call strategies for the above anomalies with put strategies, and put strategies for the above anomalies with call strategies. In commodities, calls are often king because of potential supply shortages. They often have positive call skews instead of positive put skews. This is true for stocks with large commodity exposure as well. Generally speaking, with commodities the strategy with the most risk is the short call.

Misconceptions to clear up about straight call and put positions

Remember, there are two advantages to a call purchase. They must both be seen as alternatives to buying a stock or other underlying.

■ The first is to take advantage of market gains.

■ The second is to limit exposure to capital risk.

It is inaccurate and misleading to think of a call as simply 'a chance to win', when it is equally a chance not to lose. Furthermore, if you think of an option as a 'chance', you will most likely become prey to those traders who strive to mimimize chance from their dealings.

Another advantage of a call purchase is that as the underlying advances, the call becomes a greater percentage of the underlying until eventually it trades at parity with the underlying. The alternative advantage is that as the underlying declines, the purchased call becomes less a percentage of the underlying until it eventually loses its correlation with the underlying.

Likewise, for stock holders, long puts offer the dual benefit of downside protection while preserving potential upside gains. Puts are not simply a downside chance. As the stock or underlying declines, the long put position becomes a greater percentage of a sale at the strike price until it eventually trades at parity, or the full amount of the underlying's decline. But as the underlying increases in price, the long put gradually loses its correlation with the stock or underlying, and the upside profit is maintained.

It is no coincidence that at-the-money calls and puts are priced the same. They both offer the same amount of upside and downside volatility coverage. This amount, or price, is the expected range of the underlying through expiration.

> **It is no coincidence that at-the-money calls and puts are priced the same.**

In other words, if XYZ is trading at 100, both the 100 call and the 100 put have the same price, perhaps four, because the market expects XYZ to close between 96 and 104 at expiration. If you buy the call instead of buying XYZ, you have 96 points of potential savings, and unlimited profit potental above 104. If you buy the put instead of selling XYZ that you own, you have 96 points of potential savings, and unlimited profit potential above 104.

The above relationship between calls and puts is the basis of synthetic options positions, or put-call parity. This will be discussed in Part Four.

Volatility skews

Introduction

Note: If your sole interest is in trading options on individual stocks, you may postpone reading this chapter.

We have previously discussed the relationship between implied volatility and historical volatility. We mentioned that the implied can have a life of its own based on expectations for future changes in the historical. This condition often creates variations in implied volatility from strike to strike. These variations often fall into patterns which can be plotted on a graph, and for which equations can be found to match. Such patterns in implied volatility are known as **volatility skews**.

In this chapter we will see how skews affect the profit/loss of straight options positions. We will also see that unless you are a skew wizard, your best way to reduce skew risk is to spread.

Observing skews: Bonds

Figure 20.1 shows a graph of the volatility skew for options on March '99 Treasury Bonds. Below that, Table 20.1 gives the data containing the implied volatilities used to plot the skew.

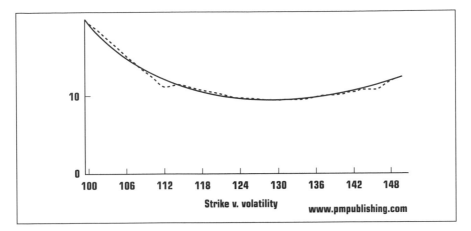

Fig 20.1 ■ Options volatility skew: March '99 Treasury Bonds Underlying futures contract at **128.01**

(Provided courtesy of pmpublishing.com.)

Strike	Call value	Call implied volatility	Put value	Put implied volatility
112			.01	11.21
114			.03	11.47
116			.06	11.21
118			.11	10.84
120			.19	10.38
122			.33	10.01
124			.57	9.76
126	3.31	9.57	1.30	9.55
*128	2.22	9.44	2.20	9.43
130	1.32	9.44	3.29	9.45
132	.59	9.54		
134	.34	9.58		
136	.20	9.84		
138	.11	9.98		
140	.07	10.45		
142	.04	10.70		
144	.02	10.76		
146	.01	10.86		

Table 20.1 ■ March '99 Treasury Bond options, 87 days until expiration, March '99 futures at **128.01**

(Provided courtesy of pmpublishing.com.)

In Figure 20.1, the dotted line is the actual plot of the implieds from strike to strike, while the solid line has been generated with an equation. Some traders use the equation to determine if an option is undervalued or overvalued. The discrepancies as you can see are very small.

The ATM implied volatility is that of the 128 strike, at 9.44 per cent. Note that the implied volatility of the 136 call is 9.84 per cent, while the implied of the 120 put is 10.38 per cent, and that both these strikes are equidistant from the money.

Calls and puts of the strike prices ascending from the at-the-money strike are said to be on the **call skew**, while calls and puts of the strike prices descending from the at-the-money strike are said to be on the **put skew**. Here, both the call and put skews have increased implieds, and so they are said to be **positive**. This type of skew is often found in longer term debt markets such as bonds, gilts and bunds.

(Personally, I refer to this type of skew as a 'parabolic' skew, because of its obvious resemblance to a parabola. This term is not in standard use.)

Observing skews: Stock indexes

Figure 20.2 shows a graph of the volatility skew for December '98 options on the OEX. Table 20.2 gives the data containing the implied volatilities used to plot the skew.

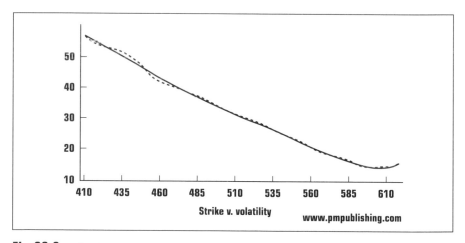

Fig 20.2 ■ Options volatility skew: December '98 OEX, Underlying index at 587.18, December synthetic future at 590.00

(*Provided courtesy of pmpublishing.com.*)

December '98 OEX options
23 days until expiration
Underlying index at 587.18
December synthetic future at 590.00

Strike	Call value	Call implied volatility	Put value	Put implied volatility
420			.13	53.67
430			.19	52.77
440			.25	51.16
450			.25	47.66
460			.19	42.59
480			.31	38.71
490			.44	37.19
500			.50	34.46
515			.81	31.92
545			2.00	25.98
550			2.38	25.06
555			2.75	23.90
570			4.50	20.56
575	21.00	20.75		
580	17.13	19.60	6.75	18.87
585	13.50	18.44	8.38	18.21
*590	10.50	17.82	10.50	17.82
595	7.75	16.98		
600	5.38	16.06		
605	3.63	15.49		
610	2.38	15.12		
615	1.56	15.05		
620	1.00	15.01		
630	.50	15.84		

Table 20.2 ■ OEX December Options

(Provided courtesy of pmpublishing.com.)

Again, the dotted line is the actual plot of the implieds from strike to strike, while the solid line has been generated with an equation. The close match-up may seem arbitrary, but because skews continue to exhibit regular patterns over the years, they are calculable.

The ATM implied volatility is that of the 590 strike, at 17.82 per cent. Note that the implied volatility of the 610 call is 15.12 per cent, while the implied of the 570 put is 20.56 per cent, and that both these strikes are equidistant from the money. Note also that the implied of the 500 strike is 34.46 per cent, or almost double that of the ATM implied.

Here the put skew is positive while the call skew, with decreasing implieds, is negative. This type of skew is found in other stock index options, such as the FTSE.

(Personally, I refer to this type of skew as a 'linear' skew. It is simply more linear than a parabolic skew. Note that the tail of the call skew flattens out.)

Observing skews: Commodities

Volatility skews in commodities have their own special properties.

Volatility skews in commodities have their own special properties. As an example, we can examine the skew for February '99 Crude Oil.

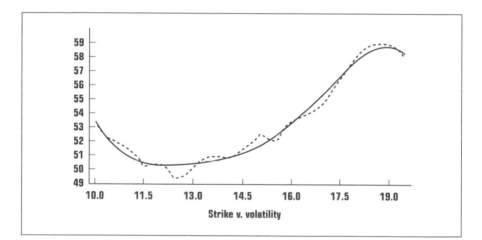

Fig 20.3 ■ Options volatility skew: February '99 Crude Oil, February future at **12.28**

(Provided courtesy of pmpublishing.com.)

February '99 Crude Oil options
51 days until expiration
February future at 12.28

Strike	Call value	Call implied volatility	Put value	Put implied volatility
10.00			.17	53.11
10.50			.26	51.97
11.00			.39	51.39
11.50			.55	50.27
12.00			.77	50.23
*12.50	.80	49.37	1.02	49.44
13.00	.62	49.98	1.34	50.22
13.50	.48	50.78		
14.00	.36	50.90		
14.50	.27	51.25		
15.00	.21	52.35		
15.50	.15	52.03		
16.00	.12	53.46		
16.50	.09	53.91		
17.00	.07	54.77		
17.50	.06	56.63		
18.00	.05	58.02		

Table 20.3 ■ **February '99 Crude Oil options**
(Provided courtesy of pmpublishing.com.)

Again, the dotted line is the actual plot of the implieds from strike to strike, while the solid line has been generated with an equation. Here, the match-up is not as exact as with those previous. Perhaps on this trading day demand was greater for the 15.00 calls than for the 12.50 calls. Those traders who are skew believers might buy this call spread, expecting the implieds eventually to conform to the equation.

The ATM implied volatility is that of the 12.50 strike, at 49.37 per cent. Note that the implied volatility of the 10.00 put is 53.11 per cent, while the implied of the 15.00 call is approximately equal at 52.35 per cent, and that both these strikes are equidistant from the 12.50 strike. Note also that the implied of the 18.00 strike is 58.02 per cent. At this time, crude oil had been in a major downtrend for many years. But like all commodities the price of crude oil can rise rapidly if demand suddenly increases.

Here both the put and call skews are positive, but the call skew is more pronounced. This type of call skew is found in many other commodities, including those on most agricultural products. When the price of a commodity is well supported, either by market demand or by government intervention, the commodity's put skew can be flat or negative.

Volatility skews versus the at-the-money implied volatility

Regardless of the nature of the skews, the implied volatility of any options contract, i.e., the implied that corresponds most closely to the current volatility of the underlying, is always the implied that is at-the-money. One can say that the at-the-money strike, however that may change, is always the focal point of both the call and put skews.

Why there are skews

As yet, there is no consensus as to why there are skews, apart from the obvious reason of supply and demand for the options. We know, however, by studying historical data that large price changes in many underlyings occur with greater frequency than are accounted for by normal distribution. At least once in a generation an asteroid hits the stock market. Skews might seem irrational, but then so do many market events.

Don't make the mistake of thinking that skews exist because brokers like to buy or sell out-of-the-money options, or because a particular house or group of houses always buys or sells certain options. One might as well say that short-term interest rates are at their current levels because the central banks hold them here.[17] Markets don't operate in this way; they are more powerful than the participants.

For whatever reasons, skews continue to appear in most options contracts year after year, and they continue to display similar patterns in each contract. Most of us by now have learned to treat them with respect.

I have personal opinions on the reasons for volatility skews. A skew is a function of variations in implied volatility. Like the implied, it indicates market expectations for the near-term level of the historical volatility. It therefore indicates what the market expects the historical volatility will be if the underlying suddenly shifts to a new level in the direction of the skew. This is a form of discounting, which all markets do.

Further, a parabolic-shaped, positive skew indicates that the implied is likely to remain relatively stable when the underlying remains in the current trading range. The belly of the skew accounts for this. The increasing

---

[17] True, central banks have in the past resisted monetary trends, but only by placing their nations' economies at risk.

slopes of the parabolic skew indicate that the implied is likely to increase exponentially if the underlying suddenly moves toward the wings of the skew and breaks through the current trading range. Again, this is a form of discounting by the market.

Most stock index and long-term interest rate contracts have positive put skews because these markets, more often than not, become more volatile as they break. There is also perennial demand for puts in these markets to protect against loss of asset value.

Many commodities have positive call skews. Commodities become more volatile as prices increase, which they suddenly do when faced with supply shortages. Corn and soybeans have had positive call skews for years. If drought conditions occur, grain dealers find it difficult to honor forward committments. Cash and futures prices, along with the implied volatilities of options, soar.

A flat or negative skew indicates that the volatility of an underlying is expected to be stable, or to decline slightly if the underlying moves in its direction. Bonds spend long periods of time with flat to slightly positive call skews during periods of interest rate stability. Commodities often have negative put skews because slackening demand results in their grinding lower. Negative call skews in stock indexes indicate that as their markets move steadily higher and the value of their indexes increases, an equivalent price change calculates to a lower historical volatility.

Skews on individual stocks are generally minimal to non-existent. This indicates that equal price changes occur with equal frequency in both directions. This can change, however, when unusual circumstances arise.

Skew behaviour towards expiration

Skews can change their degree of positiveness or negativeness. Positive skews most often become more positive as they approach expiration.

Skews can change their degree of positiveness or negativeness.

The underlying contract for this January set of T-Bond options is the same as for the previous March set of T-Bond options; it is the March futures contract. Here, the implied of the ATM call at the 128 strike is lower, at 8.14. The implied of the January 122 put is greater, at 10.42, than the March 122 put at 10.01. The January 134 call has an implied of 9.19, while the March 134 call has an implied of 9.58. While both January skews are increased, the put skew exhibits the more radical change. You may compare the implied vols strike by strike.

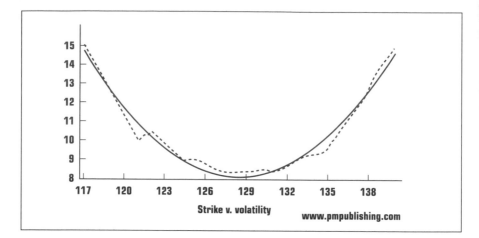

Fig 20.4 ■ **January '99 T-Bond options skew**

January '99 Treasury Bond options
24 days until expiration
March future at 128.01

Strike	Call value	Call implied	Call delta	Put value	Put implied	Put delta
121				.01	10.02	.01
122				.03	10.42	.03
123				.05	9.92	.06
124				.07	9.00	.08
125				.14	8.91	.14
126	2.26	8.59	.77	.25	8.68	.23
127	1.44	8.44	.65	.42	8.42	.35
*128	1.05	8.14	.51	1.04	8.26	.49
129	.43	8.30	.36	1.41	8.32	.63
130	.25	8.40	.24	2.23	8.46	.75
131	.13	8.38	.14			
132	.07	8.62	.09			
133	.04	9.01	.05			
134	.02	9.19	.03			
135	.01	9.41	.01			

Table 20.4 ■ **January '99 Treasury Bond options**

(Graph and data courtesy of pmpublishing.com.)

Skews' shift with underlying

Skews most often shift horizontally with the price of their underlying contracts. If an underlying drifts back and forth in a range, the skew will most often range as well. The focal point clings to the at-the-money strike, with little change to the ATM implied. This effectively changes the implied of each strike.

For example, if the above March T-Bond contract rose to 129.01 then the implieds of all the strikes would be likely to shift to the next strike upward. The January 129 calls would have an implied of 8.14, and the January 123 puts would have an implied of 10.42, etc.

This occurrence presupposes no change in the historical or ATM implied volatility. Here the underlying is most often trading in a range. Sometimes the underlying moves but the focal point of the skew clings to a strike; this occurs when the market expects a retracement.

Skews' change of degree

A skew often becomes more positive if the underlying makes a sudden move, or threatens to make a sudden move, in its direction. A bond market put skew may become more positive if an inflation report is revealed to be worse than expected. Several days in advance, the put skew may behave in the same as if the report is expected to be worse than expected.

Under these circumstances, the skew becomes more like a skew with fewer days until expiration. If and when the market's apprehension subsides, the skew may return to its former level.

A call skew in a stock index may become less negative to flat in anticipation of a Christmas or January rally, or an imminent cut in interest rates. Eventually, the skew will revert to its former position.

Skews' vertical shift

If the ATM implied increases or decreases, then the skew most often shifts vertically upward or downward. This effectively raises or lowers the implied of all strikes because the skew retains its shape. The focal point of the skew remains at the ATM strike.

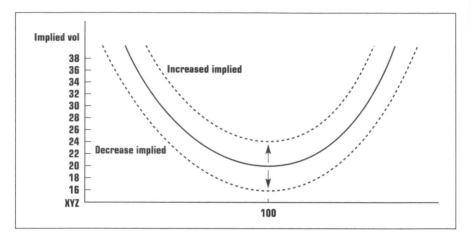

Fig 20.5 ■ **Skew vertical shift**

Caution

Do not assume that skews foretell directional moves or changes in volatility. Sometimes they do, but often they do not. A stock's put skew may be bid because earnings are expected to be bad. When the earnings are reported, they may be no worse than expected, the put skew may fall, the stock may rally and volatility may decline. Likewise, a flat call skew in a bond market is no indicator that events will continue to be dull and routine. If a shock hits the stock market, a flight to quality and so a flight to bonds may result, rapidly forcing their call implieds, and their call skews, higher.

Trading with skews

Volatility skews present additional opportunities for profit as well as additional risks.

Volatility skews present additional opportunities for profit as well as additional risks. They are additional variables which should be considered when trading options, especially straight long or short calls and puts. Their risks are lessened through spreading. The following paragraphs offer guidelines on how to deal with some of the more common, but by no means all, market situations. Skew behaviour varies as much as market behaviour.

As you might expect, there are two basic possibilities to skew trading:

■ buying or selling out-of-the money options on a positive skew.

■ buying or selling out-of-the-money options on a negative skew.

Trading options on a positive skew

The purchase of an out-of-the-money option on a positive skew, like the purchase of any option, profits if the underlying moves in its direction and/or if the implied increases. If the underlying moves in the option's direction, but meets a support or resistance level, the option profits from direction but often underperforms. This is because the focal point of the skew shifts horizontally to the at-the-money strike, causing the implied of the option effectively to decrease.

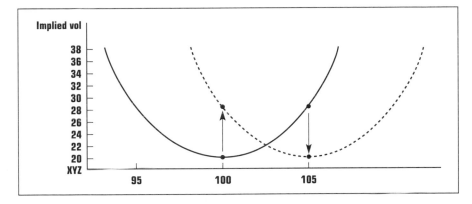

Fig 20.6 ■ Positive skew, right horizontal shift

With XYZ at 100, the 105 call is purchased at an implied that is above the at-the-money level, and as the underlying moves to the 105 strike, the option's implied effectively decreases from 28 per cent to 20 per cent . The net result is still a profit if time decay has not been too costly. Note that the implied of the 100 call and put both increase from 20 per cent to 28 per cent.

For example, suppose you pay 25 ($\frac{25}{64}$) for the T-Bond January 130 call from the set in Table 20.4. You might estimate the profit potential for a two-point rally in bonds by multiplying two points (128 options ticks) by the average delta of the call over the course of the move. This average delta is determined by the delta of the 129 call, at .36: 128 × .36 = 46 ticks profit. Your estimated new value of the 130 call with bonds at 130 is 46 + 25 = $\frac{71}{64}$, or 1.07.

By looking at the 128 call with bonds at 128, you note that the current ATM call has a value of only 1.05. If the ATM implied remains stable, then the market is telling you that a 130 call with bonds at 130 will have a value of 1.05.

Effectively then, for a two-point rally, your 130 call may underperform by two ticks. In practice, this often happens. The reason for this is that you have purchased a call at an implied of 8.40 which will be reduced to 8.14 by a horizontal shift in the volatility skew.

In this case, the underperformance is not a great amount. But if the call were purchased farther up the skew (at a higher strike), and if the skew were more positive, then the reduction due to a decrease in implied volatility would be greater.

In order to minimize this skew risk, you might instead purchase an out-of-the-money call spread. Here, you could buy the 130 call and sell the 132 call. As the skew shifts, both implieds decrease.

Another approach is simply to pay 1.05 ($\frac{69}{64}$) for the 128 call. Here, as the market rallies, the shift in the skew causes the implied of your call to increase. Using the delta of the 127 call at .65, your expected profit for a two-point rally would be .65 × 128 = 83. The new value of your call is estimated at 83 + 69 = $\frac{152}{64}$, or 2.24.

You note that the current 126 call has a value of 2.26. This is the expected value of your 128 call if bonds rally two points. Because the implied of your call increases from 8.14 to 8.59, your 128 call may, and often will, outperform by two ticks.

Still another approach is to buy the 128–130 call spread. Here, your spread's long strike profits from increased volatility, and your spread's short strike profits from decreased volatility.

You can use the preceding data to calculate the effect of a skew shift on the implieds and values of selected puts. If the underlying breaks, puts on a positive skew may underperform due to a decrease in their implieds.

Trading options on a linear skew

A long out-of-the-money option on a linear skew, or a skew that is call negative and put positive, presents a couple of possibilities. As the underlying rallies, you might expect the skew to shift horizontally, resulting in an increase in all the implieds. Often this happens.

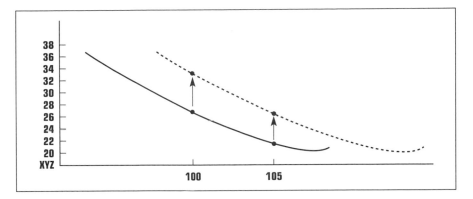

Fig 20.7 ■ **Horizontal skew shift, Negative call skew, positive put skew**

Here, as XYZ rallies from 100 to 105, all the calls and puts increase their implied volatility. Note that the reverse situation often occurs: an underlying breaks, usually on a retracement, and the skew shifts to the left, resulting in a decrease in all the implieds.

Frequently, however, on a rally the skew can remain in place, and the implieds of all strikes are unchanged. Effectively, the implied volatility decreases because the focal point of the skew moves to the new at-the-money strike. The solid line of Figure 20.7 illustrates this: XYZ rallies from 100 to 105, and the new ATM implied, now at the 105 strike, is less than that of the former 100 strike.

This situation often occurs with skews in stock indexes as they rally to former levels. The options market is unfazed by the upside retracement. This also occurs in commodities that have negative put skews as the commodities retrace from a rally; there the graph is the mirror image of Figure 20.7.

Another possibility is that on a break, the skew can remain in place. Effectively, the implied volatility increases because the focal point of the skew moves to the new at-the-money strike. The dotted line of Figure 20.7 illustrates this: XYZ breaks from 105 to 100, and the new ATM implied, now at the 100 strike, is greater than that of the former 105 strike.

This latter situation often occurs with skews in stock indexes as they break. The options market is fearful that this is the big one. When it really is the big one, then the entire skew will shift vertically upward, and the put wing will become more positive.

Conclusion

Volatility skews are indicators of market sentiment.

In all cases where a straight long or short option is chosen for a directional strategy, skew risk can be minimized by trading the long or short call or put spread.

Volatility skews are indicators of market sentiment. Positive skews indicate fear, while negative skews indicate complacence. Sentiment as we know can often be wrong, but it cannot be ignored.

Part

4

Basic non-essentials

21 Futures, synthetics and put-call parity

22 Conversions, reversals, boxes and options arbitrage

23 Conclusion

21 Futures, synthetics and put-call parity

It is possible to combine options and underlying positions in ways that simulate straight call or put positions. An underlying itself may be simulated with a combination of options. As an example of the former, a long at-the-money call plus a short underlying position has the same risk/return profile as a long at-the-money put, and is therefore known as a synthetic put.

Synthetic positions are used primarily by professional market makers to simplify the view of their options inventory in order to manage risk better. They are of little practical use to traders who take options positions based on market outlooks, but they can be studied in order to understand how options markets work.

In order to understand synthetics, it is best if you understand why they exist. Like all options positions, they are based on a relation to an underlying contract, which may be a cash investment or a futures contract. If we briefly take this subject step by step, then we will avoid future disorientation.

What a futures contract is

A **futures contract** is simply an agreement to trade a commodity, stock, bond or currency at a specified price at a specified future date. Because no cash is exchanged for the time being, the future buyer is said to have a **long position**, and the future seller is said to have a **short position**. As a result, the holder of the long position profits as the market moves up and takes a loss as the market moves down. The holder of the short position has the opposite profit/loss.

If short selling were not possible, investors would only be able to buy from those who wanted to sell physical holdings; liquidity would suffer and market volatility would increase. Most exchanges require a security deposit in order to open a futures contract, and this deposit is known as **initial margin**. The value of the contract as traded on the exchange invariably fluctuates, and so results in a profit to one party and a loss to the other. The party who has a loss is then required to deposit the amount of the loss, and this additional deposit is known as **variation margin**. Margin may be in the form of cash, or it may be in the form of liquid securities such as treasury bills or gilts, for which the depositor still collects interest. Meanwhile the party who has the profit is credited with variation margin, and he receives interest on the balance.

Futures contracts have traditionally been used in commodities markets in order to hedge supply shortages and surpluses. They are now used in stock indexes, bonds and currencies. Many excellent books describe how these forms of futures contracts operate.

An example of a futures contract

Consider the following example of a closing price of the S&P 500 index with the settlement price of the December fututres contract and the settlement prices of the at-the-money call and put on the futures contract.

S&P index:	1133.68
December future:	1140.70
December 1140 call:	34.40
December 1140 put:	33.70

Here, the S&P futures contract multiplier is $250. An investor who trades one of the above December contracts is hedging 1140.70 × $250 = $285,175 worth of stocks that track the index. The options contract multiplier is $25.[18]

We know that the December future, here with approximately six weeks until expiration, trades at a premium to the cash. This is because taking a long position in the futures contract instead of buying all the stocks in the index requires a margin deposit only. The holder of the futures position therefore has the use of his cash for the next six weeks. The value of the futures contract is increased by the cost of carrying on the stocks.

On the other hand, the holder of the long futures position foregoes the dividends payable for the next six weeks, and therefore the value of the

---

[18] The CME has recently introduced mini options on the S&P 500 at $12.50 per tick.

December future is decreased by that amount. The formula for the value of the futures contract is approximated as follows.

Futures contract = cash value of index + (interest or cost of carry on index until expiration) – (Dividends payable until expiration).

In practice, the formula is more complicated because annualized rates of carry and dividend yields are used. Here, we are simply concerned with why the above future trades over the cash.

Because current short-term interest rates pay more than current dividend yields, stock index futures trade at a premium to their underlying indexes. In the 1950s dividend yields paid more than short-term interest rates because, incredible as it may seem, stock holders were assumed to have capital at risk. This was a holdover from the stock market crash of 1929, when many stock holders' investments were wiped out. If a similar situation occurs again, then stock index futures' values will probably trade at a discount to cash.

Occasionally, shortly before expiration, there may be a large amount of dividends payable in a stock index. Then the dividend amount is greater than the interest amount and the future trades at a discount to the index.

In any event, the futures contract and the cash index converge at expiration because then there is no remaining differential between cost of carry and payable dividends. The futures contract simply expires to the current cash value of the index.

> The futures contract and the cash index converge at expiration because then there is no remaining differential between cost of carry and payable dividends.

There, the holder of the long futures contract pays the cash value of all the stocks in the index. The holder of the short futures contract receives the cash value of all the stocks in the index. The ultimate amount exchanged is determined by the value of the index at expiration times the contract multiplier.

In the case of a physical commodity such as corn or crude oil, the futures contract is deliverable to the quantity of the commodity specified in the contract at the prevailing price.

Synthetic futures contract

As we already know, a long XYZ 100 call, by virture of its right to buy, equals a long XYZ position when XYZ is above 100 at expiration. We also know that a short XYZ 100 put, by virtue of its obligation to buy, equals a long XYZ position when XYZ is below 100 at expiration. The sum of these two options positions, therefore, equals a synthetic long XYZ position with a strike price of 100. This is a result of the combined right and obligation. Consider the example in Figure 21.1.

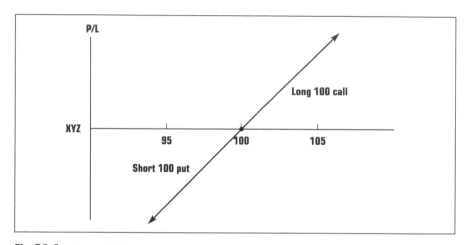

Fig 21.1 ■ **Long XYZ synthetic**

We also know that a short XYZ 100 call, by virtue of its obligation to sell, equals a short XYZ positon when XYX is above 100 at expiration. A long XYZ 100 put, by virtue of its right to sell, equals a short XYZ position when XYZ is below 100 at expiration. The sum of these options positions, therefore, equals a synthetic short position with a strike price of 100. This again is a result of the combined right and obligation. Consider the example in Fig. 21.2.

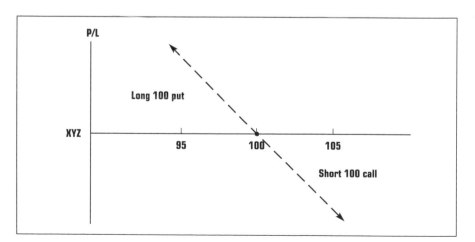

Fig 21.2 ■ **Short XYZ synthetic**

Taking the S&P 500 example above, a long December 1140 call plus a short December 1140 put equals a synthetic long futures contract valued at 1140. If you pay 34.40 for the call, and sell the put at 33.70, then you have paid a net .70 for the synthetic at 1140. In other words, you have paid .70 to go long the future at 1140. You have paid 1140.70 for the synthetic long future.

Note that the actual December future is valued at 1140.70. Your synthetic options position is valued the same, and always will be, as a futures contract.

If, on the other hand, you sell the call at 34.40 and pay 33.70 for the put, then you have sold the synthetic future at 1140.70. Here, you have the obligation to sell the future above 1140, and the right to sell the future below 1140.

The profit/loss of the two synthetics is graphed in Figure 21.3.

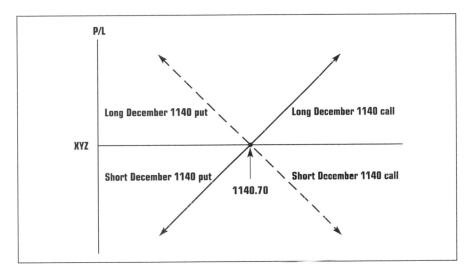

Fig 21.3 ■ Synthetic long December **SPZ** futures contract + Synthetic short December **SPZ** futures contract

Synthetics on individual stocks

In the case of individual stocks, there is no futures contract. The synthetic futures position remains, however, because the holder of a long call plus short position at any given strike controls a long stock position without having to pay for the stock. Consider our former options on Microsoft.

Microsoft at $111\frac{3}{4}$
January 110 call with 60 days until expiration: $7\frac{5}{8}$
January 110 put with 60 days until expiration: $4\frac{7}{8}$

Here, you could purchase the January 110 synthetic for $7\frac{5}{8} - 4\frac{7}{8} = 2\frac{3}{4}$. If you do this, then you have the combined right and obligation to purchase 100 shares of Microsoft at January expiration. This is the equivalent of going long one Microsoft futures contract for January delivery at a value of 110 + $2\frac{3}{4}$, or $112\frac{3}{4}$.

The difference between this synthetic futures contract and the current price of the stock is $112\frac{3}{4} - 111\frac{3}{4}$, or 1. This difference is the approximate amount that you save by placing your $110 cash in a short-term deposit for 60 days at 5.50 per cent interest, and simultaneously buying the synthetic.[19] (Microsoft pays no dividend.) In the stock options the synthetic future is often spoken of simply as the synthetic, or occasionally, the combo.

Synthetic long call position

When a long XYZ 100 put is combined with a long underlying position, the profit/loss's of the put and the underlying cancel each other below 100, leaving the upside, profit-making leg of the underlying. The sum equals a synthetic long call. For the purpose of illustration, let's assume that the call was purchased for free. At expiration, the synthetic position would be as follows.

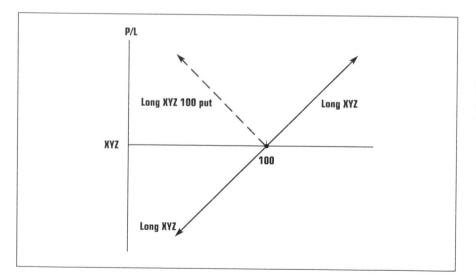

Fig 21.4 ■ **Synthetic long 100 call**

---

[19] $\$110 \times .055 \times \frac{60}{360} = \$1.01$.

Now let's return to the example based on the S&P 500 futures and options on the futures.

S&P 500 December future: 1140.70
December 1140 call: 34.40
December 1140 put: 33.70

Suppose you take a long position in the futures contract at 1140.70 and at the same time you pay 33.70 for the December 1140 put. You know that below 1140 the profit/loss of the put and the futures contract offset each other because below 1140 you have the right to sell what you own at the price at which it was purchased less the cost of the put. Above 1140 you are simply long the futures contract. Being net long a futures contract above 1140 is the same as owning a December 1140 call. The cost of your synthetic call breaks down as follows.

The futures contract costs 1140.70, and the right to sell it at 1140 costs 33.70. With your futures contract you have paid .70 more for what you own than for your potential selling price. With your put your total cost is .70 + 33.70 = 34.40, or the price of the December 1140 call. Compare the profit/loss tables for the 1140 call and the 1140 synthetic call.

SPZ	1080	1140	1174.40	1200
Cost of December 1140 call	–34.40 ----------	-----------	-----------	-----------
Value of call at expiration	0	0	34.40	60
Call profit/loss	–34.40	–34.40	0	25.60

Table 21.1 ■ Profit/Loss of SPZ December 1140 call at expiration

SPZ	1080	1140	174.40	1200
Profit/loss of long December futures at expiration	–60.70	–.70	33.70	59.30
Cost of December 1140 put	–33.70 ----------	-----------	-----------	-----------
Value of put at expiration	60	0	0	0
Profit/loss of synthetic long call	–34.40	–34.40	0	25.60

Table 21.2 ■ Profit/Loss of SPZ December 1140 synthetic call at expiration

Synthetic short call position

If instead XYZ is sold at 100, and at the same time a 100 put is sold, a synthetic short 100 call results. Below 100 the profit on the short underlying position and the loss on the short put offset each other. Above 100, a loss is taken on the short underlying position. Let's assume that the put was sold for free. The graph at expiration would be as shown in Figure 21.5.

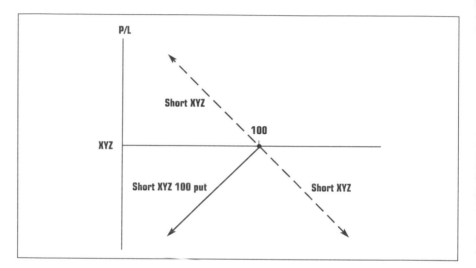

Fig 21.5 ■ Synthetic short XYZ call

Returning to our SPZ example, suppose the above December 1140 put is sold for 33.70 and a short position is taken in the futures contract at 1140.70, the result is a synthetic short call. The profit/loss is the opposite to the above long synthetic long call.

SPZ	1080	1140	1174.40	1200
Profit/loss of short December futures at expiration	60.70	.70	-33.70	-59.30
Income from December 1140 put	33.70	------	------	------
Value of put at expiration	-60	0	0	0
Profit/loss of synthetic short short call	34.40	34.40	0	-25.60

Table 21.3 ■ Profit/Loss of synthetic short SPZ Dec 1140 call at expiration

Synthetic long put position

When a long XYZ 100 call is combined with a short underlying position, the profit/loss of the call and the underlying cancel each other above 100, leaving the downside, profit-making leg of the underlying. The sum equals a synthetic long put. We'll assume that the put is traded for free. At expiration, the profit/loss graph is shown in Figure 21.6.

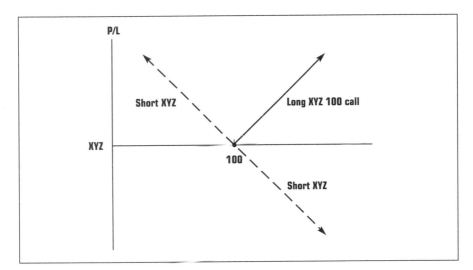

Fig 21.6 ■ **Synthetic long XYZ put**

Returning to our SPZ example, suppose the December 1140 call is purchased for 34.40, and a short position in the futures contract is taken at 1140.70. The result is a synthetic long put purchased for 33.70. Tables 21.4 and 21.5 show a comparison of the profit/loss of the synthetic and the straight put.

SPZ	1080	1106.30	1140	1200
Cost of December 1140 put	–33.70	------	------	------
Value of put at expiration	60	33.70	0	0
Put profit/loss	26.30	0	–33.70	–33.70

Table 21.4 ■ **Profit/loss of long SPZ Dec 1140 put at expiration**

SPZ	1080	1106.30	1140	1200
Profit/loss of short December futures at expiration	60.70	34.40	.70	−59.30
Cost of December 1140 call	−34.40	------	------	------
Value of call at expiration	0	0	0	60
Profit/loss of synthetic long put	26.30	0	−33.70	−33.70

Table 21.5 ■ Profit/loss of long SPZ Dec 1140 synthetic put at expiration

Synthetic short put position

When a short XYZ 100 call is combined with a long underlying position, the profit/loss of the call and the underlying cancel each other above 100, leaving the downside, loss-taking leg of the underlying. The sum equals a synthetic short put. Again, we'll assume that the put is traded for free. At expiration, the profit/loss graph is shown in Figure 21.7.

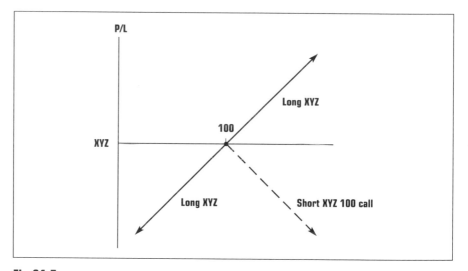

Fig 21.7 ■ Synthetic short XYZ 100 put

Returning to our SPZ example, if the December 1140 call is sold at 34.40, and a long position is taken in the underlying at 1140.70, the result is a synthetic short put sold at 33.70. The profit/loss is the opposite of the above long synthetic put.

SPZ	1080	1106.30	1140	1200
Profit/loss of long December futures at expiration	–60.70	–34.40	–.70	59.30
Income from December 1140 call	34.40	---------	---------	---------
Value of call at expiration	0	0	0	–60
Profit/loss of synthetic short put	–26.30	0	33.70	33.70

Table 21.6 ■ Profit/loss of short SPZ Dec 1140 synthetic put at expiration

The complex problem of put-call parity

The above are illustrations of **put–call parity**, which tells us that by knowing the value of the underlying, the strike price, and either the call or put, the price of the unknown call or put can be determined. The formulas for determining the value of a corresponding call or put at a particular strike are as follows.

Call minus put = futures minus strike price (34.40 – 33.70 = 1140.70 – 1140), therefore

Call = futures minus strike price plus put (34.40 = 1140.70 – 1140 + 33.70), or
Put = call minus futures plus strike price (33.70 = 34.40 – 1140.70 + 1140)

This equation can also be solved for the other two variables.

Futures = call minus put plus strike price (1140.70 = 34.40 – 33.70 + 1140), and
Strike price = futures plus put minus call (1140 = 1140.70 + 33.70 – 34.40)

All this really tells us is that a call and a put at the same strike have the same amount of time premium, or volatility coverage. If you've read this book with open eyes, you've already arrived at the same conclusion, at least intuitively. The mysterious and complex world of put-call parity is now exposed as a trifle.

> A call and a put at the same strike have the same amount of time premium, or volatility coverage.

You, the intelligent reader, have more important things to think about, such as choosing your socks in the morning.

The real problem of put-call parity is that for many options contracts it doesn't apply. It assumes that in-the-money options have no early exercise premium, which is only true of European-style options. Put-call parity works with a straight Black-Scholes model only, and only when deep in-the-money options with their carrying costs are not involved.

If the above S&P 500 options were deep in the money, there would be small discrepencies in the put-call parity values. If the put-call parity formula were applied to options on the OEX or the FTSE American-style options, large discrepencies would result due to early exercise premium. Significant discrepancies also result with American-style options on individual stocks, i.e., most stock options.

Put–call parity can be a helpful way of pricing options, but its limitations must be considered.

Questions on synthetics

1   Given the following set of FTSE December European style options, calculate the price of the missing call or put using the put-call parity formulas.

FTSE December futures contract at 5470

Strike	5325	5475	5525	5725
December calls	$306\frac{1}{2}$	?	?	$97\frac{1}{2}$
December puts	?	217	$238\frac{1}{2}$	?

   a) December 5325 put

   b) December 5475 call

   c) December 5525 call

   d) December 5725 put

2   Given the following set of December options on Intel, determine the price of the synthetic futures contract and the prices of the missing options.

Intel at 90
December options with 50 days until expiration

Strike	80	85	90	95	100
December calls	$12\frac{1}{4}$	?	$4\frac{5}{8}$	$3\frac{7}{8}$	?
December puts	?	$3\frac{5}{8}$	$4\frac{1}{4}$	?	$11\frac{3}{4}$

   a) December synthetic futures contract

   b) December 80 put

   c) December 85 call

   d) December 95 put

   e) December 100 call

Answers

1 **a)** $306\frac{1}{2} - 5470 + 5325 = 161\frac{1}{2}$

    b) $5470 - 5475 + 217 = 212$

    c) $5470 - 5525 + 238\frac{1}{2} = 183\frac{1}{2}$

    d) $97\frac{1}{2} - 5470 + 5725 - 352\frac{1}{2}$

2 **a)** $4\frac{5}{8} - 4\frac{1}{4} + 90 = 90\frac{3}{8}$

    b) $12\frac{1}{4} - 90\frac{3}{8} + 80 = 1\frac{7}{8}$

    c) $90\frac{3}{8} - 85 + 3\frac{5}{8} = 9$

    d) $3\frac{7}{8} - 90\frac{3}{8} + 95 = 8\frac{1}{2}$

    e) $90\frac{3}{8} - 100 + 11\frac{3}{4} = 2\frac{1}{8}$

22 Conversions, reversals, boxes and options arbitrage

Conversions, reversals, and boxes are used almost exclusively by market makers and risk managers to neutralize the risk of large options portfolios. At one time, they were traded in order to profit from small price discrepancies in synthetic positions, but now most mature options markets have eliminated this opportunity.

> Conversions, reversals, and boxes are used almost exclusively by market makers and risk managers to neutralize the risk of large options portfolios.

A short synthetic underlying position can be combined with an actual long underlying position to yield a **forward conversion**, or **conversion**. Likewise, a long synthetic position can be combined with an actual short underlying position to yield a **reverse conversion**, or **reversal**. The profit/loss of these positions does not change regardless of market movement, and their only practical risks are those of pin risk and early assignment.

A long box is the purchase of a synthetic underlying at a lower strike and the sale of a synthetic underlying at a higher strike. **A short box** is the opposite position. Because the box is both long and short the underlying, its profit/loss does not change regardless of market movement. Again, the only practical risks are pin risk and early assignment.

Conversion

A conversion is a long underlying plus a short call and a long put at the same strike.

If XYZ is at 100, you could sell one 100 call, buy one 100 put, and buy or go long XYZ to create a conversion. Because the sum of the position is short the synthetic and long the underlying there is no profit/loss change regardless of underlying, price movement. At expiration, the synthetic pairs off against the underlying to leave no position.

Consider again the example from S&P 500 futures, and options on futures.

December S&P 500 future at 1140.70
December 1140 call at 34.40
December 1140 put at 33.70

Here, you could sell the call at 34.40, pay 33.70 for the put, and pay 1140.70 for the future. You have then sold the synthetic at 1140.70 and you have bought the future at the same price. There is no profit or loss to this position, nor will it change for the life of the options contract. At expiration the short synthetic pairs off against the long future, and the result is no position. There is mimimal risk. Figure 22.1 shows is a graph of the conversion.

Occasionally, there is a small amount of profit to be made by trading the components of a conversion separately. For example, a trader might be able to sell the above call at 34.50, thereby making .10 profit on the whole position. This .10 is secure until expiration when all the components pair off. Some traders spend the best part of their youths trying to trade these

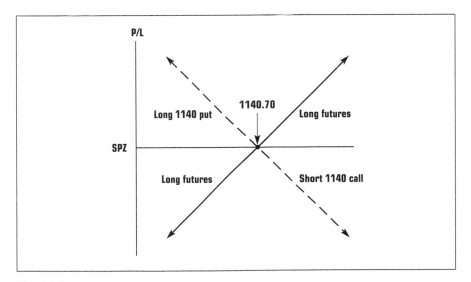

Fig. 22.1 ■ **SPZ 1140 coversion**

small price discrepancies, and it is good for the rest of us that they do so. Their form of trading is called *arbitrage*.

By keeping the conversions in line, the arbitrageurs, or arbs, help to maintain efficient pricing in the market. As a result, we benefit by getting a fair price for our options.

Reverse conversion, or reversal

A reversal is a short underlying plus a long call and a short put at the same strike.

If XYZ is at 100, you could buy one 100 call, sell one 100 put, and sell or go short one XYZ to create a reversal. Because the sum of the position is long the synthetic and short the underlying, there is no profit/loss change regardless of underlying price movement. At expiration, the synthetic pairs off against the underlying to leave no position.

With the S&P example, you could pay 34.40 for the call, sell the put at 33.70, and sell the future at 1140.70. Here you have paid 1140.70 for the synthetic and sold the future at the same price. Figure 22.2 shows a graph of the entire position.

Again, the arbs exploit the smallest price discrepancy with any of the components of the reversal. Here, they might pay 34.30 for the call, or sell

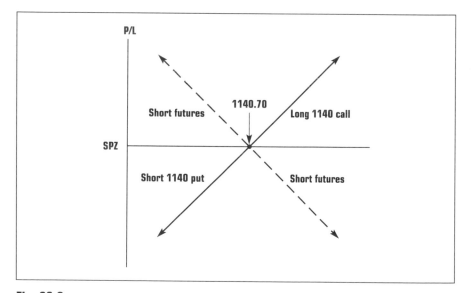

Fig. 22.2 ■ **SPZ 1140 reversal**

the put at 33.80, or pay 1140.60 for the future. Rarely is more than one component out of line at one time.

Conversion and reversals on individual stocks and on other stock indexes

The conversion and reversal markets on stocks oper-ate in basically the same manner. Remember that with stocks there are no futures contracts, but that the options combine to form synthetic futures contracts. The situation is similar to the S&P 500 cash–futures–options relationship given in Chapter 21.

> Remember that with stocks there are no futures contracts, but that the options combine to form synthetic futures contracts.

S&P 500 cash index at 1133.68
December future at 1140.70
December 1140 call at 34.40
December 1140 put at 33.70

If the futures contract were eliminated, and the options were exercisable instead to cash, then the relationship would be the same as between stocks and stock options.

The OEX options are traded in this manner, without an underlying futures contract; they are American style. Because there is no underlying cash instrument, apart from an unwieldy basket of stocks, there is no conversion or reversal tradable in the OEX.

The SPX options on the S&P 500 index, traded at the CBOE, are also based solely on the underlying index; they are European style. Traders here sometimes use the S&P 500 futures contract at the CME in order to create a conversion or reversal.

The FTSE-100 contract is a hybrid. The options are assigned to cash at monthly expirations like the OEX. There is a futures contract as well, like the S&P 500, which trades in the March-June-September-December cycle. During these four months, expiration for options and futures coincides at 10:30 on the third Friday, making conversions possible.

An example of a conversion in stocks is found in the previous set of Microsoft options.

Microsoft at $111\frac{3}{4}$
January 110 call with 60 days until expiration: $7\frac{5}{8}$
January 110 put with 60 days until expiration: $4\frac{7}{8}$

Here, you could sell the synthetic at $2\frac{3}{4}$ and buy the stock at $111\frac{1}{4}$ to create the conversion. At January expiration the short synthetic converts to a short stock position which pairs off against the long stock position. You have effectively sold the synthetic at $112\frac{3}{4}$ for a net credit of one on the total position. This credit equals your cost of carry on the stock position for the next 60 days as determined by the prevailing short-term interest rate. (Where applicable, dividends are a negative component in the long synthetic just as they are with a futures contract. Microsoft presently does not pay dividends.) During the next 60 days the difference between the synthetic and the stock will converge from one to zero.

Long box

The box is another spread that is occasionally employed by arbitrageurs in order to profit from small price discrepancies in the options markets. Again, it contains minimal risk.

If XYZ is at 100, you would go long the 100–105 box by going long the 100 synthetic and by going short the 105 synthetic. You would buy one 100 call, sell one 100 put, sell one 105 call, and buy one 105 put. The box itself always trades for a price that nearly equals the difference between the strike prices, in this case, a debit of five. Your purchase holds its value until expiration, at which time the synthetics pair off and you are credited with the difference between the strike prices.

As an example, consider again the set of options on Intel set out in Table 22.1.

Intel at 90

December options with 50 Days until expiration

Strike	80	85	90	95	100
December calls	$12\frac{1}{4}$	9	$4\frac{5}{8}$	$3\frac{7}{8}$	$2\frac{1}{8}$
December puts	$1\frac{7}{8}$	$3\frac{5}{8}$	$4\frac{1}{4}$	$8\frac{1}{2}$	$11\frac{3}{4}$

Table 22.1 ■ Intel December options

Here, the long 90–95 box is calculated as the 90 call minus the 90 put, minus the 95 call plus the 95 put, or $(4\frac{5}{8} - 4\frac{1}{4}) - (3\frac{7}{8} + 8\frac{1}{2}) = 5$. Until expiration this debit is your total profit/loss.

At expiration, the long 90 synthetic, through exercise or assignment, becomes a stock purchase at a price of 90. The short 95 synthetic, through exercise or assignment, becomes a stock sale at a price of 95. Your account is then credited with five ticks and your profit/loss is zero.

The value of the box, however, is most often modified by time until expiration, early exercise, and interest rate factors; these are discussed below.

At expiration, your profit/loss summary is as shown in Table 22.2.

Intel	85	90	$92\frac{1}{2}$	95	100
Debit from long 90 synthetic	$-\frac{3}{8}$	----	----	----	----
Value of long 90 synthetic at expiration	-5	0	$2\frac{1}{2}$	5	10
Debit from short 95 synthetic	$-4\frac{5}{8}$	----	----	----	----
Value of short 95 synthetic at expiration	10	5	$2\frac{1}{2}$	0	-5
Total profit/loss	0	0	0	0	0

Table 22.2 ■ Profit/loss of long Intel December 90–95 box at expiration

The following profit/loss graph is simply an overlay of the two synthetics at expiration. At any closing price, the sum of any two vertical points equals five:

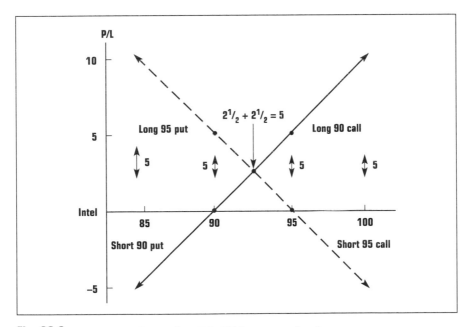

Fig. 22.3 ■ Intel long December 90–95 box at expiration

Short box

If XYZ is at 100, you could sell one 100 call, buy one 100 put, buy one 105 call, and sell one 105 put to create a short box. Here, you are short the 100 synthetic and long the 105 synthetic for a credit of five. Your sale holds its value until expiration, at which time the synthetics pair off, and you pay the value of the box to an opposing party.

For an example, simply reverse the long box transaction in Intel, above. Sell the 90 synthetic and buy the 95 synthetic for a credit of five. At expiration this credit returns to the opposing party.

Trading boxes

Boxes are seldom traded except as closing positions between market makers; we trade them close to expiration in order to clear options off our books and to avoid pin risk. But then again, the arbs try to pay $4\frac{7}{8}$ for the above box, and they try to sell it at $5\frac{1}{8}$. They often

> **Boxes are seldom traded except as closing positions between market makers.**

do this by trading the components quickly and separately. They do this in large volume, so their costs are low. The profit might be small, but once the position is on, it is almost risk free.

With contracts that have early exercise, in-the-money boxes often trade for more than the difference between the strike prices. The options that are in-the-money have early exercise premium, and the option that is deeper in-the-money has more. For example, if Intel above were a week ot two until expiration, the 95–100 box might trade for $5\frac{1}{8}$. This is because the 100 put contains the right to exercise to cash.

Early exercise premium raises the value of the boxes in the OEX and FTSE American-style options as well.

On contracts that are paid for up-front, and where there is no early exercise, the purchase of a box results in cash tied up. The box therefore trades at a discount equal to the difference between strikes minus the cost of carry through expiration. At expiration the value of the box is transferred at exactly the difference between strikes. Examples of this are FTSE European-style options contract, and the SPX European-style options on the S&P 500 which are traded at the CBOE.

Cost of carry on boxes

To be precise, a box that has no early exercise premium will always trade at a discount equal to its cost of carry. For example, an at-the-money 10-point box in Intel above, with 50 DTE, at a short term interest rate of 5 per cent, will trade at $10 - (10 \times .05 \times \frac{50}{360}) = 9.93$, or $9\frac{15}{16}$.

The sale of a box through cash-traded European-style options is often used as a means of short-term finance. If a house wanted to borrow money then it could sell the above 10-point box at $9\frac{15}{16}$. Cash would be credited to its account until expiration, and then the house would pay ten to close the position. Commissions and exchange fees would effectively raise the borrowing rate to more than 5 per cent. Only large firms that trade in large size and that benefit from low costs can take advantage of this opportunity, and most often they prefer to borrow and lend in the cash markets.

Questions on conversions and boxes

1 The current Bank of England interest rate is 7 per cent.

   a) With 37 days until expiry what is the price of a December 1,000 point box in the FTSE-100 European-style options? (Hint: the box trades at a discount.)

   b) Suppose you want to borrow or lend money for the next 37 days at the above rate in the FTSE options market. What strategy, bought or sold, would enable you to trade money at approximately 7 per cent?

   c) The December FTSE futures contract is trading at 5470, and three legs of the 4975 – 5975 box are trading as indicated below. What is the price of the fourth leg?

   FTSE December futures at 5470

Strike	4975	5975
December calls	$572\frac{1}{2}$	$35\frac{1}{2}$
December puts	81	?

2 The purpose of the following question is to help you understand how conversions and reversals form the basis of bid – ask spreads,

or markets, for options. If you get through this question, you get a double bonus.

Microsoft at $108 \frac{7}{8}$
60 days until January expiration
Fed Funds rate at 5.50 per cent

Strike	110
January calls theoretical value	$6 \frac{1}{8}$
January puts theoretical value	$6 \frac{1}{4}$

---

a) What is the value of the January synthetic future, and why is it so valued?

b) To be realistic, there is probably a bid – ask market for Microsoft of $108 \frac{3}{4}$ – 109, and it is certain to vary depending on market conditions. In order to price the January 110 conversion, the market assumes that the stock is bought at 109. At what prices must the call and put be traded in order to break even on the cost of carry on the stock?

c) Now determine the market price of the January 110 reversal. Here the stock must be sold at $108 \frac{3}{4}$. At what prices must the call and put be traded in order to receive a return equal to the current short-term rate?

d) If the prices in the options markets correspond to the current short-term interest rate, which is in fact the Fed Funds rate, what would be the minumum bid – ask markets for the January 110 calls and puts?

e) Now assume that the Federal Reserve is not in the business of trading options. But those who are, such as pension funds, bank and large clearing firms with excellent credit ratings are able to borrow and lend at plus or minus 0.50 per cent above and below the Fed Funds rate. Their interest rate market is then five or six per cent for low risk strategies such as conversions and reversals.

   As a matter of fact, the conversion and reversal market uses the strike price, and not the price of the stock, to calculate the cost of buying and selling stock. What is the cost of trading the 110 conversion?

f) If 109 is paid for the stock, at what price must the synthetic be sold in order to break even on the cost of financing the stock?

g) At what prices must the synthetic be traded in order to break even on the cost of carry?

h) Now determine the break-even cost of the reversal based on the largest institutions' lending rate, or 5 per cent. This is what they may earn for the cash received from a short stock sale. (Note that if the market was not able to earn a small amount of interest from a short stock sale, then we wouldn't be able to buy puts or sell calls.) What is the income, less costs, from trading the reversal?

i) In order to trade the reversal, the stock must be sold at $108\frac{3}{4}$. At what prices must the synthetic be traded in order to break-even?

j) For reversals and conversions at these borrowing and lending rates, what must the markets be for the options?

h) Next is the easiest question in the book. Suppose the stock is either illiquid or is trading in a volatile manner. Its market is shifting from $108\frac{3}{4} - 109$, to $108 - 108\frac{3}{4}$, to $109 - 110$. Further, only $1,000 - 2,000$ shares, or $10 - 20$ equivalent conversions are trading at each price. In order to execute legitimate size, the reliable bid–ask spread is $108 - 110$. Will the bid–ask spread for the options become greater or less?

If you have understood all of the above, then you understand what forces determine the market prices for options. You have the potential to become an options market maker because you understand that you are only able to trade at the prices that the market allows you to trade. On the other hand, if you still think that the bid – ask spreads for options represent 'profits for traders', then perhaps you do not understand the basics of finance, and perhaps you have never bought and sold an asset such as a house.

Finally, note that there are other factors that determine the prices of conversions and reversals. These include dividends, the costs of financing the options themselves, stock and options commissions, exchange fees, and the early exercise premium of the put. Most of these increase the bid–ask spread for options. In addition, conversions and reversals with different days until expiration will be priced off the corresponding forward short-term rates. In markets with high short-term interest rates, such as those in the 80s, interest rate spreads widen, causing the conversion-reversal markets to widen as well.

Answers

1 a) $1{,}000 \times .07 \times \frac{37}{360} = 7$ points discount from 1,000. The box is priced at $1{,}000 - 7 = 993$. The market for the box is probably $992 - 994$.

b) Purchase boxes in the FTSE to lend, sell boxes to borrow.

c) $993 = [572\frac{1}{2} - 81] - [35\frac{1}{2} + ?]$
$? = 993 - 572\frac{1}{2} + 81 + 35\frac{1}{2}$
$? = 537$

2 a) $110 + 6\frac{1}{8} - 6\frac{1}{4} = 109\frac{7}{8}$. The \$1 price above the stock is due to the cost of carry on the stock for 60 days: $108\frac{7}{8} + (108\frac{7}{8} \times .055 \times \frac{60}{360}) = 109\frac{7}{8}$

b) The synthetic must be sold at \$1 over the ask price of the stock in order to recoup the cost of carry. Therefore the synthetic must be sold at 110. This is possible if the call is sold at $6\frac{1}{4}$, and $6\frac{1}{4}$ is paid for the put. Obviously the call and put can both be traded at $6\frac{1}{8}$, etc.

c) If the return on a sale of the stock is 5.50 per cent, then no more than \$1 must be paid for the synthetic over the bid price of the stock. The synthetic must be traded at $109\frac{3}{4}$. $6\frac{1}{8}$ must be paid for the call and the put must be sold at $6\frac{3}{8}$. Obviously the call can be traded at 6 and the put can be traded at $6\frac{1}{4}$, etc.

d) January 110 call: $6\frac{1}{8} - 6\frac{1}{4}$, January 110 put $6\frac{1}{4} - 6\frac{3}{8}$. Both these markets may be priced greater or less to account for increased or decreased implied volatility. It is essential that their synthetic relationship remains $109\frac{3}{4} - 110$.

e) $110 \times .06 \times \frac{60}{160} = \$1.10$ to finance stock purchase for 60 days.

f) $109 + 1.10 = 110.10$, rounded up to $110\frac{1}{8}$ because no one is in the business of losing money.

g) At $110\frac{1}{8}$ the call must be sold at $6\frac{1}{4}$, and $6\frac{1}{8}$ must be paid for the put. Obviously the call can be traded at 6, and the put can be traded at $5\frac{7}{8}$, etc.

h) Interest earned via reversal, $110 \times .05 \times \frac{60}{160} = \$ .92$, rounded down to $\frac{7}{8}$, for short stock sale.

i) Here, no more than $\frac{7}{8}$ must be paid for the synthetic over the bid price of the stock, or $108\frac{3}{4} + \frac{7}{8} = 109\frac{5}{8}$. This can be done by by paying 6 for the call while selling the put at $6\frac{3}{8}$. Obviously, the call can be traded at $6\frac{1}{4}$ while the put is traded at $6\frac{5}{8}$.

j) Call: $6 - 6\frac{1}{4}$, put: $6\frac{1}{8} - 6\frac{3}{8}$

23 Conclusion

If you have read this book in its entirety, I offer you my congratulations. You are willing to make the effort needed to become a serious trader. You now know what options are and what they do. You also know how to create spreads, and you have a basic understanding of volatility. Most importantly, you have an understanding of risk. You understand how the variables interact and how to employ those variables that suit your outlook. Before you place your hard-earned capital at risk, here is some advice.

■ Learn the fundamentals cold. Even those of us who have been in the business a while are sometimes surprised by options behaviour because no two markets, and their effects on options, are alike. Never stop increasing your knowledge.

■ Paper trade before you place capital at risk. Take a position based on closing prices and follow it daily or weekly. Do this with straight calls and puts, and do it with spreads.

■ Begin trading with spreads in order to minimize skew and implied volatility risk.

■ When you first start to trade, keep your size to a mimimum, even if this makes your commision rates high. If this annoys your broker, offer to increase your size when your trading becomes profitable, or find another broker.

■ When you first start to trade, *do not sell more options contracts than you are long*. Selling naked options can take you to the door of the poorhouse.

■ Trade options on underlyings that you know, and improve your knowledge by studying the history of the underlyings and the options on them. Many data vendors, including all exchanges, have price history.

- After you have traded the basic spreads, study volatility. This is the elusive variable, and in the end this is what options are really about. Volatility data is also available from data vendors and exchanges.

- Trade options with a durational outlook; when the duration has ended, take your profits or cut your losses. Likewise, trade with a price objective; when the objective is reached (it often happens sooner than you expect), close your position and don't hope for unrealistic profits. Before you open a position, establish a stop-loss level.

- With straight calls and puts, discipline yourself by basing your options investment on the value of the underlying controlled, not on the amount of premium bought or sold.

- Analyze your trades, both good and bad. What was your outlook at the time you opened the trade? How did the market change while the trade was outstanding? What were your reasons for closing the trade?

- Analyze your reactions to trading. How did you respond when the trade was going your way or going against you? Did you make reasonable decisions, or did you make decisions based on hope or fear?

- The major benefit of trading options is that you can limit your risk. Use this benefit by choosing a risk-limiting strategy. You will then trade with confidence.

There is obviously much more to be said about options in terms of theory and in terms of trading. *Options Plain and Simple* is intented to be a practical, layman's guide to the most common strategies tradable under the most common market circumstances. Markets, of course, defy commonality, but their many variations occur again and again.

This book should be considered basic; in other words, able to impart fundamental awareness, not simply transmit rules. By rereading it, discussing its ideas with your financial adviser and following markets, options' behaviour will become second nature to you. This will be the basis of sound and profitable trading.

If you have any comments or questions, I would like to know them. Please contact the publisher and, fortune permitting, I'll include them in the next edition of this book. May probability be on your side.

Glossary

The following glossary is best used as a quick reminder of basic options definitions. Alternatively, it may be used as a source of jargon for small talk at wine bars. (Make sure you're overheard.) It is no substitute for proper learning.

American style An American style option can be exercised at any date during the life of the option's contract.

Asymmetric spread A spread whose strikes are not equidistant.

At-the-money (ATM) Calls and puts closest to the underlying.

Bear call spread Short call spread.

Bear put spread Long put spread.

Box A long box is a long synthetic plus a short synthetic at a higher strike. A short box has the opposite long-short position.

Bull call spread Long call spread.

Bull put spread Short put spread.

Butterfly A long call butterfly is a long one by two call spread plus a long call at a third, higher strike. All strikes are equidistant. A long put butterfly is a long one by two put spread plus a long put at a third, lower strike. Again, all strikes are equidistant. For shorts of these spreads, reverse the long–short positions.

Calendar spread A long calendar spread is a long option plus a short option that is closer to expiration. Both options have the same strike.

Call A call option is the right to buy the underlying asset at a specified price for a specified time period. The call buyer has the right, but not the obligation, to buy the underlying. The call seller has the obligation to sell the underlying at the call buyer's discretion.

Call spread A long call spread is a long call plus a short call at a higher strike. A short call spread is the opposite.

Combo A long out-of-the-money call plus a short out-of-the-money put, or vice versa. This is also known as the *cylinder*. The short call, long put version is also known as the *fence*. Occasionally this term applies to the synthetic underlying.

Condor A long call condor is a long call spread plus a short call spread at higher strikes. All strikes are equidistant. A long put condor is a long put spread plus a short put spread at lower strikes. Again, all strikes are equidistant.

Conversion A long underlying plus a short synthetic.

Covered write A long underlying plus a short out-of-the-money call. This is also know as the *buy-write*.

Christmas Tree A ladder.

Cylinder See *combo*.

Delta The rate of change of an option with respect to a change in the underlying.

Delta neutral Any combination of options and an underlying position whose delta sum is practically zero.

Delta price ratio The percent that an option's value changes with respect to a change in the underlying.

Diagonal spread A long diagonal is a long option plus a short option that is closer to expiration and farther out-of-the-money.

European style A European-style option can only be exercised at expiration.

Extrinsic value See *time premium*.

Fence See *combo*.

Future A contract to buy or sell a physical asset at a specified price at a specified future date. This asset can be a commodity, bond or stock. In the case of a stock index, the contract is for a cash value of all the stocks that comprise the index.

Gamma The rate of change of the delta with respect to a change in the underlying.

Hybrid spread A spread combination that is not one of the standard spreads. (This term is not in common use.)

In-the-money (ITM) Apart from at-the-money options, calls below the underlying and puts above the underlying.

Intrinsic value The amount that an option is in the money, or the parity component of an in-the-money option.

Iron butterfly A long iron butterfly is a long straddle plus a short strangle with all strikes equidistant. A short iron butterfly has the opposite long-short position.

Iron condor A long iron condor is a long strangle plus a short strangle that is farther out of the money. A short iron condor has the opposite long-short position.

Ladder A long call ladder is a long call spread plus a short call at a third, higher strike. Usually all strikes are equidistant. A long put ladder is a long put spread plus a short put at a third, lower strike. Again, all strikes are usually equidistant. Also known as the *Christmas Tree*.

Leverage The right or obligation to trade the full value of the underlying by trading only the value of the option.

Long To be long is to own. A long futures contract owns a cash or physical asset when the contract expires. A long options contract owns the right to buy, for a call, or the right to sell, for a put.

Long deltas Any combination of long calls, short puts and long underlying.

Margin Cash or liquid security deposited by holders of futures or options contracts.

Multiplier The cash amount by which a futures or options value is multiplied.

Naked A short option not spread with a long option or underlying.

One by two A long one by two call spread is a long call plus two short calls at a higher strike. A long one by two put spread is a long put plus two short puts at a lower strike.

Out-of-the-money (OTM) Apart from at-the-money options, calls above the underlying and puts below the underlying.

Parity An in-the-money option with no time premium that consequently has a 100 per cent correlation with the underlying.

Pin risk The risk of an underlying closing exactly at the options strike price at expiration. The risk lies primarily with the short option holder because he is uncertain of assignment.

Put A put option is the right to sell the underlying asset at a specified price for a specified time period. The put buyer has the right, but not the obligation, to sell the underlying. The put seller has the obligation to buy the underlying at the put buyer's discretion.

Put spread A long put spread is a long put plus a short put at a lower strike. A short put spread is the opposite.

Reversal Short underlying plus long synthetic.

Rho The change of an option's value through a change in the interest rate.

Short To short is to sell. A short futures contract sells a cash or physical asset when the contract expires. A short options contract sells the right to buy, for a call, or the right to sell, for a put.

Short deltas Any combination of short calls, long puts and short underlying.

Stop order An order to buy or sell at the market price when a market reaches a pre-specified price level.

Straddle A call plus a put at the same strike, both either long or short.

Strangle An out-of-the-money call plus an out-of-the-money put, both either long or short.

Strike price The price of the underlying that forms the basis of an options contract.

Synthetic call A long synthetic call is a long put plus a long underlying. A short synthetic call is a short put plus a short underlying.

Synthetic put A long synthetic put is a long call plus a short underlying. A short synthetic put is a short call plus a long underlying.

Synthetic underlying A long synthetic is a long call plus a short put at the same strike. A short synthetic is a short call plus a long put at the same strike. Sometimes referred to as the *combo*.

Theta The amount that an option decays in one day.

Theta price ratio The percent of an option's value diminished by one day's time decay.

Time decay The decline in an option's value through all or a portion of the option's life. Usually expressed as *Theta*.

Time premium The premium apart from intrinsic value of an option. The amount of an option's value that corresponds to volatility coverage.

Time spread See *calendar spread*.

Underlying An asset upon which an option's value is based. This can be a stock or stock index, bond, commodity, or futures contract.

Vega The amount that an option changes through a 1 per cent change in the implied volatility.

Vega price ratio The percent that an option's value changes through a 1 per cent change in the implied volatility.

Vertical spread A call or put spread.

Volatility A one-day, one standard deviation move, annualized.

Volatility, historical Volatility averaged over a time period such as 10, 20 or 30 days.

Volatility, implied The volatility that is implied by an option's price. In the case of an ATM option, this is the expected historical volatility of the underlying through expiration.

Volatility skew A pattern of implied volatility variations exhibited by in- and out-of-the-money options.

Suggestions for further reading

There are now many helpful books on options, and below are two that can be recommended. Also included are books of a more general interest in order to help you make trading decisions. They all are, or will be, classics. The list is limited because time is limited, and your priority will probably be to take the shortest route to a more advanced level.

Options Volatility and Pricing by Sheldon Natenberg
McGraw-Hill
An excellent next step

Introduction to Futures and Options Markets by John Hull
Prentice Hall
For those with an advanced mathematical background

Technical Analysis of the Futures Markets by John J. Murphy
New York Insitute of Finance
Thorough and readable

Commodity Trading Manual
Chicago Board of Trade
An excellent overview of the business.

The Gambler by Dostoyevsky
To know the difference between trading and gambling

Reminiscences of a Stock Operator by Edwin Lefevre
John Wiley & Sons
For market awareness

Index of underlying contracts

Boeing, 28, 189

British Airways, 30

British American Tobacco, 124

British Telecom, 106

Coke, 13, 23, 26

Corn, many examples
    also 133

Crude Oil, 56, 178, 226

Dow Jones Industrial Average, 107

DuPont, 42

Eurodollars, 38

FTSE-100 Index, 14, 55, 107, 176,
    177, 203, 250, 255, 259

General Electric, 12, 106

Gillette, 203

Intel, 145, 157, 204, 216, 250

IBM, 9, 11, 29, 189

Microsoft, many examples
    also 106, 243, 260

OEX, 29, 224, 255

Rolls Royce, 186

Sainsbury, 146, 156, 189

Shell Transport, 31

Short Sterling, 45

Soybeans, 15, 44

S&P 500 future, 240, 245, 253

SPX, 123, 255

Unilever, 13

U.S. Treasury Bonds, 30, 134, 222,
    230

Index

American style, 46
At the money, 39
Bear call spread, 96
Bear put spread, 97
Bell curve, 50
Black-Scholes model, 46, 56
Box, 256
Bull call spread, 94
Bull put spread, 99
Butterfly, 159
  non-adjacent strikes, 175
  and volatility, days until
    expiration, 177
Calendar spread, 185
  risks, 187
Call spread
  long, 94
  short, 96
Call and put spreads
  at different distances from
    underlying, 104
  with non-adjacent strikes, 102
Call spreads vs. put spreads, 101
Calls, 5
  in everyday life, 3
Combo, 127
Comparing call spreads, 1x2's, and
    ladders, 122
Condor, 168
  non-adjacent strikes, 175
  and volatility, days until
    expiration, 177
Conversion, 252
Covered write, 181
  risk management, 183

Christmas tree, 117
Cylinder, 127
Delta, 63
  correspondences to underlying,
    65
  as equivalent futures position, 65
  vs. gamma, theta, and vega, 196
  as hedge ratio, 66
  and probability, 67
  summary, 67
  vs. time decay, 65
  and volatility trading, 74
Delta price ratio, 207
Diagonal spread, 188
Dividends, 42
  and stock indexes, 240
Durational outlook, 215
Early exercise premium, 47
European style, 46
Exercise and assignment, 43
Fed funds, 260
Fence, 129
Futures contract, 239
Gamma, 71
  positive and negative, 73
  and volatility trading, 74
  and straddle, 74
Greeks, 63
  vs. implied volatility, 197
  vs. time, 193
Historical volatility, 54
  vs. implied volatility, 58
Hybrid spreads, 86–87
Implied volatility, 57
  changes to, 200

Index of spreads, 90
In the money, 39
Interest rate
   options component, 41
Intrinsic value, 39
Iron butterfly, 148
   asymmetric, 150
Iron condor, 152
   asymmetric, 154
Ladder
   asymmetric, 121
   long call, 117
   long put, 119
   at different distances from
      underlying, 121
   risk management, 121
Leverage, 216
Liquidity, 217
Long 1x2 call spread, 111
Long 1x2 put spread, 97
Long ATM butterfly, call or put,
   159, 162
Long ATM call condor, 170
Long ATM put condor, 172
Long calendar spread, 185
Long call ladder, 117
Long call, short put combo, 127
Long call spread, 94
Long iron butterfly, 148
Long iron condor, 154
Long option, 43
Long OTM call butterfly, 165
Long OTM call condor, 168
Long OTM put butterfly, 167
Long OTM put condor, 171
Long put ladder, 119
Long put, short call combo, 129
Long put spread, 97
Long straddle, 137
Long strangle, 142

Margin on futures, 240
Market making, 217
Misconceptions, 220
Multiplier, 8
Naked
   call, 93
   put, 26
1x2 call spread, long, 111
   for a credit, 113
   risk management, 116
1x2 put spread, long, 114
   risk management, 116
Options calculator, 57, 201
   Greeks and implied volatility,
      201
Out of the money, 39
Parity, 39
Pin risk, 45
Placing orders, terms used, 90
Portfolio insurance, 185
Pricing inputs, 56
Put-call parity, 249
Put spread
   long, 97
   short, 99
Puts, 21
   in everyday life, 2
Reversal, or reverse conversion, 254
Rho, 201
Short ATM butterfly, call or put, 164
Short ATM call condor, 175
Short ATM put condor, 173
Short call spread, 96
Short iron butterfly, 151
Short iron condor, 152
Short put spread, 99
Short option, 43
Short straddle, 140
Short strangle, 144
Stock index, 43, 44, 240, 255

Stop order, 31, 117, 215, 219
Straddle, 137
Strangle, 142
Strike price, 39
Synthetics, 241
Theta, 63, 75
Theta price ratio, 208
Time decay, 39
Time premium, 39
Time spread, 185
Vega, 63, 81
    and implied volatility trends, 83

positive and negative, 83
    risk/return, 83
Vega price ratio, 209
Vertical spread, 93
    call, 94
    put, 97
Volatility, 52
    risk/return, 59
    trading trends, 214
Volatilty skews, 102, 222
Volatility spreads introductions,
    136, 148, 159, 181